EXCLUSIVE!

EXCLUSIVE!

The Inside Story of Patricia Hearst and the SLA

by MARILYN BAKER
with SALLY BROMPTON

MACMILLAN PUBLISHING CO., INC.
New York
COLLIER MACMILLAN PUBLISHERS
London

To "the secret six," those wonderful
people I met as sources, but now
value as friends

Copyright © 1974 by Marilyn Baker and
Sally Brompton

Macmillan Publishing Co., Inc.
866 Third Avenue, New York, N.Y. 10022
Collier-Macmillan Canada Ltd.

Library of Congress Cataloging in Publication Data
Baker, Marilyn.
Exclusive!
1. Hearst, Patricia.   2. Symbionese Liberation
Army.   I. Brompton, Sally, joint author.   II. Title
F866.2.H42B34   322.420924[B]   74-16300
ISBN 0-02-506400-2

FIRST PRINTING 1974

Printed in the United States of America

Contents

Foreword

BY MARILYN BAKER

ON JUNE 8, 1974, *TV Guide* broke its long tradition of featuring only nationally televised personalities on its cover. The woman scowling out from the cover of twenty-two million copies that week was a reporter from KQED, San Francisco's public broadcasting station. Inside the magazine, a titillating headline read: "The amazing story of a 44-year-old TV newswoman who stayed two weeks ahead of the police in her revelations about the Hearst kidnapping case." Also featured were these words from Charles Bates, head of the San Francisco office of the FBI: "I wish we had that broad's connections."

I am "that broad," the "44-year-old newswoman." *Exclusive!* is the story of what I discovered while stalking Patty Hearst and the Symbionese Liberation Army—the behind-the-TV-camera story:

the secret sources, the hidden meetings, the pursuit of the truth which eventually occupied all my waking hours.

Within a week of Patty Hearst's kidnapping, I was able to report on KQED's "Newsroom" program the names of the two men who had abducted her. It was two months before the FBI would confirm my report. And on March 22, nearly seven weeks after the kidnapping, I was the first to reveal the names and backgrounds of all the SLA members. Not until mid-April did the FBI finally admit that these were the people they were looking for.

I conducted the first interviews with star players in the drama: Steven Weed, Patty's former fiancé; Chris Thompson, the stately, taciturn black man who claimed to have been the lover of several of the women SLA members, a lover they now marked for death; and ex-cellmates of Donald De Freeze (Cinque), who told me more about the man than the SLA itself would ever know.

The string of such reports that I made on "Newsroom" is what prompted Mr. Bates to envy my "connections." There were no connections in the commonly understood sense of the word; there were leads and contacts and hard work—and, most important, the dedicated, unrelenting assistance of my sons, Jeff and Chris. And important help from a man who is both friend and boss, my news director, Joe Russin.

It was a familiar role for my sons. They never complained when, as children, they moved with me from one town to another (once six times in a year) because of my need for editorial freedom at newspapers which would not grant it. Before they were out of grade school they had been part of my battles against the Ku Klux Klan and the American Nazi Party, and before their teens had barely begun, they had stood at my side during riots, learning to take pictures while other youngsters their age were out playing.

On this Hearst-SLA story, Jeff was with me twenty-four hours a day. When the last lead had been checked, the final drive-by of suspected houses completed, he would return to my home to sit up the rest of the night, a rifle across his knees, in response to the death threats I received almost every day. He wasn't alone during those predawn hours. Chris—after a full day of work at City Hall—would sit beside him, his rifle also at the ready.

A strange pair—Jeff, the hippie, with jeans and chino shirt, the uniform of the radical; Chris, the hip, with a neat razorcut and tailored suit, the clean-cut kid every parent dreams about. Two young men who have actively worked to end violence sitting prepared to resort to it, in order to protect the woman they had "raised."

Often, however, it seemed that the hunt for the story itself would finish me off long before the seven-headed SLA cobra, or its sympathizers, would get to me. From February until mid-May, there was no day off, no precious hours to laze by the pool or to curl up in front of the fireplace. No time even to water the plants I had so carefully and optimistically planted in a row of white pots a few months before. Not even time to do such mundane things as rinsing out panty hose. By summer I owned 123 pairs.

As I write this, a new threat, a death poster, has appeared during the night on buildings in the Bay Area, demanding my immediate execution. This time those who call for my death are the Black Liberation Army. New communiqués arrive, proclaiming that the SLA is not dead, and, in a sense, that is true. New variations may develop, but the SLA saga to date is already a story far too complex to be told on the television screen, too monstrous to be printed in our daily newspapers, too detailed for any slick-paged weekly. That is why I wrote this book.

One thing never seems to change—my sons always seem to pay the heavier price. They have done it all through the years, even when they were too young to know why they must pay. They are doing it again. But with all the plaudits, the banquets, the honors, the most gratifying of all is their comment: "Good job, Mom."

San Francisco
August 19, 1974

PART ONE
THE CRIME

CHAPTER 1

BERKELEY IS A CITY of 10.6 square miles and 120,000 not-so-square people. It's motherland of the University of California. World center of radical politics. Womb of campus riots of the sixties. Capital of gay militants, bisexual militants, and plain garden-variety militants. Vortex of black power, brown power, red power, gay power, and power to the people.

At eight o'clock on the night of February 4, 1974—a Monday —Berkeley's 120,000 people were living out their 120,000 different life-styles.

In the million-dollar mansions in Berkeley's foothills, maids announced that dinners were served. In Berkeley's flatland bungalows, television sets warmed up for the nightly three hours of escapism. And in the hundreds of Berkeley communes, revolutionary rhetoric grew hot while stale coffee got cold.

One of Berkeley's people is thirty-one-year-old Peter Benenson, mathematician at Berkeley's radiation laboratory. Tonight he was just able to buy his weekly supply of groceries before the Berkeley Co-op Market's 8:00 P.M. closing time. He bundled up the

3

two bulging brown paper bags and started for his ten-year-old Chevy convertible sitting in the rear parking lot. The lone mercury streetlight above the lot reflected on a few straggling Volkswagen buses and a few other rusted student-type cars. But Benenson was alone, with only the rustle of his grocery bags disturbing the evening quiet.

There was a sudden rush of sound at his side, a quick glimpse of forms—human forms—then a voice, as cold as the February night: "Shut up, don't make a sound! Do what you're told and you won't get hurt!"

The order exploded in his ear as arms reached out and grabbed the grocery bags, dumping them into the back seat; hands grabbed his wrists and pulled his arms behind him, and he felt the sting of cord binding his hands together.

Bodies pressed against him. He was dumped down onto the rear floorboards, his face rubbed raw by the worn carpeting, his legs kicked inside, cramping under his weight.

"Stay down or we'll kill you!" came another hissed warning. The front seat creaked. Three people got into the car. The key turned, the engine sputtered to life, and Peter Benenson was driven off into Berkeley's flatland. His sides ached from bumping and rolling back and forth between the front and rear seats, and he could hear little from the driver and the other two passengers except sudden whispered words he could not form in his mind. It was like being in a traveling tomb that kept going around and around. A tomb that kept moving for more than an hour.

He felt the car backing up, slanting down some incline so that he rolled with a thud against the rear seat, then the brakes being pushed down, the gentle stop. He felt the eyes of the three in the front seat turn toward him and he heard a voice: "Stay down or you'll be killed! Do what you're told and we won't hurt you!"

He never doubted the warning. He stayed down.

If Peter Benenson had looked out the car window, he would have seen he was in a driveway in front of a modern brown-shingled fourplex at 2603 Benvenue Avenue, a short distance south of the University of California campus in Berkeley, a few blocks away from the flatland communes, but still not quite into Berkeley's upper-income-area homes.

If Benenson had looked up, he would have seen a white woman and two black men slide out of his car, holding the doors

4

until they closed with a single small metallic click. All three moved in silence, though all three wore combat boots.

They were going into combat.

The woman's slim body was hidden in the tattered folds of a long dress that brushed against the scuffed boots. Her face was hidden behind her long black hair, now whipped across her face by the cold night wind. She didn't bother to brush it back. It was her mask. She moved quickly, fluidly, only her right arm staying rigid, her hand beneath the folds of the dress clutching a .38 automatic revolver.

Both men held automatic rifles pressed tight across their chests. The taller man had wide, flared nostrils and a mouth thick with bitterness. He pressed his narrow shoulders flat against the brown shingles and looked over his shoulder. He could see a waiting white Chevrolet station wagon, its occupants hidden by the night. A dark blue Volkswagen was behind it, its driver also screened by darkness. His comrades were waiting, ready for the start of the "combat action."

The other man was a good three inches shorter than his six-foot comrade. His body was chunky, his shoulders hunched down inside his dark pea coat. He wiped the cold sweat off the mustache that ringed his wide mouth. His hands reached up to the red bandanna tied around his short Afro hair, sliding it a little higher so that it was tighter, the cloth firm and solid around his perspiring head. He didn't bother to look toward the waiting cars of his comrades. He knew they'd be there, in place, ready. His knuckles whitened as he tightened his grip on the rifle.

The three slid down the narrow concrete walkway, past the two units in front of the fourplex, past windows ablaze with lights from the rooms behind them. In seconds they were at the patio in the middle of the four two-story apartments, the patio where each unit's sliding glass front door opened.

A large pottery jug held growing bamboo, and they crouched behind the needle-sharp leaves and slender reeds. The two men looked at the woman; she nodded and slid forward past the small screen of bamboo into the patch of light from the front door of Apartment 4. They had reached their target: the apartment where Patricia Campbell Hearst lived with Steven Weed.

Steven Weed was relaxed. He stretched out on the long sofa, leaned back and soaked up the sound from the stereo. The music was good, the dinner had been satisfying. His life was as neat as the white-duck pants he wore so often.

The only other sound was the rush of water from the upstairs bath where Patty Hearst stepped out of her shower and started toweling her slim five-foot, three-inch frame. Her long, light-brown hair turned up at the ends from the steam and waved across her face from the center part. She slipped into a pair of nylon underpants, pulled on the dark blue robe from I. Magnin's exclusive fashion shop, and passed back down the shiny hardwood stairs to Steve. Tonight was a quiet night, like most nights they shared.

Just forty-eight hours before, on Saturday night, some woman had rapped on their glass front door. She'd looked bedraggled and shabby, and the tall, thin, light-skinned black man with her had stood silently by her side. Patty still thought they had been panhandlers. There are so many in Berkeley they even have a special title: street people. Street people live by their wits and the alms of others. But Steve had said they just asked about a vacancy among the four apartments. There was no vacancy. Maybe Steve had been right—they were trying to find a place to rip off. But that had been forty-eight hours ago. Now it was 9:00 P.M. on Monday. Patty didn't even think about that strange couple at their door. By ten tonight, it would sting Steve's mind with horror.

Now, tonight, there was another rap, a gentle one, almost unheard among the sounds of the stereo. But Steve heard it. He got up, walked toward the glass front door and the darkness beyond it. Patty stopped, standing in the narrow hallway a few feet behind the front door, waiting to see who was there. She was certain it wouldn't be anyone they knew. Their few friends didn't just drop in—they called first. And Patty Hearst and Steve Weed were not activists in either the social or campus community.

Steve slid back the front door; the screen door outside it was already ajar. The first thing that flashed through his mind was "panhandler."

The woman's head hung down, her face hidden behind the mass of black hair, her voice muffled in its thickness. "Had accident in car—need phone," Steve thought he heard. But he still didn't want to let her in. She was so disheveled, he'd later explain.

He didn't get the opportunity to refuse her admittance. Before the woman had finished her mumbled words, two men jumped from behind the potted bamboo plants and crashed into the doorway, sending the skinny Steve sprawling onto the floor. He had only a glimpse—"But that's all I needed. I could see the long barrels of guns across their chests. I thought, 'Oh, God, we're being robbed.'"

"Keep your face down or you're dead!" the taller man snarled into Weed's face, as he shoved it into the cool hardwood floor.

"I laid there, he kicked me, punched me. I could feel him tying my hands behind my back. I thought, 'My God, why don't they just rob us and not kill us?' And I saw them grab Patty's wallet with her credit cards out of her purse. They took my passport too. I thought we'd die," Weed would later recall of those minutes of terror.

"I felt this blow—it crashed into my skull again and again. The blood was running down my face into my eyes. He was beating me with a full bottle of wine Patty and I had on the bookshelf near the front door. I couldn't see, between the blood in my face and the beating that kept my face smashed into the floor. But I heard. I heard Patty struggling, screaming, then whimpering in the kitchen just a few feet from me. Then I heard the woman's voice say, 'Shut up or we'll have to hurt you.'

"That's when it hit me: 'This is no robbery. They are doing something else, not robbing us.'"

But Steve Weed says he still didn't know what was happening; all he knew was that he heard the sharp click of the rifle bolt snapping into position for firing; the click seemed to explode in his ear.

"I knew they'd kill me—I had nothing to lose now, so I jumped up, screaming. I just ran, ran around the living room, smashing into furniture, overturning the lamps, anything at all, screaming, screaming all the time. I saw that tall black man standing there, watching me run around like a crazy man screaming. He had the rifle pointed straight at me—he could pull that trigger at any time. But he just stood there, almost smiling.

"I didn't scream words, not like *help* or *police*, just sounds— just screams. I didn't know what to do—I was almost crazy. Then I saw them, the white woman and the shorter black man. They

7

had Patty. She was still struggling but they were carrying her out the hall, out to the front door.

"That's when I ran out the back door, still screaming. Somehow, while I was the madman in the living room, I had worked my hands free. I ran across the backyard, over the fence. I don't know where or when I stopped running or when I stopped screaming."

It was three backyards away, three fences later, that neighbors finally calmed Steve Weed enough to silence his screams and stop his running.

Other neighbors heard the screams and the crashings and rushed toward the apartment to help. A young Asian was grabbed as he came around the corner from his front apartment. The tall black man grabbed him, slammed him into the floor already soaked with Steve's blood, and pounded his head with the same bottle that already dripped with the blood of Steven Weed.

Two young women living directly next door rushed out their sliding glass front door. They saw Patty struggling, her robe ripped from her breasts, her body being hauled away like a sack of coal by the stocky, short black man and the slender young white woman. The taller black man rushed from the apartment where the neighbor lay unconscious, the apartment Steve Weed had fled. He turned and saw the two women—bullets from his rifle splintered the shingles next to their heads. The women screamed, rushed inside, stumbling as they raced toward the telephone to call for help.

The three figures in combat boots rushed toward the waiting convertible where their first kidnap victim, Peter Benenson, still shuddered on the floorboards. The trunk lid flew open, Patricia Hearst was thrown inside, and the lid slammed down on her weakening whimpers.

Benenson felt the car rock from the sudden weight in the trunk. He'd also heard the crack of the bullets, and now he waited for the one he was sure would pierce his brain. The doors were flung open, the three jumped inside. Motor roaring, the car spun out of the driveway, careened around the corner and raced toward Derby Street, which leads into the Berkeley foothills. The old white Chevy station wagon roared off behind the kidnap car, the dark blue Volkswagen right behind it. Two blocks away, the three-car caravan, with its cargo of two victims, slowed to normal speed, all eyes watching the side streets and looking behind them. Was anyone following? They drove silently by the California School for the Deaf and Blind.

They swung around a side curve and turned into block-long Tanglewood Drive, the street of Berkeley's finest old mansions, hidden from the peasantry by towering hedges and higher walls. The lone streetlamp was an old-fashioned one, preferred for its romantic glow, not for its functional illumination.

All three cars slowed, then stopped. Peter Benenson had now been rolled around his own floorboards for an hour and a half. Again, he heard the trunk of his car snap open, felt the convertible's gentle roll as a weight was lifted out of it. He heard a voice hiss down on him: "Stay down, stay put, and you won't get hurt! Look up and you're dead!"

He didn't look up. If he had, he might have seen the no-longer-struggling form of the half-naked Patty Hearst being carried to the waiting station wagon and then dumped inside by the two black men. He would have seen the woman in the front seat of the wagon lean over and pull a worn, soiled blanket over Patty Hearst's huddled body. The woman from the combat trio jumped into the wagon, the two men raced to the Volkswagen, and both cars drove off.

He waited minutes, hours. He didn't know how long. He just knew his body was shaking with terror, his muscles screaming from their long-cramped position. His head throbbed with pain. His hands were cold and numb from the cords that bound them behind his back. But he didn't move. Only his mind raced on.

Were they waiting across the street, ready to shoot his head off as soon as he raised it to window level? Were they standing right over him, just outside the car, the gun aimed at him, ready to send a bullet smashing into his skull? Had they really gone off in the other two cars? Or were they still here, holding the power of life or death over him?

But pain and cold and terror can overcome the urge to live. Peter Benenson finally gave up; he edged upward, leaning on the back seat, not breathing, waiting for the impact of a bullet.

There was only silence.

He leaned higher, onto his knees, his head above the seat

level, silhouetted against the dark night—a perfect target. He waited for death. It didn't come.

He crawled, fell, pulled, until he was out of the car, stumbling as he tried to stand on the legs that had been warped under him. All he knew was that he had to get away, away from those silent people hauling bodies in and out of his car, away from the guns and the bullets they spit out. He walked down Tanglewood Drive, down the same streets the three cars had earlier climbed. He walked past the quiet elegance of Berkeley's mansions, into the hum of the student apartment centers, down to the flatlands and its dirt and grime, around the green edge of the campus. He crossed Hearst Avenue and kept walking. Two, three, four miles. By now his hands were free. Somewhere, somehow, the cords had slipped off. He didn't bother to think of or question their absence. He just kept walking.

At the other end of Berkeley, he reached his sister's house. He knocked and she opened the door to his terror-stricken face. The words spilled out of him—the guns, the bodies, the sounds, the hours. She asked if he wanted the police. He looked at her and said, "No, I can't; they'd kill me."

So it would be dawn before police found the empty convertible with its trunk standing open on Tanglewood Drive. They had known of the Patty Hearst kidnapping within minutes, but they couldn't follow any trail. They didn't know Peter Benenson had been the first abduction victim. The "all points bulletin"—APB of police radios—crackled across the Bay Area, alerting the police in San Francisco, Oakland, San Jose, reaching up into the vineyards around Sonoma and near the state prison at Vacaville.

"Be on the lookout—a white female, two black male Americans. Driving a 1962 or '63 Chevrolet convertible; hostage, Patricia Campbell Hearst, white female American, nineteen years old, five feet, three inches, a hundred and ten pounds, long brown hair, brown eyes, mole on right side of chin. Last seen wearing a blue bathrobe; may be nude."

Police knew all this from neighbors and from hospital interviews with Steve Weed and the bloody and beaten neighbor who had tried to help.

The police brass called across the Bay to Hillsborough, to the home of the victim's parents, Randolph and Catherine Hearst. They told them the bare-bone facts: "Your daughter Patricia was carried screaming into the night by a white female and two black males. They all had guns; they fired bullets at neighbors."

The police didn't add that small dark stains had seeped out of the spent bullets, stains the police already feared might prove to be cyanide.

In Hillsborough, the Hearsts did what little they could to cope with the horror that confronted them. They asked police not to divulge that their daughter had been living with Steven Weed. They were shocked that she was half-naked—and police took steps to keep that out of their reports. But was half-clothed any more acceptable than half-naked?

The San Francisco office of the Federal Bureau of Investigation geared up. This was their meat, their specialty. They were ready. They would stand by the family, stake out the place of the ransom payoff, and grab the kidnappers—just as they had so many other times.

A gag order went out: no press coverage. Most of the news media were locked down for the night anyway. Television's 11:00 P.M. news is seldom more than a warm-up of the 6:00 P.M. news. Radio stations rarely monitored police radios all night, and it was only the urgent APB, echoed in newspaper city rooms, that brought any puzzled inquiries from a few police-beat reporters.

"No coverage. Hold the story—or you'll endanger Patty Hearst's life."

That was the constant word for the next twelve hours, and reporters rushed back to their editors to warn them not to use the biggest story in the state. Editors checked to see who had put the lid on the Hearst kidnapping; no one would say, and rumors rumbled that Randolph Hearst had pushed it down, demanding no coverage of his daughter's abduction. Police hedged, refusing to say whether the stricture was the result of parental or police concern. But the news media accepted it. By the next morning there was talk of little else inside Bay Area newsrooms.

No one reported the kidnapping. So no one knew that the white woman and two black men they might drive by on a freeway were now the subjects of the biggest manhunt in California's history. The lid stayed clamped down through the night, past sunrise. Then at 9:00 A.M., former U.S. Senator William F. Knowland called the Berkeley police. He was the owner-publisher of *The Oakland Tribune,* the major daily newspaper of Berkeley and its neighbor city, Oakland. He warned them his afternoon paper would headline the kidnapping. Police pleaded with him to keep on the gag. The FBI warned solemnly that any news coverage would endanger the ransom drop. Had there been a ransom demand? No, they admitted, but it must be on its way. After all, that's routine in all kidnappings, the local agent in charge, Charles Bates, assured others from his FBI office in San Francisco's Federal Building.

But the old man who had served in the Senate for decades wouldn't give in. It's news, it's to be reported, he ordered. (Before the month ended, Knowland himself would be found floating in a river, his death labeled a suicide.) Police scrambled to alert the rest of the media, the ones who had quietly agreed to be gagged. They called KGO-TV, where Jim Dunbar had just finished his morning television talk show and was about to gear up for his three-hour hitch as the communicaster on KGO Radio. He sat in the tiny cubbyhole of a broadcast booth waiting for the phone lines to light up with callers. Instead he got the call of the kidnapping—by noon it would be on the streets as *The Oakland Tribune* headline. He turned on his mike and broke the story: Patricia Campbell Hearst, nineteen-year-old daughter of publisher Randolph Hearst, had been kidnapped twelve hours earlier.

CHAPTER **2**

EVERY TIME there was a major break in the Symbionese Liberation Army story, I was sitting 250 miles south in the town of
San Luis Obispo at a renovated army camp, trying to teach
flint-faced law-enforcement officials "how to deal with the news
media."

I'd been there the day Oakland superintendent of schools
Marcus Foster was murdered, returning to San Francisco only
minutes before he was gunned down.

Then, when the story of Patty Hearst's kidnapping was blast-
ing out in headlines and television news bulletins, I sat in San
Luis again. It didn't really matter. So far, on February 5, no one
had connected the abduction with the SLA, and all I knew about
the Hearsts was that "The Chief," William Randolph Hearst,
had scandalized the nation, built a newspaper empire, and died
nearly a quarter of a century earlier.

Between February 4 and the end of May, I'd begin to feel
as if I'd crawled inside the very skin of Patty Hearst. So much
so that by May 30, her fiancé, Steven Weed, appearing on the

"Dick Cavett Show," would tell a national television audience that "Marilyn Baker and Patty came from similar backgrounds and I think Marilyn understands Patty."

Of course, I'll never really understand Patty Hearst, but we did share similarities that only emphasized Weed's comparison. She had gone down a road and I was trying to follow her.

An obvious similarity was that we both had fathers who adored and indulged us. But my generation was of God Bless America and beach parties; Patty's of the peace movement and pot.

I was an only child, raised in the bosom of middle-class security. It was a patterned life—private schools, country clubs, and divorced parents before I was ten. Patty was the middle child of five sisters, but she may well have been an only child. She was the pet of the family—from parents to servants—and her life revolved around private schools, country clubs, and social circles.

While I was the child pictured as the urban creation, the product of a broken home used by one parent against the other, Patty was a picture postcard of the good life in America.

Her mother, Catherine Campbell, was a southern belle when she married handsome Randolph Hearst in 1938. She was the perfect helpmate for the son of the protected Hearst publishing empire, their union the whipped-cream final fade-out of the Hollywood movies of the thirties.

The year Patty's parents set the social pace with their wedding, mine provided their country club with gossip of their divorce. My father—strong, individualistic, and charming—would come to represent little more than Christmas and birthday presents, and those generally through impersonal checks, as though the dollars and cents he gave could replace the time and attention I'd lost.

Patty's was the best of both worlds. Her father Randy was the smiling, pleasant father who met all her friends and kept any disapproval buttoned up inside his double-breasted suit. He was the constant support for the demands of Patty's mother, Catherine. The tall man who would have been called an Arrow collar ad in the thirties was now the statesman who kept peace in a mansion of females where Patty reigned supreme.

Mrs. Hearst wanted her daughters reared as Catholics. Randy

had converted to Catholicism when he married his southern beauty. But Patty had rebelled at the stern discipline of the convents, and so her father had convinced her mother to let their sun-kissed child attend other schools, equally private and expensive, but where the whims of the rich are catered to and not considered unacceptable.

I had changed schools just as frequently, but not by choice. The pattern of my divorced mother was to move every four months, whether we needed to or not. I never knew when I left for school at 8:00 A.M. if I'd be living in the same apartment when I returned at 3:00 P.M.

Patty never had to question where her home was. It was within the high walls around the twenty-two-room mansion in Hillsborough, with its formal dining room, Persian rug, swimming pool, and cabaña.

Whereas my mother demanded that I become the Second Coming of Shirley Temple, Catherine Hearst demanded only that her daughters be ladies, well-mannered and graceful. It seemed little enough to ask of a child named Hearst. Just "conduct yourself with dignity and keep your name out of the newspapers." In this family founded on newsprint, the only acceptable times their names could appear in print were at birth, marriage, and death.

The Hearsts today are private people, not like the man who sired them, William Randolph Hearst. His business was news and his life made news. Only Hollywood maverick Orson Welles dared to film *Citizen Kane*, a celluloid-veiled biography of the old man himself. I'd sat through the film ten times, absolutely enamored of this mammoth man who toppled countries, created movie stars, and ignored convention—a man bigger than life, bigger even than Hollywood's magic lantern could encompass.

There was the story of how he had sent a photographer to Cuba to cover the Spanish-American War. The befuddled photographer wired back: CAN'T FIND WAR. Hearst shot back a cable with the terse message: YOU FURNISH PICTURES, I'LL FURNISH WAR. Hearst was as good as his cable.

It was The Chief, as the reporters nicknamed him, who had built San Simeon, a castle no king could afford. There he'd enthroned his movie queen, Marion Davies, the love of his life, while his socially correct wife, Millicent, stood firm, refusing the one thing the giant wanted—a divorce. Hearst's gifts to Marion Davies were legendary, but the one I remembered most was his order that whenever her picture appeared in a Hearst newspaper, it was to be one of the Hollywood glamour shots taken in the 1930s. This unspoken rule continued into the forties and fifties. The Chief gave Marion the ultimate gift—eternal youth, in newsprint.

But all that was history, buried with The Chief in 1951, three years before Patty was born. It was history that Patty's mother and father had studiously ignored and that Patty had shown no interest in at all. She didn't need a Hollywood film to tell her who she was or what genes had created her. She was a Hearst. That was enough.

At fourteen I had attended a private girls' school where I fell in love with the boy who delivered the morning paper. When Patty was fourteen, her suitor was the socially correct heir to a fortune as established as the Hearsts'—sixteen-year-old Stanley Dollar III of the steamship millions.

Patty at that time was chafing under the stern discipline of the Santa Catalina Convent, hidden behind the twisted pines along California's rocky coast. Young Dollar was ensconced in the Robert Louis Stevenson Boys' School just a few miles away.

Theirs was a love via letters, each writing the other almost daily. But Stanley Dollar's letters were more of the underage Elizabeth Barrett Browning kind, while Patty's tended toward O. Henry—scribbles of how much she loved Stanley but managing to peel off the luster of the words with a final jibe or joke. They wrote each other about their problems, problems that stemmed more from their being among the chosen few of their generation than anything else. Patty was appalled by the hippie cult, telling her sixteen-year-old boyfriend that she could never become one, that she couldn't stand their filth.

"There is no hope for me in this 'turned on' generation," she penciled in one letter, covering pages with her rejection of drugs of any type. Young Dollar was crushed. He wanted his love to be honest and pure, so he wrote back and admitted the worst: He'd smoked pot. Patty's immediate reply was sizzling. It was all over. She was through: no boy who smoked pot for proper Miss Patty. Stanley did what others in the same situation have done for centuries: He wrote back and lied, claiming it had all been a joke; he'd never touched the stuff. Patty's answer was swift. She forgave him, she'd take him back. But that was the last letter he ever received from her.

Now, five years later, Stanley Dollar III sits in a house in a vineyard in the northern outlands of California, musing over the girl he once loved, telling reporters from *Newsday* that Patty's smile obsessed him.

For Patty, it was on to new and bigger conquests and still another new school, having already convinced her father to intercede with her mother to take her from the convent. She enrolled at Crystal Springs School, still private, still peopled with two hundred other Patty Hearsts, but a school not as demanding, slightly more tolerant of the whims of children of the rich.

Even there Patty demanded more than her share of privileges. Other girls were not allowed to bring a car to school. Patty did. Other students had to wear uniforms, the great equalizer among the rich. Patty didn't. She wore her own clothes, despite grumbles from both students and faculty.

And there, in the heart of the safe and secure Crystal Springs campus, came the ultimate challenge for Patty Hearst: to win the man that two hundred of her contemporaries were battling over, the twenty-four-year-old shaggy-haired math teacher, Steven Weed. He was one of only three men on campus and, as the youngest, the "prize" the girls fought for, some laboring to win his favor by good grades, others hatching elaborate schemes to see him after class. Patty initiated her own campaign.

She didn't take one of Weed's classes, but she was always there. For the first few weeks, she intrigued him with tales about the difficulty of bearing the Hearst name. It worked. After all, he'd never known what it was to struggle under the load of a legendary name.

But he wasn't exactly head over heels in love. As he would later recall, for the first six months he could take her or leave her. But Patty didn't leave him. She spent the weeknights at his apartment, inventing excuses why she wasn't in the virginal dormitory where the young ladies were supposed to be tucked in safely every night.

Before the year was out, Patty had snared the plum, the love of the rather nondescript flaccid young man, Steve Weed. She didn't even bother to gloat. After all, wasn't it only natural for the prize to belong to a Hearst?

Steve Weed was what Patty wanted, and Patty got what she wanted. It was as simple as that. Weed is shy, soft-spoken; his attention never goes beyond his own narrow boundaries. Patty slid into his world and made it hers without a ripple. Weed was no match for this seventeen-year-old.

Her parents were furious. Steve Weed was not their idea of the ideal match. Her mother pleaded with Patty, "Go on to Stanford University." Patty would have none of it. She was going to Berkeley, to the University of California, where her mother is a regent and a street bears the family name. Besides, that's where Weed had decided to go for graduate study. Patty may have been only seventeen, but she was wise enough to know her hold on Steve might slip if she were separated from him by two campuses. To Patty the solution was simple. She would move in with Weed. Then her prize would be safe from aggressors.

The notion of their favorite daughter living with this gangly young man who slunk about their home sent shivers down the Hearsts' spines. They demanded, pleaded, cajoled, and bribed. But after seventeen years of pampering, it was too late to start laying down restrictions.

It was her father who finally gave in, asking only that Patty try not to let it leak to the newspapers that she was living with this man. Her mother remained outraged, but was unable to do anything against the combination of the daughter backed by her father.

Patty had been getting along well on a $100-a-month allowance and a stack of credit cards signed by Randolph A. Hearst for emergencies, whatever she might believe them to be. She gently reminded her father that now she'd be sharing the rent and home upkeep with her twenty-four-year-old lover. The hint was heard. Her allowance was jumped to $300 a month and she moved out, still carrying the cushion of daddy's credit cards in her purse. It was a cushion that softened the hard knocks for a young couple starting out.

Weed had selected their home, one of four modern apartments in a brown-shingled building, just south of the Berkeley campus. The rent was $250 a month, an astronomical sum for most struggling students but hardly beyond the range of Patty Hearst. There were two bedrooms, a living room, dining alcove, kitchen, and bath in a campus community where one private room per person is rare.

But no similarity can be drawn between the love affair of Patty and Steve, and that of her late grandfather William Randolph Hearst and Marion Davies. Patty and Steve quickly turned into Mr. and Mrs. Upper-Middle America. While all around them street people scammed for pennies, radicals plotted revolutions, and students staged sit-ins, Patty and Steve collected antiques.

By my eighteenth birthday I had been a reporter on William Randolph Hearst's *Los Angeles Examiner* for two years. My father told me how proud he was that I was so self-sufficient. On Patty's eighteenth birthday, her father gave her an $8,000 check. That money helped turn her and Steve's two-bedroom apartment into a small niche of affluent America, a civilized enclave in the midst of the teeming humanity of Berkeley.

"One day I saw them strolling across campus. They were hand in hand, like they always were. You never saw one without the other. Patty was in white sharkskin slacks, knife-sharp creases in them, and a flowered blouse. Weed wore those white-duck pants he favors. It struck me that they belonged in an F. Scott Fitzgerald novel, not on this campus of jeans and sweat shirts and radicals," a professor later recalled.

Their friends would agree. An evening with Patty and Steve was straight out of yesteryear. Good food, cooked by Patty who prided herself on her culinary talent, and vintage wine, not the mountain red Gallo that graced other Berkeley tables. A few classical records on a fine stereo player. Oriental rugs on the floors, fine china, and silver. Conversation that could be heard back in Hillsborough more often than in Berkeley. As for politics, Weed would say, "We just never talked about that. Patty wasn't interested. In fact, she was rather annoyed by the street vendors and peddlers in Berkeley and the political radicals. She thought they had no right to block the sidewalks."

One of my earliest breaks in the Patty Hearst news coverage was getting the first in-depth interview with Steven Weed. It was just a couple of weeks after the kidnapping and he'd been avoiding the news media entirely, staying with the Hearsts in Hillsborough where a law-enforcement official would describe him as "just creeping about from one room to the other."

The interview was hardly the cloak-and-dagger stuff the rest of the journalists tried to turn it into. I called the Hearst home and asked Mrs. Hearst if she'd have Weed ring me so that I could interview him. She and I seemed to get along. In fact, if there was to be any one hero or heroine in the SLA story, it was Catherine Hearst, a tiny woman with an iron will and great dignity.

"Marilyn, I'm sure it's all right for you to talk to him. Randy and I both admire so much the way you've been reporting on all this," she answered. And as good as her word, within five minutes Weed was on the phone from Hillsborough. His personality is less than scintillating. On the phone he had all the verve of mush. But he agreed to the interview, adding, "I have no car. You'll have to pick me up here." Buses don't exist for the likes of Weed or the Hearsts.

Bob Huestis, cameraman and the best of video-journalists, took off, drove straight to the Hearst home, picked up Weed, and brought him back to KQED.

The press corps continued to toss a football back and forth in front of the Hearst home.

Weed turned out to be no more than his front-page photos had promised—reedy of limb and body and voice, concerned lest he appear less than sincere on camera. We spent two days talking. It seemed impossible that this cool, calm, unemotional man could be the lover of the kidnapped Patty Hearst.

Weed probably never saw the walls go up in Berkeley. He'd been a semipolitical activist back at Princeton, having actually roomed with the president of the campus chapter of Students for a Democratic Society, a high-sounding title for a group that spawned violence.

By the next day he had agreed to talk in front of the camera. Again Bob Huestis picked him up at the Hearst mansion and spirited him up into the hills above Hillsborough to the home of KQED's Jim Raeside. As he talked to me it was obvious it had never occurred to him that Patty hadn't shared his life; he had shared hers. It was Patty Hearst who had spelled out their lifestyle during those past two years in Berkeley, not Steven Weed. And it was Patty who was dominant, not Steve.

Now, as I interviewed him, Weed seemed more preoccupied

with the problems of being a guest in the Hearst mansion than distraught over where the love of his life might be. He offered examples of his ordeal: "We were all just sitting around in the living room and Catherine got up and started pacing and she was so agitated. She clenched her fists and almost screamed, 'If I could just get my hands on them [SLA], I'd strangle them with my bare hands.'"

I silently answered Catherine Hearst, saying, "I'll help you."

Weed droned on. "Can you imagine anything so ridiculous?"

Yes, I could, I thought. And if it had been either of my sons in Patty's place, I probably would have said exactly what Mrs. Hearst had said.

But Weed wasn't finished. "Then she turned, with me sitting right there, and she demanded, 'Whatever happened to the real men in this world, men like Clark Gable? No one would have carried my daughter off if there'd been a real man there.'"

Weed looked at me, "Can you imagine her saying that with me right there?"

I wanted to shout out loud, "Right on, Catherine!" but Bob Huestis took one look at my face and quickly changed the subject. He realized that Weed was not about to sit still for an interview with a reporter who appeared less than totally sympathetic.

But Weed hadn't even seen the flare of anger in my face. He went right on, still occupied with his hassles with the Hearsts, seldom mentioning the vanished Patty. "Patty and I always thought her mother was so hypocritical. She'd say one thing to your face and another behind your back. Like, if you asked her if she liked a new dress, she'd tell you how beautiful it was, then you'd hear her telling the cook 'Isn't it awful?'"

Again the thunder in my head. Hadn't he ever heard of tact, or would he tell you to your face your new dress was awful? Yes, he probably would.

When you can't communicate, you settle for small talk. I asked the obvious: "How long will you be staying with the Hearsts?"

"Oh, I already left and stayed with friends for a week. I just couldn't take it. Do you know, the Hearsts have cookies brought in by the box from the bakery every day; they don't even have home-made cookies?"

21

Horrors! What an ordeal this young man must have suffered, I thought, and bit my tongue for the thousandth time in two days. Try another tack. Surely he would want to sing the praises of his love. "What was Patty like?" I asked.

"Oh, she's pretty, you know, the prettiest of any of the Hearsts' daughters. But then, none of them are raving beauties.

"She's a bright girl too. Not brilliant, of course, but reasonably bright. She's a simple girl. The simple things please her. She rarely got angry and then it would all be over in a few minutes. She has a very good character too."

Dear Lord, was this person he described actually the woman he loved, the one who had screamed, "Not me, oh please, not me!" in the night at her captors?

Maybe the description of the girl was accurate. She would have been a fitting partner for Steve Weed. But could this be the child of Catherine Hearst of the clenched fists, the passion, the fire and brimstone? Or the child of Randolph Hearst, decent, trying to please, a man of his word? God knows it was not the granddaughter of old William Randolph Hearst. If the SLA had ever dared kidnap him, he undoubtedly would have given them exactly five minutes to surrender to him, or else.

And about the only similarity between the Hearst of legend and this mustachioed man sitting beside me was that both had little regard for others. When our host, Jim Raeside, offered a glass of cold cream soda, I said I'd love it. That's one of my favorites. Weed asked for water with ice, adding, "I always wondered who drank that cream-soda shit."

I cringed at the insult to our host, much as I'm sure Patty's mother would have cringed at such an insult, but Weed mumbled right along, as though insulting one's host were an acceptable act.

I tried to listen, but my mind was too busy trying to conjure up an image, an image of what had brought Steve and Patty together.

Had any wonderful, low animal moans of satisfaction strained through Weed's mustache or shuddered out of the thin pressed lips that looked out at me from the picture of Patricia Campbell Hearst?

For me love had been a rolling, rocking embrace that stretched the muscles, seared the blood, and melted the bones.

What was love to Patty and Steve?

Yet there must be something besides strolling through antique shops, sipping vintage wine, listening to music, sharing an upper-middle-class life in an semi-upper-class apartment.

In all that Steve Weed said, I could find only one thread of blood and guts and determination: Patty's stand that she be allowed to move in with Weed. That was a slender thread at most, almost a Victorian revolution in an age when group sex can be found in the classified ads.

But at least Patty had done it; she'd taken that decisive step outside the leafy walls of Hillsborough into the campus caldron of Berkeley. Once inside the caldron, it appeared that she and Weed had quickly manufactured their own mini-Hillsborough.

To me, Patty Hearst still seemed more paper doll than person. A pretty face seen in fuzzy focus in a high-school yearbook.

A girl-child playing at conquests.

A lover without orgasm.

CHAPTER 3

By dawn on February 6 the "lid was off" the kidnapping of Patty Hearst.

A million electronic wires carried the bare facts from the news-service offices to their eager subscribers—newspapers, radio stations, television outlets. The long rolls of yellow copy paper covered with the hieroglyphics of journalism spewed out on city-room floors around the world. Everyone wanted to know what had really happened in the campus town of Berkeley. London, Munich, Rome, Paris, Hong Kong, Rio de Janeiro waited. And small towns and other campus communities like Ames, Iowa, Claremont, California, and Bloomington, Indiana, also waited.

It meant more news to crack into already bulging front pages, the meaning plucked and played with until only the bones remained.

Yet there was so little to speculate about in this new worldwide headline story:

> Beautiful heiress Patricia Campbell Hearst, 19,
> daughter of publisher Randolph Hearst, was kid-
> napped Monday night in Berkeley. Two black

men and a white woman dragged her screaming into a car. Miss Hearst's fiancé, Steven Weed, 26, was taken to the hospital badly beaten by her abductors.

No mention of why Patty Hearst had been at her fiancé's apartment. No word that she and Weed had shared it for more than two years. Not a word that her bathrobe had been ripped from her body, and that, except for the nylon panties, she was nude as she struggled against her fate. Not even any long summations about who Randolph Hearst really is, or about the father who had sired him and become a legend.

For Berkeley's Police Chief Charles Plummer, there didn't have to be any of that information in a newspaper. He knew it already. Just one month in the chief's small corner office and he has this kind of case to cope with. Damn! Why didn't it happen last month, Christmas, or any other time? Why just when he was given the chief's badge that Bruce Baker had worn so long? Oh, Plummer knew, all right. Baker had retired. It hadn't come as any surprise. Not after the good citizens of Berkeley had elected a City Council, half of whose members had run on the radical platform. Not after that same City Council started up all that nonsense about "police review boards" and "citizen input," whatever the hell that was supposed to mean.

Charlie Plummer knew why Baker had resigned all right. Right now, sitting at the shiny-topped desk in the two-by-four office of the chief, he wished he were with Baker up in Portland, Oregon, still second in command. Baker had it made—pension from Berkeley, plus being police chief of Portland.

But it was no good to think about that. Charlie Plummer had a crime on his hands. Not any run-of-the-mill crime, but the kind every cop in the country has nightmares about.

Victim: Daughter of one of the city's—no, the nation's—most prominent families.

Facts: Obscure. You can't say where she lived. You can't admit that the fourplex at 2603 Benvenue was more than the scene of the snatch. You can't tell the press what she was wearing.

Her father controls one of the major newspapers in the whole of the Bay Area. Thank God for small favors. At least Old Man Hearst had been dead more than twenty years. The cops could be grateful for that, anyway.

The old man, William Randolph Hearst, had built an empire on the very thing the police feared: the news media. And built it with bricks of money that seemed to come from some endless supply. The great William Randolph Hearst, the man who used the clout of that money and media to make, or break, anyone, from movie stars to presidents. He'd even played a major role in the rise to glory of Billy Graham.

At least his offspring, Randolph Apperson Hearst, didn't try to play God, like his old man had. Randy was a decent enough guy, from all Chief Plummer had heard. But that didn't change the fact that Plummer sat there, police chief of Berkeley, where a street had been named Hearst Avenue, and that he had to get the daughter back, the kidnappers caught, and the whole mess solved, while making sure nothing leaked out that could tarnish the magic name of Hearst. Like the fact that Patty was living with Steve Weed. What nineteen-year-old girl in Berkeley wasn't living with some guy? Maybe her father should be glad it was only one. Berkeley isn't known for its puritanical ethic—or it's work ethic either, for that matter.

And work was what this case demanded. Chief Plummer started in. Call in Lieutenant David Johnson, crack man in the detective bureau, and team him with Detective Dan Wolke. They had worked together before, and well. Let's hope their record holds.

Dave Johnson is a tall, solid man with Madison Avenue good looks. If he weren't a cop, he could be a model for the tweed sport coats he favors. Dan Wolke is quieter, slightly shorter, with a professional air about him, in solemn colors with a solemn face above them. They have great respect for each other.

They geared up. One tiny glass-walled room, with the department's open line sitting next to an unlisted phone. Quick calls to the snitches who would turn in their mothers for a guarantee of no hassle on their next bust. Get all the reports, the statements. The statements of neighbors and Steve Weed and anyone else who might have seen something. Go over the statement of Peter Benenson again. It sounded weird. Was he telling the truth, that he just stayed down on the floorboards through the whole thing? That he just walked four miles to his sister's house when it was all over?

Berkeley was ready, the push was on. And both Johnson and Wolke kept the thought at the backs of their minds: The ransom demand will hit soon. That's the first key to unlock Patty Hearst's cage of captivity.

Oakland is south of Berkeley; the city limits of one ends where the city limits of the other takes up. That's about all they have in common. Oakland, sprawl of industrial sites, heavy black population, run-down shops facing torn-up streets. Gertrude Stein had said it all years ago. "There is no there, there in Oakland." Oakland is a city where no one comes from and where few go.

But Police Captain Joseph Lothrop was in Oakland. Tall, stocky, craggy Captain Lothrop sat in his empty office, running a hand through the tight gray curls that cover his head. His eyes, set in a million squint wrinkles, were thoughtful.

He knew that the Berkeley police and the FBI were just waiting for a ransom note. They were certain it was money that was behind the kidnapping. Why else would anyone grab the daughter of one of the Hearsts?

Lothrop wasn't quite so sure. He'd been on the case since the police first learned that the small evil-looking stains left by the bullets fired into the brown-shingled home of Patty Hearst were actually cyanide. Cyanide-laced bullets—just like the bullets that had killed Marcus Foster back in November in Oakland. That's how the Oakland police got into this act, an act Lothrop wished they had no part of.

But what other law-enforcement agency knew anything about the self-styled Symbionese Liberation Army?

John Lothrop knew about it. This SLA had written two letters. The letter dated November 6 and delivered to the *San Francisco Chronicle* claimed responsibility for the vicious murder of Foster. It had warned: "This attack is also to serve notice on the fascist Board of Education and its fascist supporters that The Court of the People have issued a death Warrant on All Members and Supporters of the Internal Warfare Identification Computer System. This shoot-on-sight order will stay in effect until such time as all political police are removed from our schools and all photos and other forms of identification are stopped."

The letter ended: "Death to the fascist insect that preys upon the life of the people."

And Lothrop knew they weren't crackpots. That SLA letter had referred to the cyanide-tipped bullets. It was the cyanide the Oakland cops had kept so quiet about. Fortunately, they had good enough relations with the media that no one prodded it out onto a prime-time news show. Cyanide was the password—they'd known when they'd found the murderers by that sticky clear stinking stuff in those bullets they'd probed out of Marcus Foster's dead body.

And when the first letter came, they knew, all right. The SLA said there was cyanide. No one but the cops—and the killers—knew that.

Lothrop knew the cyanide was more a calling card than an effective killer. It would take thirty-five bullets to put enough cyanide into a man to kill him.

But it didn't take thirty-five bullets to kill Marcus Foster. Lothrop will never forget that night—November 6, 1973. Election Day. Rain kept crying down on the Bay all that day. The cold winds whipped it into faces, swirled it around feet running to polling places and back to the mobile safety of cars.

By seven that night, the voters had one hour left to cast their ballots. On the Golden Gate Bridge, linking San Francisco and Marin County, the car jam that had tied up the bridge since five was just starting to break. The Bay Bridge, the double span that reaches first from San Francisco to Yerba Buena Island, then tunnels on through to still another span stretching from the island to Oakland itself, was still heavy with traffic, snail's-pace cars afraid of the slick left on the blacktop by the constant rain.

In Oakland, just off the freeway that links to the Bay Bridge, the old brick building of the Oakland school administration was one bright spot in the sea of rain and night. Windows blazed, the heavy glass front door was in a constant swing. The school board was meeting. Dr. Marcus Foster had to be present, but he probably would have been anyway. He had lived and breathed education ever since his days back in Philadelphia when he was known as the "first black man to reach such a high position in the school system." That's when he'd first started seriously working with dropouts, trying to wheedle them back into classrooms, using threats, promises, anything—just to make them get some education. It wasn't always rewarding. Many came back, only to drop out again in a day, a week. A few stayed. It was those few who made Marcus Foster's reputation: the man who could turn the losers around, win back the dropouts, save the ghetto child.

Then, just a year ago, Oakland started its search for a school superintendent. Oakland, once known as the All-American City, home of the Oakland "A's" of pennant fame. Oakland, now almost entirely black, whose few remaining white citizens had moved closer to the hills behind it, pulling back from the ever-spreading black of the city itself.

There had to be a black school superintendent. It was the only way. But the one chosen also had to be a good school administrator. That was the yardstick—black and good. The yardstick took the measure of Marcus Foster and the job was his.

But black students and black parents weren't automatically pacified just because the head of their schools had skin the same color as theirs. Despite Marcus Foster's coal-black shiny skin, he quickly became "honkie"—the enemy. He didn't want drugs on campus, and he didn't much care what had to be done to keep twelve-year-old kids from sticking needles in their arms or to keep eleven-year-olds from popping pills into their innocent mouths. He wanted the pushers out of the schools.

But Dr. Foster was caught in the crunch that had stopped so many before him: How do you police a school with no police? He was emphatic. "There will be no uniformed officers on our campuses. No police, not while I'm school superintendent."

He did take one small step—identification cards. Simple, small, wallet-sized cards, with a student's signature and a Polaroid picture. Then, when the bearded Super Flys hit the grade schools, one quick question—"Where's your student I.D. card?"—could be the reason for tossing them out. Dr. Foster never even considered these small white cards a problem. Hadn't the students actually been paying to have one for years? It got them into the movies for half-price. Let them ride buses for less. It assured them a seat at the weekend football games. It was, in fact, a magic key that opened the door to any student activity.

But Marcus Foster hadn't reckoned with the seething hate in Oakland.

As soon as the first public hearings were held, back in April 1973, a group sprang up to battle it. The Coalition to Save Our

Schools was a title with a faint odor of the John Birch Society about it, but this time, it represented the other side of the coin. The Coalition was battling the use of I.D. cards. Coalition spokespersons labeled their issuance as "police tactics," branded the plan a method of bringing the "Gestapo" into the classroom.

And Marcus Foster was caught in a dilemma—constitutional rights versus drug-free schools. How many times had some do-good plan gone down to defeat because equally visionary do-gooders demanded that every letter of our Bill of Rights must be adhered to?

By November, Dr. Foster was almost ready to quit the fight. Forget the I.D. cards that were so acceptable to every school district but his own. Find another way to fight the drugs that turned his young charges into zombies before they were out of the eighth grade.

It was almost daily that Marcus Foster made another firmer announcement, "No cops on any campus." But the Coalition didn't hear, or didn't want to.

They attracted more and more supporters with the rallying cry, "Keep the cops out of our classrooms." It wasn't the first—and it wouldn't be the last—time a political group would use the slogan that would get it the most attention instead of the slogan that was the most accurate. After all, why would the Oakland-based Coalition to Save Our Schools be any different from the national political parties?

So the ball went back and forth. "I won't put cops in the classrooms." "Keep the cops out of the classrooms." But it was the children who were being batted to and fro.

As in any game, the longer it went on, the more heated it became. By the cold and rainy night of November 6, tempers were ragged among all the players.

Dr. Foster finished talking to the board and started out the rear of the old building. It was desolate. The freeway to the west; a parking lot on the east; tall trees, heavy with rain water, to the north; and the front entrance, with it's empty old stores, to the south.

Walking next to Foster was Robert Blackburn, the intense young white man who had been Foster's aide back in Philadelphia and who had come to Oakland to try again to help this man he idolized. They talked of the constant school problems, the problems that tonight appeared to have no solutions.

They walked down the flight of worn concrete steps into the dank alleyway under the old trees and turned east, toward the parking lot. Each had a car there. One of the few advantages of heading up Oakland's schools is that one gets a parking space with one's name stenciled on it. "Reserved for Dr. Marcus Foster."

Death waited in that alley.

All his life, Dr. Foster had fought against narcotics, for equality, and, ironically, against violence. But he had no chance to fight for his life.

Three murderers waited for this gentle man as he walked toward death, his loyal assistant at his side.

They waited in the shadows, two men, knit caps pulled low over their ears, lounging against the cold, wet bricks of the school administration building. Their comrade stood behind a tree, its gnarled trunk her cover, her hair hidden under the same type of knit cap as they wore. All three wore dark pea coats over their worn jeans. All three moved silently in their combat boots. And each appeared to have a dark complexion.

First, the woman behind the tree stepped out into the path of Foster and Blackburn with a shotgun leveled at them. A blast of fire spit from its barrel—and it ripped the life out of Marcus Foster.

The two male comrades jumped forward, no longer idle loungers. Their hands held .38 revolvers that fired into the already dead school superintendent.

Robert Blackburn spun around, just in time to catch some of the bullets aimed at his friend. They bit into his flesh, and blood spewed out, blood that quickly turned pale in the puddles of rain.

Silently, the three ran toward the street and other comrades waiting in a car to whisk them to safety, a safety where they would not see the blood leaving Marcus Foster's body, where they wouldn't continue to hear the echo of the shots smashing into the night or smell the burned flesh of their victim.

As the assailants ran toward the parking lot, Blackburn staggered toward the stairs he had walked down just seconds before.

Later, doctors would wonder how this grievously wounded man had walked at all. But fear and terror can hold torn flesh together. He climbed, each step an agony, not knowing if still another bullet would crash out of the blackness into his back, his head. Each step brought him closer to safety and closer to the confirmation of Marcus Foster's death.

The people inside were all but incoherent. They couldn't believe it. Marcus Foster could not be lying out there, nothing but a mass of torn and bleeding flesh. No longer a man at all.

Yes, Captain John Lothrop remembered that November evening well. He and Chief Charles Gains had been there within seconds. They'd wondered how KQED-TV, the public television station for the Bay Area, had known. They'd already heard the terse announcement on the nightly program, "Newsroom," on KQED: "We have been informed that Dr. Marcus Foster, superintendent of the Oakland school system, has been killed." The first announcement over KQED's Channel 9 was just minutes after seven, minutes after the guns first barked their message of death.

Peggy Stinnett is a stringer for KQED. Her prime job is reporter for a small weekly paper in the Oakland Hills called the *Montclarion*, but she also does weekly reports on "Newsroom." She had been with the city and school officials, seen the faces turn white, heard the whispers—"Foster's been killed!"—and rushed to a phone to alert "Newsroom."

Captain Lothrop remembered the swarm of cameras and microphones and people, standing in shock in the rain, that had quickly surrounded the death scene. He remembered Chief Gains, already retired, packed and ready to move to a new job in a quiet Florida city, standing in the rain, trying to make some statement about something no one understood. Gains had just four weeks left. He'd served his twenty-five years in Oakland—he had the pension, now the new Florida job. Despite his pleas that the press look to the new acting chief for comment, they wanted red-haired Charlie, the chief they knew and trusted.

Chief Charlie Gains had built a solid reputation since the 1967 antidraft riots, when he took over from a chief who had retired. His term in the big glass-walled office heading the Oakland law enforcement had started during those riots. Now it was ending with still another crime that would rip apart the city he had lived in and loved so long.

I was there, with the KQED video truck, standing in the middle of the street. In fact, I had been in on the antidraft riot too, standing next to Gains then as gas mains were broken, windows were smashed, and 5,000 rioters took over downtown Oakland.

Gains hadn't worried about me—he knew I could take care of myself in the mob. But my son, seventeen-year-old Chris, was another matter. He stood in the vortex of the mob, holding a sign reading, Ask Not What Your Country Can Do for You, But What You Can Do for Your Country, a remnant of the John F. Kennedy era somehow still hanging on in the violence of the late 1960s.

It's a wonder that kid wasn't killed, Gains said later. That sign and Kennedy quote were bad enough, but he had to carry a five-foot American flag too.

Gains had listened to my explanation; he told me he'd never forgotten it. I'd said: "My oldest son, Jeff, is in Vietnam right now, and we stand here while these creeps pass the hat, collecting money to buy the Viet Cong bullets—bullets that may kill my son, his brother. I'm damned proud Chris is out there, and God help anyone who tries to take away his right to say what he thinks."

But nobody had. Oh, there'd been scuffles. The cops managed to look the other way if Chris was winning. And he generally did. He had an incentive—his marine brother. There was the young man who had joined him, on crutches, one pant leg neatly pinned up. He'd left the leg in Vietnam. He came down from the hospital to stand with Chris after the first television news showed the lone demonstrator against the riot. There was also a tall, gangling black kid, already enlisted, just waiting for the army to take him away. He'd stood on the other side. He'd been one of two towering big dudes on the scene, well known to Gains and his men as Black Panther activists, but the Panthers were having no part of the 1967 antidraft riot. That was a white middle-class riot. So each Panther had stood near a Baker—one with Chris and one with me.

Gains had grinned when he'd seen me trotting those two Panthers right into the garage where the cops had their command post. Some of the guys bristled, but I told them, "These men are helping me. They're not your enemy. Not today."

And I felt Chief Charles Gains didn't think they were the enemy on November 6, as he looked at the five-foot-wide stain of red that had been the blood of Marcus Foster. True, witnesses kept saying "dark-complexioned." That should mean black. But Gains didn't think it did. The description of features wasn't Afro. Dark-complexioned. That could mean Chicano; it could mean anything. Even that night, as Foster's blood still spread through the continuing rain, Chief Gains thought it might mean damned little.

Captain Lothrop was already in charge. Gains would deal with the media; Lothrop, the crime. The first descriptions were garbled. "All three were small, under five feet six inches." Maybe women? It's possible, Lothrop grudgingly admitted. Women killing people? The thought was almost obscene.

News stations crackled with excitement. Election returns were all but forgotten as the murder of the Bay Area's outstanding black leader preempted other news events. The usual hackneyed phrases were repeated: "It's only a matter of time until we apprehend the killers. . . . There is no known motive. Dr. Foster was loved by everyone."

Radios and televisions hummed in homes all over the Bay in Oakland and San Francisco and Berkeley and the small towns that fringe their more cosmopolitan sisters at the hub.

Some news editors were apprehensive. Suppose Foster wasn't really dead? They hedged in the traditional manner—"KQED 'Newsroom' has reported the murder of Dr. Marcus Foster." If the report was wrong, let KQED "Newsroom" take the lumps.

I was soaked to the skin and tired from a round-trip flight to San Luis Obispo where I'd spent the day holding my news-media class for the law-enforcement officials. The only reason to be at the station at seven on November 6 was to handle the election news. Now I was with the TV crew on a murder story. The KQED truck maneuvered to get its spotlight shining down the alley, to get a shot of the actual murder scene. I dragged Chief Gains out in the rain, out of the building where witnesses were trying to stop crying long enough to give statements. He told me what I had already heard: Foster was shot by three assailants. No known motive.

34

Rumors were rife among the curious who had been drawn to the school administration building:

"It was a right-wing plot to kill off the first black ever to head a major educational district."

"It was the Nazis, putting action behind their racist words."

Other reporters poured out the description of the killers—small, dark-complexioned. But since dark-complexioned meant black, many just said "black," so the confusion grew. Why would a black kill a leading black man, a black man who had fought all his life to help his people?

KQED "Newsroom" stuck with "dark-complexioned"—not "black." Not for any valid reason, but rather from a gnawing gut feeling that "black" wasn't right.

But all that was last November, and Captain John Lothrop was not a man to dwell on the past. This was February 6, and Patty Hearst had been held by her abductors since the evening of February 4. Now the cops knew those abductors were the same ones who had killed Foster—the Symbionese Liberation Army of the cyanide-laced bullets.

Now we all waited for the ransom demand.

True, they hadn't murdered Marcus Foster for money. They claimed they had gunned him down just because he was instituting I.D. cards for students in Oakland schools.

But why abduct Patty Hearst? Why kidnap an heiress if you don't demand money?

Everyone knew the Hearst name meant money. When old William Randolph, the kidnap victim's grandfather, was alive, he'd owned 550,000 acres of timberland and a silver mine in Mexico. And if that weren't enough, he'd also owned another 212,000 acres of land in California. That's where the Hearst castle stands—San Simeon, the castle that is now a state landmark, where for a few dollars tourists can wander its marble halls, whose walls were imported from Spanish monasteries; see fountains that splash fifty feet in the air, a swimming pool surrounded by invaluable Greek statuary. A castle that was thinly disguised in Orson Welles's movie classic, *Citizen Kane*.

A simple fact sheet of Hearst holdings listed real estate in eight major cities across the nation, a paper company in the rocky state of Maine, four radio and television stations in four different states. Then there were the newspapers and magazines—a publishing empire that included nine daily papers and eighteen best-selling magazines, including five published in Britain.

There were the priceless antiques the victim's grandfather had prized so highly; most went to museums when he died in 1951. His sons couldn't pay the inheritance taxes. San Simeon went to the state. So did the wild-animal skins, 157 in all, collected long before the subject of endangered species became popular.

But there were no animal-skin rugs in son Randolph Hearst's home in Hillsborough. Just one Persian rug, and that a gift. A collection of antique vases, already deeded to museums, a collection too priceless to leave any child.

Despite the magic name of Hearst, Randolph was not the multimillionaire his father had been. He lived in comfortable affluence, not opulent luxury. The millions had all been left in an iron-clad trust fund called the Hearst Foundation. Randy's possessions were a few acres of land in California, a home in Hawaii, and the house in Hillsborough, the house that would become the backdrop for the saga of the century. Even it is something of a white elephant. It has been on the market a year at the asking price of $385,000. But there have been no takers, even at a lower price. No one really needs twenty-two rooms today, and in Hillsborough it is one of the lesser homes, its paint faded, its gardens not quite groomed.

Randy Hearst is his father's son in that he presides as publisher over a Hearst newspaper. But unlike his father, who stormed his way through life building castles, buying up newspapers, and lavishing luxuries on his mistress, Randolph Apperson Hearst hung onto his money.

A wealthy businessman recalls visiting Hearst in his office in the big granite Hearst building on San Francisco's Market Street. "As I was leaving," he says, "Randy told me to be sure and have my parking ticket validated downstairs, or the garage next door would charge me. So I reassured him, 'All right, I will.'"

About then the elevator arrived, but before the businessman had a chance to step inside, Randy Hearst was in the hallway, calling out a final warning, "Make sure you get that ticket validated. If you don't, the garage will charge you seventy-five cents."

That 75¢ was important to this man whose father had lavished millions on whims; Randolph didn't have those millions. Just two weeks before she was kidnapped, Patty had asked her fiancé, Steve Weed, "What do you think my father's worth?"

"About twenty million dollars, I would guess," Steve recalled answering. Months later he'd muse, "It's funny, I really thought that then, but once all this SLA thing happened, I started doing some checking on my own—Randy's lucky to have about two million actually. But I didn't know that then, and neither did Patty."

But whatever the expected ransom note demanded for the return of his daughter, Randy would meet it—with his entire fortune if necessary. Or, if that weren't enough, with the millions he would borrow from the Hearst Foundation.

Everyone at the Hearst home waited for a ransom note. So did the Berkeley police. So did the FBI, anxious to get its teeth into the type of crime it handles best. So did the media, now swarming in front of the Hearst home in big Winnebago news vans bulging with reporters who whiled away the hours of waiting with gin rummy games or a few tosses of a football. Cameras and microphones webbed the front of the house, all aimed in expectation at the double front door. Telephones linking the "scene of the suffering" with city desks around the world sprang up— phones under bushes, in suitcases, trailing out of trailers, even nailed on trees.

A tall loose-limbed man with a lived-in face arrived. His suit was the uniform proper to the circumstances: dull color, narrow lapel, narrow dark tie, and spotless white shirt. Even his jewelry was right—a small metal American flag in the lapel. Charles Bates, the local agent in charge of the FBI, had arrived to wait with the Hearsts for the ransom demand. He didn't know then, on February 6, that it would be the first of almost nightly visits, visits that deteriorated into silent sips of Scotch and meaningless words.

Today he walked briskly past the pink roses around the house, sure-footedly climbed the stone steps, rapped on the door with an authoritative air. He was certain that he and his agents would quickly wrap this up. Why shouldn't they? They'd made all the right moves: agents in position around the Bay, the repeated public statements that "Patty's life comes first. We will do nothing to harm her." Even the statement that if they "knew right now where the SLA was, we wouldn't move in if it would endanger Patty."

Everyone waited. Charles Bates, with the American flag tightly pinned to his lapel. Randolph Hearst, trying to be decent about the whole thing, terror not yet quite on the surface. His wife Catherine attending to the amenities through her fears.

In Berkeley, Dave Johnson and Dan Wolke waited, impatient to get going, to solve this horrendous crime in their city.

In Oakland, Captain Lothrop waited, checking as he did so, unsure that the Symbionese were going to demand money, uncertain whether this was going to be another feather in the cap of the FBI.

And in "Newsroom," the second floor of a dilapidated warehouse cum television station, others waited. They sat in the old leather chairs where mice had chewed through the stuffing; they drank the cold rancid coffee made hours before. Joe Russin, news director, coiled like a spring ready for action. His mind was racing with notions of how to cover the kidnapping. He'd be ready. Within the news business, Joe Russin was known as the best—the brightest kid in any classroom. The man who could cut through the nonsense to the meat of any news. The tall lanky Wyoming cowboy who could ride herd on his reporters—and did.

Now we were on the trail of the SLA, but the trail didn't seem to lead anywhere.

CHAPTER **4**

THE FIRST AND ONLY major break in connection with the
Symbionese Liberation Army was the arrest of two of their soldiers on January 10, 1974. I had grinned reading the news
bulletin. It had happened just as I'd said it would—not because
of any super sleuthing, à la Efrem Zimbalist, Jr. and television's
"FBI," but by something as penny ante as the soldiers driving a
van around the block once too often. Too bad Hollywood seldom
tells the story of how crimes are really solved—because someone
runs a stoplight or overparks or doesn't pay a utility bill.

The point was it had happened. Now the seven-headed cobra
kill-cult wasn't just a faceless symbol spitting its venomous
cyanide. It was two flesh-and-blood men, Joe Remiro and Russell
Little. They had been stopped at 1:30 A.M. by Deputy Sheriff
David Duge of Contra Costa County, who became suspicious after
he noticed their white van circling the block several times. The
men claimed they were looking for a family named DeVoto on
Sutherland Court in suburban Clayton. Sergeant Duge checked

with headquarters and found there was no listing for a DeVoto at the address.

Duge ordered the men out of their vehicle, and then Remiro allegedly drew a gun from his belt and began firing. Duge shot back. Little was hit in the shoulder but escaped in the van. He was arrested several blocks away by another patrol car. Remiro escaped on foot and was picked up four hours later when police found him hiding behind a bush in a driveway.

The reason Remiro and Little had tried to resist arrest soon became clear. Not only did they turn out to be SLA members—their van was littered with SLA documents—but the revolver Little had used in the shootout with Duge was a .38— the same caliber as one of the weapons used in the murder of Marcus Foster.

The police were elated. So was I. After two months of investigation involving endless legwork and talking to hundreds of people, it looked as though the Foster case was about to break wide open.

Then at 6:00 P.M. of that same day another bombshell burst: A fire—obviously set deliberately—broke out in a house on Sutherland Court in Clayton—only two blocks from where Remiro and Little had been arrested. SLA literature was strewn about inside. Cyanide was found in the attached two-car garage, as well as metal filings, as though bullets had been hollowed out on a workbench there. It didn't take any great brain to figure out that this was the "safe house" of the elusive SLA, the hideout where they made their revolutionary plans and had plotted the murder of Marcus Foster.

Now the tracking started.

Grab the directories, the city's, the one that lists by phone numbers; get the voter's registration office on the phone, have them pull all the Littles and Remiros. A total madhouse, of course, coffee spilling over papers, phones ringing with run-of-the-mill tips, and calls such as "My dog was killed at the pound —can't you do something?"

"No, lady, I can't. Sorry." And I really was. I love dogs.

"Mrs. Baker, I know about corruption in a nearby city's police department. Can you expose it?"

"Sorry, sir, I'm already on an assignment."

And I'm especially sorry about that: Corrupt cops tend to rot the good ones around them. But I was assigned the SLA story; I had no time for anything else.

Four different city directories later, I found it. "Joseph Remiro," an address on 48th Avenue in San Francisco's Sunset district. It figured. The house Remiro and Little had been arrested near—their safe house—is in the heart of a middle-class white area. So is the Sunset district—all row houses, marching hip to jowl over what was once rolling sand dunes, west of Twin Peaks, out in San Francisco's fog belt.

But the number had been disconnected. The tinny metal recording sent my hopes crashing, until I heard the last sentence: "That number has been changed to . . ."

That new listing was my hot lead. I immediately shared my break with Joe Russin. He agreed: Get on it.

I spent six hours on it. The fact that the number was listed to a young attorney living at the other end of San Francisco Bay in Fremont, another bedroom community, didn't daunt me. Couldn't Remiro have an attorney for a front? It seemed logical.

Walt Bjerke, who would handle the videotaping today, tossed the camera into the panel truck, and we clambered up the big steps to the front jump seat. Jim Raeside sat behind me and Bjerke took the wheel. Damn. Why was Bob Huestis sick today? I was used to having Huestis on camera, always sure of his genius.

By the time we reached the sprawling apartment complex where our mysterious new phone number had led us, we were convinced we'd found the lair where the seven-headed cobra coiled. We tramped up the steps to the second-floor unit. There was no answer to our repeated knocks. Were they hiding from us? Raeside was tall enough to look into the kitchen window.

"There's butter on the table . . . and it isn't even melted."

The trail was hot. They couldn't be far ahead of us now, not if the butter hadn't melted. Going downstairs and through the parking lots, we were on the alert for suspicious cars. They all looked suspicious. We scribbled license plate numbers on scraps of paper we would never look at again.

The apartment manager was right out of Central Casting—rigid in a too-tight girdle, too-curled hair, and too-heavy makeup. We asked to see the lease on the apartment.

"It is not our policy to give out information about our tenants." She bit off each word.

"Would you rather talk to me or to the two hundred cops who will show up if we tell them about the phone number in that unit?" I shot back.

It always works. The rental agreement magically appeared. The young attorney was working for a Fremont law firm. Raeside, Bjerke, and I scrambled, dragging the clunking cables of the videotape camera, hauling the tools of our trade back to the van and taking off for the offices of respected civic-leader attorneys.

I wasn't about to let their ten years of prominent law service throw me off the track. The attorneys had to be connected with the cobra kill-cult and we were ready to cart back the seven heads as trophy for "Newsroom" that night.

Once again, we saddled up, camera in position, mike at the ready; the three of us marched off. The law firm was nonplussed. It had never been so invaded before.

The two senior partners agreed to "tell you anything at all you want to know" if our camera would just not poke down their throats.

"Okay, Raeside, stay in the van. But be ready," I warned.

But something was wrong. The young attorney was attending a funeral in Southern California, and they were able to reach him by phone. He sounded honest. It didn't fit; as we'd figured it, he was supposed to be the legal mind behind the SLA. He told me where he'd lived in San Francisco before he moved to Fremont. It was near Remiro's 48th Avenue address.

"So you knew Joe Remiro, did you?" I demanded in my most intimidating manner.

"I've never even heard the name," he answered.

A small annoying bell started ringing in my head. This nice young attorney, who was trying to explain himself via long distance to this nosy reporter while his two senior law partners sat next to me in stoic silence, may have innocently been assigned the San Francisco phone number after Remiro had moved. Could good old Ma Bell have screwed it up? She sure as hell could have—and had!

The attorneys suggested I return the next day when my red-hot suspect was to be back in town. I managed to walk back out with a degree of dignity, despite the initial charge I'd made into their leather-book-lined sanctuary.

"Is he the one?" Raeside whispered.

"Maybe, maybe not. Who the hell knows? This whole thing is too weird to know anything."

"Should we go back and check out his apartment some more?"

"No, I think the Forty-eighth Avenue address in San Francisco is our best lead. That's where we should go."

It was Walt Bjerke who chimed in, "Don't you think we'd better call the assignment desk first?"

I knew, of course, that I should call the assignment desk, but I didn't want to. While I was doing the bit with the city directories, the assignment editor had been harping all morning, "Go out to the burned-out house in Clayton. Have something on that for tonight."

I didn't want to stand in front of any burned-out house mouthing something as asinine as "This is Marilyn Baker from in front of the former SLA house." What else could we do out there? By now the house would be sealed tight as a drum, with armed police at the front and back. So what was the point of traipsing all the way out there? It was a good hour's drive, just to get a tired piece of videotape that would look as though I should have been wearing a trench coat. Everyone has seen that piece of footage. I wasn't about to do that routine, not when I had this hot lead on an old address in San Francisco's Sunset district.

But Bjerke called in anyway, and again the order: "Go to the Clayton house!" It was screwing up my whole plan. How could I catch the cobra while I was running around a burned house under the noses of a dozen cops?

If I'd been alone, I probably would have ignored the command. I wouldn't have even called in. But Bjerke is an organization man who goes by the book. So we went—past Berkeley, past the Oakland Hills, over the "big divide," out past Concord to the fringe of the city limits. There sits Clayton. A thousand look-alike houses, all of California ranch design, all built at the same time, sold at the same time, and inhabited by the same kind of people. Plastic-wrapped middle America.

We pulled up in front. The only signs of the arson attempt were the smoke-stained picture window, with one cracked pane, and a rifle case lying on the brown grass.

"Hi, Marilyn, what brings you here?" It was a plainclothes cop from Oakland.

"Oh, just thought we'd look around this place. I don't suppose we can go inside, can we?" Stupid question to ask; of course, they wouldn't let us inside.

"I don't know. I'm just doing a door-to-door check of the area. I'm not here on the house."

"Could you check for me and see if we can go inside?"

"Sure thing, Marilyn. I'll check when I get back to the office."

Great. That would be a good two hours from now and it was already 3:00 P.M. Well, at least I'd tried. "Newsroom" couldn't fault me for that. I was already rehearsing, "Don't blame me because we couldn't get inside"—ready to spit it out at the assignment editor the moment we got back to KQED.

The plainclothesman wandered off down the street and we stood there in Sutherland Court, a short cul-de-sac, with no more than six houses. The usual trikes tipped over in neighboring driveways, a station wagon per family, the proper statistical 2.4 children, one dog, kittens, and housewives in curlers. So much for the scenery the SLA looked out on behind the clapboard house at 1560 Sutherland.

After ruining the hot lead on the young attorney in Fremont, then getting sent out on this dead end—street as well as story— the ultimate happened: The video camera wouldn't work. We couldn't even do a silly stand-up, as those pieces are called in this trade known as television news. It was too much. I didn't know whether to laugh or cry; I swore instead.

Bjerke fiddled with the camera, poking one wire, prodding another. "It just won't work."

I stalked off to the front of the house. What the hell. Now, after all the trouble and travel, we wouldn't even have a picture. Damn the SLA and their seven-headed cobra and safe houses out in the sticks.

That's when I saw them. Kids, young kids, eight- and nine-year-old kids, grinning like clowns and waving at the camera van we'd parked in front. You could almost hear their shouts, "Hi, Mom, I'm on television!" But they were waving and grinning from inside the house, behind that smoke-streaked front window, inside the SLA hideout itself.

"Get that goddamned camera working and I don't care how

44

you do it," I yelled to Bjerke, and started around the side yard, trying to find how those kids had gotten inside the SLA treasure trove. It was too good to believe. Some of the flat six-foot boards of the side fence were knocked down, the tall weeds trampled, and the imprint of tennis shoes led me straight to the sprawling backyard. No grass, no flowers—nothing but raw dirt and two dead trees—a huge, yawning yard, aching for a barbecue and kiddies' swings. It was empty now, except for the mashed-down weeds that reached right to the sliding glass door that opened onto the kitchen. The door was wide open.

A quick look inside showed dishes and bottles, spices and books, posters and clothes. Some were charred, others smoke-stained, but right at my hand was solid, tangible evidence that the SLA had eaten and read and slept and lived here.

I skidded on the weeds as I ran back along the path, over the fallen fence, out to the front lawn, yelling at the two men still huddled over the inert camera, "Get the damned thing going and get it in here NOW!"

Raeside did the only practical thing under the circumstances. He gave the camera a whopping kick. A whirl went up, then it settled down to a steady, reassuring whine. The video camera was working.

Bjerke was senior man, according to union protocol, so that meant he got to do the actual camera-shooting. Raeside was relegated to carrying the backpack and hauling the cords.

All I could think was, "Damn Huestis and damn the union." This was going to be heavy. We'd have to shoot like mad—everything in sight—and pray that no cop walked in while we were doing it. It was one thing that neighborhood kids were playing inside among the evidence. It would have been another for a news team, that knows better, to be caught inside.

In the side yard, Raeside couldn't quite make it past the slat-board fence. The space where the fence had been broken wasn't wide enough for his tall wiry frame and the hump on his back that was the spinning videotape machine. He smashed into the fence, bringing it down with the backpack, sending the last of the standing boards flying in all directions. We marched on—past the backyard, where two freshly dug holes intrigued us but didn't slow us down—right inside the house, into the bowels where the Symbionese had festered from last October until the night before—Thursday, January 10—when they'd tried to torch the house and had then fled. The fact that the house was only two blocks from the site of the arrest of Remiro and Little explained the torch job. They'd undoubtedly figured the cops would be down their throats in no time at all. They had no way of knowing that, when Deputy Sheriff Duge was told by his dispatcher that there was no listing on Sutherland Court for anyone named DeVoto, the police would figure the whole story was a phony and wouldn't even bother to drive the two blocks to check on it. That's what had given the SLA those extra hours—from dawn until 6:00 P.M.—to decide what to do. The decision had been to burn the house and flee.

Now, less than twenty-four hours after the cobra cult had occupied the house, we were here, along with every kid in the neighborhood.

It was souvenir-hunting time in Clayton that day. Kids carted off bayonets, bottles, papers, posters, record albums by the armfuls. Their mothers weren't far behind. They came in their housecoats and curlers, carrying their babies. They took glasses and dishes and clothes and towels and anything else that wasn't secured. They talked in whispers:

"This is right where they slept. I wonder who slept with who?"

"Look at the filth. My God, they lived like pigs."

"Don't use that word, dear, to these people it means police officers."

"Can you believe it? I talked to the woman here only last week. She told me her husband was away a lot—he was in the army."

What a great touch. A husband "in the army." I wanted to know more about the woman, so I stopped my own gawking long enough to interview the neighbors of the cobra clan.

"What did the woman look like?"

"Oh, she was a pretty little thing. About twenty-four or twenty-five years old. Only about five feet tall, thin, with big eyes and a nice smile. She looked just like any of us, maybe a little prettier. She wore pants and clean white blouses and all that. But her hair—well, she didn't keep that up much. It would just hang down on her shoulders, but then she was young and I guess all the young ones wear their hair that way now."

"Did you ever see her husband?"

"Just once. They came over to borrow our jumper cables. She

did all the talking. He just stood there. She said they couldn't start their van, but they had another car they could use to start it if we'd just lend them the jumper cables."

"Did you lend them?"

"Of course. This is a neighborly place. She said she had to learn how to do these things herself when I offered to come over and put on the cables for her."

"Did she explain why she had to learn that herself?"

"Oh, yes. She said her husband was in the army and away a lot."

"Can you describe the husband?"

"Yes, he was dark-haired, his hair was short. He looked like a military man, but he sure never opened his mouth, not around her anyway. She did all the talking. He just stood there."

So the woman was the dominant one. That was logical. From all the bits and pieces I'd been able to dig up about the SLA since last November, it appeared that women were leading it.

Except for smoke-streaked windows and the plasterboard walls popped by the heat, the house was virtually undamaged by the flames. Someone had simply poured gasoline on the carpeting and tossed in a match. In one bathroom, tightly bundled newspapers were singed in the bathtub. Whoever had tried to torch this place obviously didn't know a thing about setting something afire.

Within a week, Nancy Ling Perry would send an SLA letter declaring that she had set the blaze, that she was the tiny brown-haired woman in the house known as DeVoto, claiming that the fire had been set simply to "melt the fingerprints."

We stumbled around, trying to dodge the kids and their mothers, the vultures picking the carcass. We didn't interfere with their treasure hunt until one kid started out the door with several bottles of pills.

"Hey, you can't take those. Put them back where you found them."

"Fuck you, lady," he yelled, and his chubby legs took his chubby body in its Boy Scout uniform off down the street.

So much for my maternalism.

First we videotaped the kitchen where the seven-headed cobra had fed. It was filthy—filth would become almost as much a trademark of the SLA as the cobra they drew on all their writings and posters. Dishes still soaked in the sink, scum floated above them. Obviously they'd been submerged in this murky mess for days, not just twenty-four hours. A rack stood nearby with some dried cups and saucers. No two were alike—all chipped, cracked, the discards of any flea market or garage sale.

Grease was so caked on the stove that I could have carved my name in it. The wall behind the stove had its own layer of grease, just as thick. A lopsided table stood against another wall, with rows of spice jars and seasonings alongside it. Someone in the SLA had taken on the role of cook, but obviously no one had cared enough to clean up.

There was a wooden salad bowl coated with grime, empty bottles for plum wine and Tokay; and empty beer cans, four full bags of them, all neatly rinsed out, ready for recycling. These people were into ecology.

Cardboard boxes were stacked with flour and sugar and corn-flakes, as though someone had packed them, then decided food was not the vital thing to carry away. The cupboards contained cans of soup and a jumble of odds and ends of plates and bowls. No organization at all. No "woman's touch" to put the place in working order. Whoever the SLA members were, they were disorganized, dirty, and obviously unable to make quick de-cisions. Otherwise, why pack half a dozen boxes to move, and then leave them all behind? They'd had a good twelve hours' head start on the authorities. Remiro was arrested around 5:00 A.M.; the SLA hadn't run from the licking flames until 6:00 P.M.

What about the living room? We wandered into it. It had a lone chair that would have long ago been discarded by even the lowliest thrift shop; a floor lamp like some relic from a Roaring Twenties movie; a pillow, it's stuffing spilling out; a cardboard box piled with phonograph records—acid rock and more acid rock.

That was it. The total furnishings of the SLA living room. How dismal.

The fireplace had no ashes or logs. The ashes were in the middle of the floor where they'd tried to start the fire to burn down the house. A thin wooden shelf was the only mantel. It was stacked with pocket books, every title that every radical had to own, if not read. George Jackson's *Blood in My Eye*, a tome titled *How to Fight a Revolution*, another on *Police Methods and*

Practices, poems by radical women, at least two dozen paperbacks, all proper titles to grace the shelf of the proper revolutionary, Berkeley style.

There was an eight-by-ten glossy picture tucked between the paperbacks. A tall black man, good-looking, wearing jeans and a chino shirt. A hand was on his arm, a white hand, with a white cuff jutting out from the business-suit sleeve. Someone had drawn an arrow pointing to the hand and penciled a notation: "A cop's arm."

Why? Maybe the man in the picture was another black convict the SLA planned to spring from prison. Or maybe the picture was just another element in the childlike game they'd concocted, a game of secret codes, hidden names, and silent messages.

There were three bedrooms down a narrow hall. In each was one double mattress, flat on the floor, without bedsprings or headboard. The mattresses stank, not only from the stench of smoke and water, but from sweat and grime. They were so dirty we prodded them only with our shoes, not wanting to touch the vile, molding pads. The blankets were little better. Ragged, discarded, torn, burned, stains spreading across them. They were tossed into tangled heaps in a corner, almost like discarded bodies, shapeless, no longer usable.

In one bedroom stood a metal chair, its leatherette seat torn and drooling cotton, and an old table, its black paint scratched down through the other three coats that had preceded this latest effort at decor. A wallet, false drivers' licenses, phony I.D. cards. Another trademark of the SLA. Hardly original. It was all out of an underground book called *The Paper Trip.*

We poked in the first closet, Raeside flipping the heavy cables to bring the camera closer. Bjerke worried whether or not he was in focus, while I prayed he was, and cursed that he probably wasn't.

The closet was a shock. No revolutionary dressed like this. There were women's primly tailored suits with the best San Francisco labels hemstitched in their collars. And a satin dress, made for prom dates or penthouse parties, and blouses with tiny Peter Pan collars that would turn any face into a cherub's.

And the shoes. No combat boots. No hippie sandals. No run-down heels. But demure Florsheim pumps, three-inch stack heels, spotless brown leather gleaming. The shoes of the debutante lunching in the city. These shoes hadn't walked the alley where

Marcus Foster had been killed. They were the shoes of an elegant California matron. But there they stood, quietly at attention, toe to toe on the shelf above the neat row of clothes.

Only the male clothes fit the filth and debris of the SLA lifestyle: shabby jackets, threadbare car coats, pants that had never known a crease, and tennis shoes rancid from years of wear by sweating feet.

Along the closet floor was a jumble of suitcases and trunks. How I wanted to open each and sort through the things that might yield some clue to the SLA! But we were racing against our own judgment of police competence. They were bound to be back. Cops swarming in, demanding explanations of just what we were doing deep inside the SLA house, their first vital clue in the manhunt for Marcus Foster's murderer.

It never occurred to us that the police wouldn't come, that it would be another twenty-four hours before this vital link to the SLA was sealed off from prying neighbors and probing journalists. So we rushed. Another mistake on my mental list of What I Did Wrong in Covering the SLA.

Another bedroom, the same scene. The mattress curled up on the floor. A three-mirror vanity table that would probably prove to be an antique if anyone sanded off the numerous coats of paint that now hung in peels from it. A woman's jewelry case of imitation leather—the kind you buy as a gift when you don't really know the woman or like her—spilled out its contents, a horde of costume jewelry.

No hippie had worn these. There wasn't a peace symbol in the lot. Not one Indian headband. Not a single tinkling bell to tie on a bootstrap. These were matched costume pieces of a middle-class matron. Neat pearls, with matching earrings. Single strands of gold-mesh chain, with a brooch of the same looped chain. Dainty bracelets that would accent cashmere sweaters. And a wedding band, thick with gold engraved flowers, that shouted "married" from ten feet away.

More closets, more clothes. Raeside remarked, "These sure don't look like what I've seen hippies wearing. Do they to you?"

The final bedroom, the master's suite with its own bathroom, was chaotic. Boxes and papers and bayonets and battle bandages littered every square inch of the small room, piled across the mattress flat on the floor, spilled over the two pillows whose striped ticking lay bare to the world.

Here the SLA was unmasked. This room had been their arsenal. Gas masks, new and in working condition, stared back at us from empty sockets. Ammunition boxes piled like bricks—all empty now, their former .30- and .45-caliber lethal contents gone with the SLA. The heavy metal cartridge-belt case for the machine-gun bullets was empty, its belt missing, taken by the SLA. Books again—on how to treat battlefield wounds, how to build a better booby trap, how to kill.

The three of us stopped in our tracks, all staring at the crudely lettered poster tacked on the wall, at eye level if you lay on the vile mattress.

REVOLUTION . . . NIGGER

Only those two words. Dark, dank colors of blue and brown and black swirled around the letters. Was that supposed to be a rifle just under the word *Revolution?*

"What does that mean?" Raeside asked.

"Damned if I know. They use the word *nigger*, yet claim they are Third World revolutionaries, with black and brown and all races in their ranks?" I asked right back.

"Get a tight shot of that poster. No one will believe us if we don't," I said to Bjerke.

Raeside pulled more cable, like a long snake, after him, and we started looking for some list, some address, that would lead us to the next SLA hideout. There was nothing but garbage. Pads of paper scribbled on without rhyme or reason. One crayon drawing of a tiger stalking through a jungle. Some tot's toys that waggled their heads as you dragged them by their cords.

A map—someone's backyard? Two trees, a fence, all penciled in thin wavy lines. Was it the alley where Marcus Foster had been gunned down?

"Maybe that's where they'll kill the next victim," Raeside said. If only we knew, we would be able to warn someone. Who? This silly drawing could be of any backyard, any home.

As the kids and neighbors paraded by clutching their Symbionese trophies, I kept pulling more papers from under the pile on the bed. A sheaf slid out, at least ten pages, all covered with not-very-good typing—there were typographical errors in almost every line. But here were the "Federation Papers of the Symbio-nese, Statement of Purpose"—in their own words, corrected by one of their own in a petite hand.

I hesitated for only a moment. These papers were undoubtedly evidence. It was wrong to cart off evidence. But then I heard the whoops and cries of the children as they continued their scaveng-ing of SLA artifacts. I could not permit the same thing to happen to these papers, could I? I stuffed them inside the jacket of my pantsuit, turning my bustline into an improbable profile.

Raeside saw what I'd done. "You want me to stash them?" he asked. But I couldn't let him take the heat from the police who I still thought couldn't be more than a minute away.

"No, they'll have to call a matron to search me, so I'll carry them," I answered with more confidence than I felt.

We inspected the two bathrooms. Scouring powder had never been used on them. Cough drops—did reciting all their rhetoric make them hoarse? Hand lotion—to keep smooth the hands that held the guns that killed Marcus Foster? Pills—no prescrip-tion labels, just bottles of pills. More than half a dozen. Several of them were codeine, no doubt to dull the sting of the bullets these paranoid terrorists probably believed to be only a day away. The others were Temaril, a drug that stops itching and is used primarily in jungles for insect bites or bad cases of poison ivy.

Then I saw the makeup. It was a whole dime-store collection. The pancake makeup was in the darkest possible shades, almost black. Yet the neighbors had said the petite woman who lived there was fair-skinned. Black eyebrow pencils, worn down to a nub. From the heavy penciling of black eyebrows where none grew? Eye shadow—a whole palette of colors, all dark, blues and browns and purples, all worn by the brushes lying next to them. Boxes of powder, the sweet smell spilling out into the grime of the basin. Dark powder, dull finish, the kind that takes the shine from any face and turns it into an indistinguishable blob of flesh.

Supposedly, two facts never vary about revolutionaries: They have no sense of humor and the women involved never wear makeup. The second fact is so hard and fast it is almost as if their plainness is a weapon in their war against the pretty and stylized masses.

52

Yet, there in the heart of the SLA safe house was a substantial supply of makeup. Then a huge book with its hundred full-color illustrations slipped from the wall it had leaned against at my feet—*Makeup for Television and Films.* I thumbed the well-worn pages. How to look like an Indian. A Mexican. How to pass for black.

"My God, they deliberately tried to put the blame for Marcus Foster's murder on the blacks! They tried to make us believe blacks had murdered a black man!" I exclaimed.

"It makes sense. It's the first thing that has," Raeside answered.

It did make sense. Now the vague descriptions from witnesses on November 6 came flooding back: "dark-complexioned." Something had made them believe the killers were dark. But something had also made them believe the killers were not black people. I remembered one cop saying, "No one is describing any Negroid features. If they were black, they sure didn't have any facial characteristics of blacks."

Of course they hadn't. They were white. White killers painting black pancake makeup on their faces, drawing in the black eyebrows, turning themselves into a blackface masquerade to murder the black educator.

"We better get the hell out of here. I don't even know if the camera's working. The light's lousy," Bjerke said.

"If that tape doesn't turn out, I'll have his head," I vowed silently.

The papers inside my jacket were scratching and creasing. I had to get them out, read what I'd found, see what the SLA said about itself.

"Okay, pack up, let's go. But put a blank tape in a box, so if the cops do stop us and demand the tape, we can give them a blank one."

Raeside had done it before I finished the sentence.

The kids were still squealing with delight with the sudden new toy on their block, a pad to play in. But we packed up anyway. Let the cops find only the kids. We had to get back, get this video ready for the air by 7:00 P.M., when "Newsroom" would begin, complete with its rinky-tink-piano theme song, "San Francisco."

Only after the camera was stored, the backpack unstrapped from Raeside's aching back, and we were back in the van, did we breathe a little. Bjerke drove off, away from the tidy little court with its SLA hideout. But we weren't out of the woods yet. We had no sooner turned onto the main street, to head west to San Francisco thirty miles away, than a sheriff's car pulled in behind us, keeping our pace.

So after hustling these papers out of the house, getting the first actual written statement of the SLA, one they hadn't flowered up for public consumption, the whole thing could be lost now. We'd end up in the slam, booked at the least for obstructing justice. Or maybe it was a felony. With KQED's constant fiscal slump, who would post our bail? Is bail even allowed for a crime like stealing evidence?

"Slow down, let him pass," Raeside ordered. Bjerke slowed. So did the sheriff.

"Speed up a little, stay in the right lane, give him room to pass on the left," came another Raeside maneuver. Bjerke complied, but the car with the big star on its side stayed behind us.

We stuffed the SLA writings under the dash, then decided against it. They'd certainly search the van. We tried to put them in the camera, but it wouldn't work. The twelve pages were too bulky. They went into my purse. But suppose they didn't bother to call a matron before they searched my purse? I put them back into my jacket.

Would Joe Russin back us? Would he agree we should have carried off the SLA writings? What if he didn't? We were now going in the wrong direction—east, not west—and every mile we traveled took us farther and farther away from KQED, away from that rigid 7:00 P.M. deadline and "Here's 'Newsroom' . . ."

The cop had to know we were from KQED-TV. The van had letters the size of baseball bats on both sides and on the back. "Maybe he'll think we're on our way to another story since we're going away from San Francisco, not toward it," Bjerke hoped aloud.

We were too scared to try a U-turn, so we just kept putting more miles behind us, more miles away from where we needed to be.

I finally gave in. "If we're going to be busted, let's get it over with. If we keep going like this, we'll miss the news tonight. And anyway, what's the point of having the tape and the SLA papers if we can't get them on 'Newsroom'?"

"Here's a restaurant. Turn into the parking lot, like we're going for coffee," Raeside commanded.

Bjerke turned. We stopped breathing, waiting for the wail of the siren, the flashing red light. What we saw instead was the sheriff's car roll right past us.

By the time we stopped laughing, we were back at KQED, watching the tape, seeing the filth and debris and bayonets and gas masks and all the terrorist toys we'd held and examined two hours before.

"Okay, Bake, what's with that shit-eating grin?" Russin barked at me. Funny, he always knows when I've done something that doesn't adhere strictly to the rules. I pulled open my jacket and dumped the papers on his desk.

"Jesus Christ, you stole the goddamned evidence," he yowled, as he quickly read through the pages.

"It's a great show-and-tell for tonight," I explained. After all, wasn't he always reminding me that television is a visual media, not like the newspapers I'd labored on for so many years? Wasn't he the one who kept urging me to have something to show as well as tell?

Well, tonight I had something to show. Something no other reporter had. And I was absolutely gloating.

"You can't show this stuff on camera, for Christ's sake, Bake. Your ass will be in jail before we go off the air," Russin fumed.

I couldn't believe it. He wasn't going to let me show these treasures we'd risked arrest for!

"But, Joe, you said to get visuals."

"Not the goddamned evidence in a murder case."

"Well, what was I supposed to do, let some other reporter cart them off?"

"How do I know? Christ, what a mess! You better get on the phone and let the cops know you have them and get them over to the cops before they come in here and toss you in the slam."

What a blow. All that hassle for nothing.

"Joe, I've got to use them. Hell, one page is even singed from the fire. It's great to show. And how else can I report what these creeps are thinking if I don't report what they write?"

"You can't do it, Bake. It's illegal. It's a fucking crime to steal evidence, you know that."

"Well, could I just sort of read from them? I'll keep them down at my side, so they don't show on camera."

"How the hell will you attribute them? Where will you have learned what you read?"

"Oh, I can say, 'It's believed' or something like that. Damn it, Joe, I don't want to go to all this hassle for nothing but a lousy videotape of a burned-out house and no more."

Russin said to write the story. He'd think about it. It didn't take him long. Within minutes he walked over to my desk on his long cowboy legs, his voice turned into that country-boy drawl that always means he is about to put someone on.

"Ah been thinkin', Bake, and Ah would guess that you can read what those papers say, as long as you don't show them and as long as you've already turned them over to the proper authorities—as soon as you finish making Xerox copies."

I could have kissed him!

I could use my exclusives, and still stay out of jail. I dialed the Oakland police station. A gentle-voiced sergeant came on the line and I explained my predicament, hedging slightly by claiming some kid had handed me a fistful of SLA writings, instead of saying it had been my own hand that had dragged them out from under a mattress. I calmly told him that as a good citizen, I wanted to get the papers to his department with all possible haste, but as a journalist, I couldn't afford to have my name connected with turning anything over to the police. He was the soul of understanding.

We agreed that I would put the originals in a plain brown envelope and have it hand-delivered to him within the hour. As I was hanging up, his sense of humor came through as he quipped, "Send them along just as soon as you finish making your copies."

"You got yourself covered with the cops?" Russin asked as we walked down the rickety stairs to the "Newsroom" roundtable.

"Of course. In fact, they're glad to get the papers. And it turns out that Oakland thought the Contra Costa County sheriffs were guarding the house, and the sheriffs thought that the Oakland police were guarding it, since the SLA are Oakland's suspects in the Foster murder. So what happened? No one was guarding the place at all."

"You think they'll get someone out there now or could we go back?" Russin asked.

"Joe, I would guess a cop was on his way to seal that place before I hung up the phone."

He grinned. "Okay, ace, go on and tell the world what you found." It was all the reward I needed.

Seven o'clock and the theme started. "Newsroom" was on the air. The videotape rolled. The SLA hideout. Gas masks, guns that were target pistols, a target on the hall wall. Pills and powder and books and bayonets. We had it all.

I tried not to let the excitement get in my voice. Stay calm and authoritative, I kept reminding myself. Wasn't that what made Walter Cronkite rich?

I reported, for the first time in any of the news media, that "the murderers of Dr. Marcus Foster may have disguised themselves with dark makeup to try to put the blame on black people."

Russin grinned as we reported, exclusively, what the SLA first intended the seven heads of the cobra to symbolize: black, brown, yellow, red, white, young, and old. And that their name *Symbionese* was from the word *symbiosis,* meaning dissimilar organisms living together in harmony.

And now for the zinger that would start our phones ringing, reporters from all over the country asking, "How do you know . . . ?":

"Women are the dominant force, the leadership of the Symbionese Liberation Army."

We couldn't say how we knew. But it was there, in their own handwriting, on the purloined papers. The only major editorial correction that appeared in them, again and again, was the reversal of the order of *man and woman* and *men and women* every time they were typed. Also, when they had written of the Ages of Man, *Man* became *people.* The woman always came before the man in Symbionese rhetoric.

No man would have made those editorial changes, and few women would have either, even the most radical women's libbers. We were beginning to see the human forms behind the seven-headed snake.

SYMBIONESE LIBERATION ARMY
Western Regional Adult Unit
February 4, 1974

Communiqué #3   WARRANT ORDER:
SUBJECT: Prisoners of War   Arrest and protective
TARGET: Patricia Campbell Hearst   custody and, if
              Daughter of Randolph Hearst   resistance, execution
              Corporate enemy of the people

On the above-stated date, combat elements of the United Federation Forces of the Symbionese Liberation Army armed with cyanide-loaded weapons served an arrest warrant upon Patricia Campbell Hearst.

It is the order of this court that the subject be arrested by combat units and removed to a protective area of safety and only upon completion of this condition to notify Unit #4 to give communication of this action.

It is the directive of this court that during this action ONLY, no civilian elements be harmed if possible, and that warning shots be given. However, if any citizens attempt to aid the authorities or interfere with the implementation of this order, they shall be executed immediately.

This court hereby notifies the public and directs all combat units in the future to shoot to kill any civilian who attempts to witness or interfere with any operation conducted by the peoples' forces against the fascist state.

Should any attempt be made by authorities to rescue the prisoner, or to arrest or harm any S.L.A. elements, the prisoner is to be executed.

The prisoner is to be maintained in adequate physical and mental condition, and unharmed as long as these conditions are adhered to. Protective custody shall be composed of combat and medical units, to safeguard both the prisoner and her health.

All communications from this court MUST be published in full, in all newspapers, and all other forms of the media. Failure to do so will endanger the safety of the prisoner. Further communications will follow.

S. L. A.

DEATH TO THE FASCIST INSECT
THAT PREYS UPON THE LIFE OF
THE PEOPLE

The pompous declaration that Patty Hearst was a prisoner of war was no great shock. The police had already admitted to me that a cyanide-tipped bullet had been found in the living room of the Berkeley home she shared with Steve Weed. The cyanide was the kill-cult's calling card, just as the seven-headed cobra was its emblem. No doubt it was their notion of the cobra's venom; however, it seems little more than a theatrical effect.

The communiqué read like a movie script—all that rhetoric about a court of the people deciding Patty had to be snatched. The frightening part was that the media seemed to be accepting at face value whatever the SLA said. Suddenly editors were chewing their copy pencils in a frenzy to "not endanger that poor girl's life." Attempts by two or three reporters to strike away the snake's mask and reveal the cobra clan were quickly vetoed by the same editors who earlier had beaten their breasts about the constitutional rights of a free press when the Nixon administration had claimed that to reveal the Pentagon Papers would endanger thousands of lives. But there wasn't time to reflect on the shortcomings of my profession. Not today. I'd just had a call from one of my best friends, a civic leader whose contacts span the world.

Months ago he'd hinted that he had close friends high in law-enforcement offices. I had snapped at the invitation. "Could you introduce me?"

"I've mentioned it to them, but frankly they don't seem to want to meet with any reporters. They keep dodging my suggestion we get together for lunch."

That was the routine answer each time I asked, month after month.

Now came a sudden change of heart. My friend, whom we can call VIP, telephoned me one day around noon.

"Don't make any plans for lunch tomorrow."

It was cryptic at best. "Why not?" was my rejoinder.

"Well, you're about to have a contact no other reporter in this whole city has. My friends just called. They want one of their men to meet you and they want to do it right now, tomorrow, for lunch."

"Why the sudden interest, when they've brushed me off for so long?"

"How the hell do I know? All I know is they called just minutes ago and said, 'Set it up. We want to meet with Baker.' They said no one else was to be there, except me, of course," and he chuckled.

But why now, out of the blue, would these top-placed police officials agree to meet with me? What did I know that they wanted? All I was sure of was that they knew a lot that I wanted to know.

It was back in a huddle with Joe Russin, off in the tiny nook that passes for an executive office for the news director of KQED's "Newsroom." He was as puzzled as I. "Why you?"

"How should I know, except I've been needling VIP to introduce me to them?"

"How the hell does he even know people like that?"

"VIP knows everybody."

Russin agreed the lunch was an unexpected opportunity. We just hoped some contacts would come out of it that would lead us to news stories. Russin added, "Don't mention it to anyone. It's better to keep it to yourself."

I agreed. We had had a few news leaks before in "Newsroom." You can't keep a secret among some forty people, half of them volunteers who come and go with the changing of the calendar.

Promptly at noon the next day, February 8, I walked into the private elevator that whisked me straight up to the penthouse restaurant Empress of China. It had been VIP's idea, and he was picking up the tab. Fair enough.

He was waiting with the contact. I had expected some hard-faced, stuffy male egotist, his coat bulging with hidden pistols, carrying a trench coat over his arm. Instead, there stood a most pleasant-looking man with a warm wide smile and not a badge in sight.

By the time we made our way through three of the ten courses of Chinese delicacies, it was obvious that my new friend was sharp-witted, keen-minded, and exceptionally bright—a professional who knew his job and respected my right to do mine. We can call him Badge.

As VIP poured endless cups of tea, Badge and I verbally took each other's measure. First and foremost, would he respect the secrecy of my sources?

"Does that mean if you knew where the SLA was hiding you wouldn't tell me?"

Of course not, I assured him; no press credential took precedent over citizenship. I'd tell him if I found the SLA. That was hardly the problem. And for all I knew, they could be in Africa.

"But suppose I have a source who tells me where the SLA is. Will you insist on knowing the source if I pass along the information?" I asked.

"Absolutely not. We will respect your sources. All we ask is that you give us some idea of how reliable your source is. We don't want to go chasing to hell and back on the word of some unknown. We'll accept your judgment on whether or not you consider your source solid." Badge was emphatic and reassuring.

The ice started melting, and we were suddenly putting the facts on the table next to the Won Ton and tea.

"There's a special investigation going on of gambling payoffs in Chinatown. What do you know about that?"

That was his opener. It was a hard one, but thanks to some honest, hardworking street cops, I was able to sketch out some of the details of how Chinatown gamblers paid off the few crooked cops cluttering up the San Francisco Police Department.

Badge wasn't surprised. In fact, hours later, it occurred to me that he had already known everything I had told him and more. Undoubtedly, it was his way of seeing if I had the right information on the situation—a test. Evidently I passed.

"What's your reading on this SLA?"

Now we were down to the reason for the urgency in our meeting, the sudden change of heart after all those months of "No, we won't meet her."

VIP slid out of his chair as though the question itself had startled him. "I think I'll take a stroll and let you two chat," and he vanished.

I looked at the wise face across the table from me. He wasn't kidding. He really thought I knew something vital about the SLA. Now if I only knew what he thought I knew.

"Well, it's run by women." It was a question more than comment.

"Right on. You're on target there."

I was? Those editorial transpositions placing *women* before *men* in the SLA writings had meant something after all. My confidence grew, and I decided to try another half-question, half-certain remark.

"I think at least some of the SLA came out of Venceremos, the radical group that was into busting blacks out of prisons."

"How in hell did you find that out?" He was honestly amazed. So was I. It had been a shot in the dark, and it had hit the bull's-eye.

I decided to gamble the big one. It would make or break the contact: "Do the names Bill and Emily mean anything to you? Or Angela or Willie the Wolf?" It all came out in one breath and I sat back and waited.

He stared, long and hard. Then came a grin that would have

been almost boyish if it hadn't been for the penetrating eyes above it. "Lady, I don't know how you know, but you sure as hell know."

I felt like dancing on the tabletop—I knew! It meant those long talks I'd had with the radical leaders in Berkeley hadn't all been in vain. Emily and Bill and Angela and Willie Wolfe had been right-on information. Thank God for the radicals who still draw the line at murder and SLA tactics.

My newfound friend looked at me and shrugged. "Look, I know this has to be a two-way street. I can't just ask information and not give any." I waited expectantly. His information was a long time coming.

"Try checking out where Little and Remiro lived, the people at a Bond Street house in East Oakland, where Little and Remiro both were, along with Willie Wolfe, and the house known as Peking Man House. That's a commune near Berkeley in West Oakland. Little and Wolfe lived there."

I could hardly wait to race back to Russin and head for those two houses. All kinds of angles spun in my head. Check out who owns the places, call them: Whom did they rent to? What did their tenants do for a living? Check with the neighbors: Who came and went? Who were their friends and/or comrades?

It wasn't that we hadn't known about those two houses. We had. Both had been searched less than a month ago, right after Remiro and Little were arrested on January 10. But what I hadn't known was that anyone remained who might know what the shadowy SLA was or what it was after.

Badge promised to keep in touch. It was a needless promise. I wouldn't let this one get away. It was the opening I had needed, a place to check out the rumors, whispered leads, and fuzzy clues that pile up from street people, underground journalists, and just plain folks, who rang me about every suspicious neighbor they saw.

VIP had been right. This was the contact every reporter dreamed about. It was a short-lived elation.

The lunch conference with Badge had lasted four-and-a-half hours. When I walked into the station, the assignment editor was standing there, a scowl creasing his face. "Where the hell have you been all afternoon? For Christ's sake, how the hell am I supposed to get out the fucking assignments when the reporters don't even bother to call in?"

After that outburst, he got to more serious complaints, all directed at me. As usual I sought Russin. Why hadn't he covered for me? He knew I was going to this secret meeting. Why hadn't he set up some cover for me? Russin himself was nonplussed. He didn't know how to deal with these recurring outbursts. Nor did he want to undercut the authority of the assignment editor by openly siding with me. The "country boy" twang came back into Russin's voice as he started pacifying me. It didn't work too well. I was furious, tired of the tirades that were heaped on me.

But if that Friday night was miserable, it was only an omen for the weekend ahead, and every weekend for the next several months. Weekends that no longer would serve as tidy dividers between working days and nonworking days. Every day was a working day now. "The SLA doesn't take the weekend off" would be Russin's constant reminder. It would be months without definition. Days running into nights, weeks without end, one month slipping into the next.

Weekends were the worst, when I yearned for a hot herb bubble bath and a book. But conscience prevailed, and it was back to the car and off to Berkeley to meet with bearded radicals who publicly disavowed me but privately fed me information. Or dropping by the Berkeley and Oakland police departments— weekends were best for those visits; there was more time for talk, and the cops were less cautious with less brass around.

I followed up on the two houses I knew Remiro and Little had lived in. I was less than welcome. The Bond Street house was like a Grandma Moses picture: a tiny, white frame house, set behind a larger house, with an all-American white picket fence separating the two. Trees shaded the windows, daffodils poked about in the knee-high grass. The only occupant was a spaniel-sized dog with Great Dane teeth by the name of Amos Moses. He turned out to be my only friend at that address.

I knocked on the door of the front house. After all, the rear one was vacant, two of its three tenants in jail, the other, Willie Wolfe, underground and being sought as an SLA soldier.

The woman who answered my knock, Jean Dolly, refused to talk to me, claiming she'd never heard of Remiro, Little, Wolfe, or anyone else, not even the person who owned the dog in her backyard. Actually, according to the police, she and the man who shared the house with her, Robert Hood, *had* known them. In fact, Hood had been active in Vietnam Vets Against the War with Remiro and my older son, Jeffrey, who had returned disillusioned from his service in Vietnam.

Jeff had been my secret weapon from the start of the SLA story. The day Little and Remiro were arrested, he told me he had also known Remiro, or G.I. Joe, as he was called, when they went to the same college. Jeff had then told me about the VVAW —how he filled out a membership card, but that Remiro never told him where or when the meetings were being held. About the time when the group marched against the Alameda Naval Base, and Jeff had taken up the chant of the peace movement— "One, two, three, four, we don't want your fucking war"—chanting the numbers right up the line—"ten, eleven, twelve, free your sisters, free yourselves."

"Remiro turned to me and said, 'Hey man, that's brothers, not sisters.' That amazed me. After all, we radicals were supposed to support women's lib, too, but Joe sure didn't," Jeff had said.

So while I prowled East Oakland, Jeff, in flowing red beard and shoulder-length red curls, prowled Berkeley, blending into the commune scene in a way I never could.

Students on campus would talk to Jeff, but they wouldn't be caught dead talking to me, a pig reporter who talked to the cops. They told Jeff about Remiro and his friend "Hymie," and how they had joined La Raza and attempted to control it. But the campus Chicano movement would have none of that. They politely but firmly declined the pair's involvement, but not before their treasury vanished. "We still figure it was Remiro's friend Hymie who got it, but whenever we'd ask where he was, we'd be told he was in South America. I guess that's where our money went, too," they told Jeff.

After checking the Bond Street house and finding only Amos Moses, I was off to the Peking Man House. This time Russin was with me, camera at the ready. Neither of us looked very Berkeleyish. Russin might pass. He had on his cowboy boots, sport shirt, and jeans. But I never would, not in a tailored pantsuit. The fact that we didn't exactly fit in didn't daunt us. A sign in front of 5939 Chabot Road, the Peking Man House, said "Yard Sale."

"That's it, we'll go in and pretend we're looking at things in the yard sale," Russin immediately exclaimed. I was game, if skeptical.

We wandered into the backyard, which was nothing but a wide path of dirt in front of a dilapidated rear house where two bearded men sat in tilting kitchen chairs, enjoying the noon sun.

While we browsed, a woman opened the rear-house door an inch and peered out. Could it have been Patty?

We were both interested in a shiny red Volkswagen parked in this backyard of dirt. It had been a dark blue Volkswagen that had been the stakeout car at Patty's kidnapping. Now we'd found this shiny red VW parked behind Peking Man House, where at least one hard-core SLA member had lived, perhaps more. Why else would the paint be so shiny, unless it had just been painted red to hide its true role in the SLA?

Russin wandered back toward our two lounging observers. Luckily they kept their eyes on him, which afforded me the opportunity to scratch at the red paint with a dime.

The paint flaked off, but no blue showed. We were wrong again.

"Enough of this, Russin," I exploded, "let's knock on the front door!" He was almost as tired as I, so he gave in. We marched up the front steps to the door, pounded away, and got nowhere. A man at the door simply said, "I don't want to talk to you." Then a car pulled into the driveway, and out jumped David Gunnell, who headed the commune.

He took one look at us and said, "You're Marilyn Baker and you're Joe Russin. What do you want?" Our cover was blown.

"We want to talk to you about Russell Little and the SLA," I said. Russin put on his friendly face and started his cowboy voice rolling. "Ah know you all must be havin' a lot of folks bother ya."

Gunnell was unimpressed. He'd obviously seen razor-sharp Russin too many times on "Newsroom" to believe his cowpoke routine. And he certainly wasn't eager to sit and chat with me. I just kept saying, "We have to talk to you." He finally decided it was better to agree than to get hassled on his front porch.

"Come back at seven tonight and we'll talk," he grudgingly agreed.

Russin and I took off, proud of our success. It was short. "Hey, as long as I have the camera, let's take a picture of the house right now," Russin said. It made sense. We drove off to circle the block and get a running shot of the place.

Just as we reached the house, the car stopped. Dead. Right in front of the place. A woman sunning herself on the front lawn stared at us.

I told Russin, "That woman saw us. We have to say something now. We can't pretend this didn't happen."

He agreed. We parked and went back. She was not overjoyed at our approach. But I was the one she was mad at. "Why were you taking pictures of this house?" she demanded.

Before I could answer, Joe said, "We just wanted to have a still of it."

The woman, called Jean Wa Chan, huffily informed us she too would talk to us at seven that evening. We went for coffee, to wait for the meeting.

When we returned, Gunnell didn't even wait for us to knock. He met us on the walk. "We had a meeting. We refuse to talk to you, because you took pictures of Jean Wa Chan today," he snarled.

That's as far as we got. We were ordered off the premises.

A day later Russin did get into the house, with another reporter the Peking commune considered "more sympathetic" toward them. But all Russin got for his hours of talk was a lot of mis-information and flat-out rejections. Nothing solid at all. No mention of the gun classes held there, which we had heard of from a man who had actually been a live-in member of the Pe-king Man commune. No word that they knew Nancy Ling Perry or any of the other SLA members. Nothing but political rhetoric.

We would have to start backtracking. Surely the street where the SLA had changed cars would yield some clues. Someone on it might have seen or heard something. We covered Tanglewood Road and drew another blank.

Jeff had had better luck. He had pinned down the information that people once active in the East Bay Venceremos were thought to be SLA members. He came up with the vital links, the names: Emily, Angela, Bill, and Willie Wolfe. It was time to put people and faces on the names.

PART TWO

THE CRIMINALS AND THEIR DEMANDS

CHAPTER **6**

On February 12, 1974, the first of many taped messages was delivered to a Berkeley radio station by the Symbionese Liberation Army, messages it demanded that the news media carry in full. The media became its de facto captive, obeying all the terrorists' demands.

A copy of the tape and the envelope's contents were picked up by KQED. In the original large, plain-brown envelope, which I saw days later, was also an eight-page letter. Nancy Ling Perry, who had adopted the SLA name Fahizah, claimed she wrote it. The return address, printed in large block letters by the SLA, was:

MARILYN BAKER
KQED 1011 BRYANT STREET
SAN FRANCISCO, CALIFORNIA

Why had the SLA singled me out, when reporters from all over the world were camped around the clock at the Hearst Hillsborough home? I had only to read the tirade in Nancy's letter to know the answer. She was furious that I had reported on "Newsroom" that the SLA murderers of Marcus Foster may have resorted to dark makeup to put suspicion on black people.

Nancy raged on about "all Third World people being represented in the SLA." It was typically middle-class of the SLA to rant against "capitalist oppressors," and then put faith in the U.S. Postal Service and chance my name for the return address. Ready to destroy the system but at the same time relying on it to deliver their notes of destruction.

But the brown envelope with my name on it wasn't nearly as intriguing as its contents.

The newsroom came to a halt as we huddled around a small white plastic radio and listened to KPFA play the tape recording. For the first time, for as long as I could remember, there was no sound of typewriters, no shouts of reporters berating the production staff in the continuing battle about content and visuals. The only interruption was the ringing telephones, the ceaseless rhythm that never quiets in a newsroom.

This was probably the first time anyone besides her captors had heard Patty Hearst's voice since her last scream had faded into the night on February 4. Now, eight days later, the voice seemed tired and heavy, hollow with the ache of drugs; but it was a voice her parents easily recognized, though they pointed out, "It sounds like Patty sounded when she was very ill a few years ago and the doctors had to give her drugs." It was a weary voice, one so low we strained forward toward the radio, barely breathing in an effort to catch her every word.

I had half-expected Patty to reassure her parents, to lessen the terror they must be suffering. If that was her purpose, however, it was half-hearted. "Mom, Dad, I'm okay. I had a few scrapes and stuff, but they washed them up and they are getting okay. And I've caught a cold but they are giving me some pills. I am not being starved or beaten or unnecessarily frightened."

Then, in a voice that bordered on apology for her abductors, Patty said, "I've heard some press reports and know that Steve and all the neighbors are okay and that no one was really hurt. And I also know that the SLA members here are very upset about press distortions of what has been happening."

Somehow it didn't seem possible that the kidnap victim was more concerned about the press reports of her abductors' demands than about her parents' fears for her well-being. Yet there it was, in Patty's own voice, words that immediately cast a shadow of doubt over her and turned public opinion more toward the theory that she had been part of the SLA from the start and had planned her own abduction.

"Why is she apologizing for the kidnappers if she wasn't in on it?" became the most frequent question by the "man on the street," a question I heard from cab drivers, waiters, doctors.

I didn't believe she was in on it—not because I thought the tape from Patty dispelled such doubts, but for a much more practical reason: Wouldn't a woman planning her own abduction wear more than just underpants and a bathrobe? Perhaps she had no choice in those first words—the SLA carefully scripting what she could say and not permitting her to offer one word of comfort to her distraught parents. Or perhaps Patty already believed in her captors. "These people aren't just a bunch of nuts. They have been really honest with me, but they are perfectly willing to die for what they are doing."

Then a thin nasal voice with an affected accent identified itself as "General Field Marshal Cinque." It seemed to be a black man's voice. In pompous tones, he listed the SLA's demands:

"Each person with one of the following cards is to be given seventy dollars' worth of meats, vegetables, and dairy products: all people with welfare cards, Social Security pension cards, food-stamp cards, disabled-veteran cards, medical cards, parole or probation papers, and jail- or bail-release slips."

A quick estimate of the cost of such a handout came to the staggering amount of $400 million, a sum that would have been far beyond the reach of The Chief himself, let alone his son Randolph. The demands were so ludicrous that it was obvious the SLA didn't give a damn about feeding the hungry. They wanted Patty's parents to forfeit their dignity. On "Newsroom" that night I said as much, and the first of a series of threats began to accent my life.

At six o'clock that morning I had received a call on my unlisted home phone. It was one of my sources, whispering, "The two blacks are Wheeler and De——, escaped cons." Then a click. The line was dead.

Wheeler and "De"-something. I was half-asleep and the second name could have been anything from Defis to Debreeze. It had been more a sound than a name—a roll of the tongue, a slur of letters, and the phrase "escaped cons."

By 9:00 A.M. Russin and I started piecing the puzzle together. I told him that the early-morning tip had come from a solid, reliable source. Russin accepted that and we started the endless chore of finding people to fit the two names—faces, backgrounds, facts.

Could the squeaky voice of the self-styled General Field Marshal Cinque be matched to one of the names? The name Cinque itself was a clue. Whoever had adopted it as a reborn name—a not-uncommon practice among militant blacks—hadn't known much history. Cinque was a black who had been among a cargo of slaves brought to America more than a hundred years ago. He had led his fellow captives in mutiny and taken over the slave ship. But then he had turned captain himself, keeping command of the slave ship he had pirated and making many more trips across the Atlantic, bringing more slaves for sale. He was hardly a hero figure for a black man.

With these slim threads, I began to weave the fabric of the first public report of who the two black men were who had dragged Patty Hearst off the week before.

I made a quick call to Sacramento, to an official of California State Prisons, a man I'd known since covering San Quentin's last execution in 1967. He was always honest and direct.

The question I put to him was: "Do you know of any black male convicts who have escaped with the last name of Wheeler or one that sounds like De Feese?"

It was a long wait. My friend came back on the line; he had pulled the records. "Try Vacaville for Wheeler, Soledad for the other."

Vacaville is called a medical facility, because it houses the criminally insane and processes other prisoners who pass through it for "psychological evaluation." After such tests many of the prisoners go on to one of the regular state prisons, such as Soledad.

Telephone calls to both prisons found their superintendents unavailable. Russin checked in with me. He had Tom Devries, a former "Newsroom" reporter, out on the streets in Berkeley, trying to turn up leads. Devries had quit the year before, to live on a small farm near Mariposa. But he was, first and foremost, a good

74

reporter. This story was too gripping to pass up. He came down from his retreat to help.

Russin began, "Devries just called. Some black dude has been going around Berkeley for about six months, claiming he escaped from Soledad." It was another thread, another piece of the fabric slowly being pulled together. "Devries was also told," Russin went on, "that this dude came on so strong that some of the left-wing groups thought he must be an agent provocateur. He called himself Cinque."

I finally got through to Alf Christenson at Soledad. He said he was the "prison official." It became clear that, in our enlightened prison age, the word "warden" is no longer acceptable.

Again I asked a simple question: "Do you have an escaped convict listed with a name that sounds like De Feese?" And again the long wait.

"You must mean De Freeze. That's Donald David. He escaped last March; was in for assault, robbery. He was working in a boiler room outside the main compound and he walked off." He sighed. "That's how most of them escape."

The General Field Marshal on the tape had talked of being a father. Did De Freeze have children?

"Why, yes, I believe he had two or three. Maybe they are in Los Angeles. That's where he was from, where he was convicted. He was at Vacaville before he came here, just a couple of months before his escape."

"By the way, Mr. Christenson, do you happen to know if De Freeze had a nickname, or any other name he was known by— an alias?"

"Now that you ask, yes, he did. He was known as Cinque. That's what he called himself."

It all fitted. Donald David De Freeze had to be the self-appointed leader of the SLA and a captor of Patty Hearst. I put in a call to a law-enforcement official who had access to the artist's sketches of the two black men and the white woman who had abducted her. This man would have access to prison mug shots of De Freeze as well.

We met at our usual table in the rear of a greasy spoon, the kind of restaurant frequented only by winos. He had the artist's sketches and the mug shots. They were a perfect match. The sketch drawn from the witnesses' descriptions couldn't have been better if De Freeze had actually posed for the police artist. There was no doubt about it—De Freeze was Cinque.

Calls to Vacaville produced the name Thero Wheeler, black, militant, once a member of Venceremos, the revolutionary group that had been the vehicle for some of the cult members in pre-Symbionese days. I compared the police artist's sketch of Wheeler with the prison mug shots. Wheeler had an exceptionally wide mouth and nostrils that flared out toward his ears. The artist had not exaggerated these features as much as nature had. Yet there was a strong likeness, even though the sketch was not as perfect as De Freeze's.

I asked my friend if he knew there were two black men wanted for Patty Hearst's abduction. He smiled, glanced down at the pictures, and said, "If I was a reporter, I'd figure I was on the right track."

Back at KQED Russin was doubtful when I said I wanted to break the story on "Newsroom" that night. Maybe we should wait for more proof. We argued. What more proof was needed?

"Call Vacaville, get more on Wheeler," Russin snapped.

The record was precise. Wheeler had been under consideration for parole. He had renounced Venceremos, the revolutionary group. The prison officials hadn't wondered why. The previous August, when Wheeler had been nearing his parole date, he was mowing the grass at a Little League field just outside the prison. He had walked away. His family is from San Francisco. His brother, Billy Wheeler, is a San Francisco policeman.

The Venceremos group of which Wheeler had been a member was headquartered in Palo Alto, the campus community for Stanford University, just a stone's throw from the Hearst home in Hillsborough. Prison officials recalled a white woman who had constantly visited Wheeler. She said she loved him. She had been there twenty-four hours before he had escaped. She had close ties with the law firm that represented Joe Remiro, one of the two Symbionese soldiers charged with Marcus Foster's murder. It was more than coincidence.

Since Wheeler's brother Billy absolutely refused to answer any questions at all about his family, I lugged the city directories over to my desk to dig out whatever information they could provide. I finally found an address for the mother—a hotel in North Beach, in the center of San Francisco's topless joints. But she had moved and left no forwarding address.

By calling Sacramento again, I was able to find out who had visited De Freeze and Wheeler in prison. Wheeler's visitors were primarily San Franciscans, none with ties to Venceremos or the SLA. De Freeze had had only one visitor, a young woman from Berkeley. Yet when he went before the parole board in November 1972, two people had written letters recommending he be given his freedom—Russell Little and his sister Jo Ann. Now Little awaited trial with Remiro for the Foster murder, and both had been publicly identified by the SLA as two of its soldiers.

Each name, from prison visitors to former neighbors, was another lead to follow through on. Voters' registrations provided home addresses; motor vehicles, physical descriptions; city directories, places of employment. It all came together. De Freeze and Wheeler. But in coming together, it opened up another trail to follow—the remnants of Venceremos. Had they really disbanded after one of their inner circle had been charged with murdering a guard in a prison escape in Southern California? If there was no longer a Venceremos, had its splinters come together as the Symbionese?

The matter would have to wait until tomorrow. Tonight we would name the two black men. One question remained—about Wheeler's first name, Thero. I thought it might be wrong, that there was another name he'd been known by. So I decided to use only his last name in writing the script for "Newsroom." Russin read it, made editorial corrections, and sent it through. Tonight we'd break it.

"Maybe you'd better let Hearst know what you're going to do," he said.

He was right. I had to call Randolph and Catherine Hearst, and I could almost hear their question now: What about Cinque's whining threat that any effort to identify the SLA would bring death to their prisoner? We knew the SLA was capable of murder. The bullet-torn body of Marcus Foster proved that. Was the story serving journalism or risking Patricia Hearst's life?

One fact was clear. As long as only Patty could identify her captors, they had every reason to wish her dead. If I went on television and identified them, even the SLA couldn't believe it could murder half a million viewers. But I frankly wanted the decision to come from the Hearsts. I had strong empathy for what they must be living through. My son Jeff had spent a year in Vietnam and I knew the terror of wondering each hour if he had been killed the hour before, and I didn't even know it yet.

Randolph Hearst immediately took my call and told me what a fine job he and his wife thought I was doing, reporting on the SLA. Briefly, and as undramatically as possible, I read him the script I had just finished, read him the names and prison records of two of his daughter's three kidnappers.

"Oh, my God. Oh, no . . ." Now he knew that his daughter's abductors had a history of violence and were indeed capable of murder. Before I could ask if he wanted the story held, he asked me to repeat the story to a man who was with him.

A male voice came on the line and mysteriously said, "I can't tell you my name or what agency I'm with but you can trust me." For a second I wanted to toy with this cloak-and-dagger player. He is an FBI agent and I knew his name. But I decided against any charade and read my story to him, then asked that he put Hearst back on the line.

"Please, just call me Randy," Hearst said quickly, setting the tone for our future conversations, which became almost a daily occurrence.

"Do you want me to hold the story or not?"

"Well, I just don't know. If we're dealing with bad ones, like you say, I don't know what to say. I can't ask you not to do it. After all, you got the story. I know the news business. I can't ask that of you. I guess you'd better go ahead and do it. I know the *Chronicle*'s been trying to put something like this together, but I don't think they have it all like you do yet."

As I started to thank him, he broke in. "Let me give you the unlisted numbers we have here. The first is used by quite a few, but the second number just rings in my room. You call at any hour, whenever you want," he offered as a good-bye.

I went back to Russin. "Hearst says to go with it." He looked up as though he couldn't quite believe it.

The evening news rundown was changed—the Hearst story had to lead. I sat at my desk, rereading the script a hundred times—the names, the records, the histories—words that would strip the SLA of its seven-headed cobra mask. I had no doubts now that the story should be told. I believed it was the best life insurance policy possible for Patty Hearst.

The hands of the clock crept forward, the hum of the studio quickened with the sudden burst of adrenalin that hits any newsroom before a deadline. By 6:50 P.M. the six reporters took their places at the roundtable, the lights glared, sweat started dripping down faces tired from a ten-hour day. The mugs of ice water turned lukewarm, speckled with the dust stirred from the overhead rafters. Only one chair was still empty. Mine. I sat with Russin as he told me, "Mrs. Hearst just called me. She was crying, she was hysterical. She pleaded with me to kill the De Freeze piece. I killed it. What the hell else could I do?"

"Absolutely nothing, Joseph, don't sweat it. It's their daughter who's on the line."

"Damn, I hate to lose it, but she was crying the whole damned time, saying they'd kill Patty."

I thought for a minute. "How about my open letter? Can I do that instead?"

"Okay, do it," Russin agreed without enthusiasm.

I had written an open letter that afternoon because I felt so angry with this radical group. How dare they expect to be taken seriously! How dare the media take them seriously! Someone had to remind the public that these people were killers. No one volunteered, so I spoke out. I began: "You continue to try to hide your violence, kidnapping, and murder behind the rhetoric of political action. And you talk of the people's court and your pledge to free the oppressed. But *YOU* are *NOT* 'the people.' Who gave you the right to decide the life or death of another human being?" I added a line to Cinque: "You claim you care about children. When was the last time you tried to do anything for your own?" And I finished: "It is you who are the fascist insect preying on the people—and it is the people who will destroy you."

Russin had read the letter. It was concise. The SLA was composed of murderers and kidnappers; but Russin couldn't help a gut reaction, a hold-off-don't-do-it feeling. The clock ignored the decision-making. It kept its steady pace toward seven. In the control booth Cordelia Stone, the director, started the stopwatch, readied the opening tape of the rinky-tink piano that would splinter out the theme song. The slate, a battered three-by-three-foot board lettered "Newsroom, February 12," was held before the camera; the red eye above the camera's gaping lens winked on. Decision time was past.

"Newsroom" opened with the report of the tape and the ransom demands. I said my piece about how the SLA should try to find jobs for the poor, then waited for my turn on camera again to read the open letter. I never got the chance. A message, slipped to me from Joe Russin, said: "The open letter is dumped. Shut up."

I sat silent for the rest of the program, disappointed, wounded, and wondering what was going on. I didn't know that minutes after my first blast at the SLA, a male voice had telephoned the station and said to Russin, "Shut Baker up—or else." And cool, calm Russin had taken the threat seriously enough to repeat it to the FBI.

The FBI took it seriously enough to insist I have a police guard. For a week I had armed cops escorting me home from work and looking under the bed before they'd leave me for the night. And every morning they'd escort me back to the office. I have no illusions about my safety. If a bullet could reach John F. Kennedy, one could certainly find me.

So I didn't read the open letter that night. And I didn't report to the viewers who the man behind the title General Field Marshal Cinque was. Catherine Hearst's tears had canceled the disclosure.

I was determined that my open letter, at least, would air tomorrow night. And it did.

By 8:00 A.M. a hum was starting in KQED's second-floor offices. It was a day to pry one more small fact out of the state's records, to pick up one more bit of gossip from Berkeley's street people, to put the final polish on the story revealing Cinque.

Old contacts were brought into play. One was a Los Angeles law-enforcement official who had been one of my students in the Specialized Training Institute and who remembered me as his "teacher." He also remembered that I had leveled with the class, had told it what the media didn't like about cops. So he leveled with me. They had the record of Donald De Freeze.

The record was stark in its simplicity, one that could belong to a thousand other drifters in the black community—De Freeze had been picked up half-a-hundred times as a suspect in muggings, small-time crimes, strong-arm robbery. Each the kind of crime that was an everyday fact of survival in the ghetto of his black victims. *And all his victims had been black.*

There had been a roust in the summer of 1969, when he was picked up while riding a bicycle. The makings of a bomb were in the bicycle basket. De Freeze was never a part of the militant black movement; the police had enough intelligence on him to know that. The bomb wasn't destined for political action, as the militants called their killing of cops. It was more a giant fire-cracker, the kind thugs use to break open back doors of Mom and Pop stores to steal pennies from cash registers. Soon after De Freeze made bail and was back on the streets, he was picked up again for questioning on recurring crimes, the kind that make statistics but not headlines.

I remembered the taped voice, the affected lilt, the attempt by a ninth-grade dropout to sound intellectual—Cinque's voice declaring the equality of women, the importance of women, the dignity of women.

The official voice at the end of the phone in Los Angeles continued: "Then there was this last bust. He was out on bail from the bomb thing; he picked up this black prostitute, took her to a motel at Forty-second and Broadway down in the black area of Los Angeles. He made it with her, but when she asked for her money he beat the shit out of her, slammed her into the wall, and got a gun out of his jacket. He held the damned gun on her while he turned her purse inside out, took all her money and a government check she had, then opened the motel-room door and threw her out. She told us he said: 'What can you do, you black cunt? You can't call the pigs.' "

I could hear the official laughing. "Man, that woman was mad. She said she may be black, she may be a whore, but she sure as hell had some rights. So she called the cops and told them the whole story. De Freeze had been so certain that a prostitute couldn't do a damned thing that the cops found him still in the motel, boozed up, asleep on the bed, with the goddamned gun still in his hand."

He had been booked on new felonies—assault, armed robbery, and possession of stolen property. The cops started digging. The revolver was one of three that had been stolen in a burglary a few months earlier. They grilled De Freeze. This time, they told him, the victim would testify. This time he wouldn't beat the rap. He started talking.

"He said," my source continued, "if we'd take him to his house he'd show us where the other guns were and other stuff he had burglarized. We fell for it. The house was an old two-story job and De Freeze had a room upstairs. Well, we're walking around that room, he's talking a blue streak, and all of a sudden he dives right out the damned window—right out that damned window! We chased him, but he just rolled over on the grass, got up, and took off. It took us twenty-four hours to find him again, still hanging around the same street corners he always hung around. The dude just wasn't too bright."

After that arrest, there had been no way for De Freeze to save his skin by a leap out a window. The cops started questioning him again, pointing out that he now had four felonies against him and that spelled life behind bars. But De Freeze tried once more to save his skin: Wouldn't the cops like to nail his partner in the burglaries?

It was the usual thing. Squeal on a buddy so the court will let you plead guilty to a lesser charge. There was no reason for the cops not to go along with him. After all, despite their ominous threat of a life sentence for De Freeze, the cops knew he would probably be back on the street within three years. Why not go along with the lower sentence and get two birds at the same time?

De Freeze spilled everything, talking on and on, piling words on words until he'd built a solid case around a black brother, Ronald Coleman, his partner in crime, his buddy. Both went to prison in 1970. De Freeze was assured of an easy sentence and a quick switch to a semi-trustee position. Coleman was bitter because his capture had been brought about by a black man, not the cops.

Weeks later I checked with some of the men who had been De Freeze's cellmates at Vacaville, one of the prisons he had spent time in. They told me, "He was the asshole of the mainline"—the prison snitch, the dude who would turn in anyone for a pack of cigarettes. He was hated by the inmates, especially the black inmates. Man, they didn't dig a snitch—and that's all this punk De Freeze ever really was, a two-bit hood and a snitch.

It was five minutes before airtime on Thursday, February 14, when I got the call from Randy Hearst. His message was simple, direct, and despairing. "The *Chronicle* is going with a story tomorrow on who Cinque is. Since you had it first, and held it up for us, I thought it only fair to let you know. You can go ahead and do it."

"I don't need scoops that much. Do you want me to kill it anyway?" I asked, afraid he would say yes.

But his voice got stronger. He said, "No, after all, at least you're reporting all of it. You aren't trying to whitewash the left with this story."

I ran across the newsroom to Russin's desk. "It's go for tonight—Randy says okay!" I yelled.

Russin stared, not sure he had heard right. "I want to talk to him myself," he grumbled, and he himself called Hearst for confirmation.

Huddled at Russin's desk again to rewrite the story of how the identity of Patty's two black abductors had become known, we decided to concentrate more on De Freeze's background, not using too many details, but saving some for later. Of course, there was more checking to be done for backup information other than that from police sources, followed by a cross-checking of all the sources. The "rule of two" was in force—a rule that has held throughout the SLA coverage. We always make sure our information comes from at least two sources. Street and cops—or friend and foe. Only actual eyewitnesses were believed, but even their quotes were salted down to simple statements.

That night I identified the two men who had kidnapped Patty Hearst. For the first time, there were unmasked humans behind the Symbionese Liberation cobra. My revelations made me a part of the SLA story, and reporters from other television stations were outside the newsroom door when we went off the air, waiting to interview me. And there were calls from New York, Canada, and the Midwest.

I called my radical sources, those who publicly disavowed me, labeling me "pig lover" and "reactionary" while privately funneling me information. "We think these SLA are a bunch of nuts. They're doing more to harm the cause of the oppressed than to help it. We want them caught. The women run it. The SLA is women. Try checking heavy lesbian contacts."

The calls kept coming into KQED-TV, in San Francisco's

industrial slum. In every fifty calls, there was at least one person who would say, "Yes, I heard about this SLA thing. Try so-and-so; they may know." I kept trying until the rule of two held. Yes. Women controlled the SLA.

"Newsroom," February 18. We were on the air when the silent phone at Russin's elbow began winking. He picked it up, his face turned pale, and at the next break, when a film clip took over the screen, he leaned over to me and whispered, "There's been a bomb call. A man. He said it was a plastic bomb, set for eight-seventeen P.M. He said: 'It's meant for Marilyn Baker.'"

Russin glanced around the roundtable at the other reporters. None of them looked too pleased. He looked back at me and said, "We've called the cops. Stay on the set, right here."

Within minutes blue uniforms were moving around silently behind us. Cops walking on tiptoe, so that the audience wouldn't know there was anything happening besides the usual weeknight telecast of "Newsroom" with its familiar faces around the table.

I could see police sliding under the camera lens, as they searched for some sign of the bomb. By 8:00 P.M. beads of sweat were trickling down all our faces. The final credits were still rolling on the tube when a cop rushed over to me and demanded, "Where's your desk? Quick, show us!" We ran upstairs, but one look at my desk defeated them. It was stacked three feet high with papers, books, files, and the paraphernalia of investigative reporting.

"A plastic bomb can be as small as a pack of matches. There's no way we can find one in this mess," grumbled a police sergeant.

"Damn it, Marilyn, think!" another cop shouted.

"Think of what? How in hell do I know where someone would put a bomb?" I shouted back.

"Where would you normally be at eight-seventeen tonight?" In my car, on my way home, or to whatever new lead I had to follow. Yes, I was certain. At 8:17 P.M. I was almost always in my car.

Out in the street black-and-white patrol cars double-parked all along the front of KQED. We ran along the street to my car, parked on the corner. The hood was open, gaping like an angry wound. Two officers hauled me off and shoved me into the back seat of a patrol car. They got in and drove off, tires squealing. "We're getting you away from here," one called over his shoulder.

We stopped at a spot where we could watch the activity

around KQED from a safe distance. Red flares were set up for a block around the station, patrol cars swung across traffic lanes in front of the red glare, stopping all cars; and the bomb squad, their bodies hidden by massive chest guards and their faces lost behind heavy masks, slowly started pushing the hood of my car higher up.

It was 8:15 . . . 8:16, one minute left. We sat. No one talked. We kept watching. Nothing happened.

By 8:45 P.M. they allowed me to look at the car. Wires had been ripped out under the hood. The motor wouldn't even start. The squad had been all over the car, but they weren't satisfied. "Don't drive it tonight at all. A plastic bomb could be anywhere —under a fender, inside a door. We just can't be sure and, from the inside of that engine, someone's tried something here."

I didn't need a second warning. A patrol car drove me home.

CHAPTER **7**

IT IS USUALLY QUIET in the newsroom at 8:30 in the morning.
Only a few of the staff struggle in that early. On this particular
day, it seemed a good time to catch up on what the newspapers
have been printing on the Hearst kidnapping.

The headline story was about a mystery witness appearing before the grand jury in the Foster murder. The reason behind the
grand jury probe was to try to indict Remiro and Little, the
SLA soldiers, directly, without going through the laborious pre-
trial steps of arraignment demanded by our court system. If the
grand jury were to return indictments, the two would go straight
to trial. I dreaded that trial. It would be like watching summer
reruns on television. I could already see the cast of characters,
the picket lines around the Alameda County Courthouse in Oakland, just like the lines formed to protest the trial of black Huey
Newton in 1968. I didn't want to get stuck covering that circus.

Besides, I hadn't the foggiest notion where to start searching
out mystery witnesses. My work was aimed at the hard-core SLA,
the members still on the loose, the ones holding Patty Hearst cap-

tive, not the two SLA soldiers smirking at the cameras from their cells. Jeff had told me all I wanted to know about Joe Remiro anyway.

The ring of the telephone interrupted my reading. At the other end of the wire, a man's voice said, "This is Gordon Reynolds, an attorney in Oakland. I have a client who would like to talk to you."

"Oh? What about, Mr. Reynolds?"

"About this SLA thing."

"Well, what does your client know?" I'd been receiving at least a dozen calls a day from people who wanted to talk but had no substantial information. I didn't dare not talk to them. There was always the possibility that one of them had a vital clue, a piece of the puzzle that would make all the odds and ends fall into place.

"My client is Chris Thompson."

I'd never heard of him.

Mr. Reynolds continued, "He's the witness the morning newspapers are talking about, the secret witness before the grand jury."

I tried to keep the excitement out of my voice, "Oh. Well, I think I'd like to interview him. When would be a good time to come over with a camera crew?"

"How does Monday seem to you?" Reynolds asked.

Of course, Monday seemed light years away, but my instinct told me not to push it. I calmly answered, "That sounds fine; Monday it is. Is noon good for you?"

"Yes, that's fine. Chris will be here." He gave me his address, in downtown Oakland, three blocks from the courthouse where the grand jury was meeting.

So Chris Thompson would be on Monday; but today there was another lead. I had had a phone call a few days before—it was the same muffled voice that had rocked me out of sleep at 6:00 A.M. a few weeks ago, the voice that had said "Wheeler and De Freeze." Now I heard another whispered name, even less understandable than De Freeze's had been. All I could make out was something that sounded like "Sol-tie-sick," which, my mysterious caller said, belonged to a woman, "the brains of the SLA." The voice added, "Ms. Moon." That was all.

The garbled name kept me busy the rest of the day. It carried me across the Bay Bridge to Oakland, to the cool cellar of the County Building, where the voter's registration records are. I spent hours poring over them, checking every name that began with the letters "Sol," every one that had the slightest foreign sound. I ran through hundreds of voter cards, none quite right, none matching the phonetic identification humming inside my head. Suddenly there it was: Patricia Monique Soltysik. Even the address seemed right—2135 Parker Street, Berkeley. There couldn't be two names with that same phonetic ring—and in Berkeley, the backdrop of the SLA.

The Parker Street house was not what I expected. It was no musty commune nor a paint-peeling shed. There weren't even any rusted cars as front-yard decoration. It was quaint and picturesque, a small yellow bungalow behind the older front house.

Two young men now shared the ground-level apartment where Patricia Soltysik had lived, the apartment with leaded-pane windows, red-tile floors, a kitchen that cried for simmering pots, a fireplace that beckoned, and bookcases. It was a house I could happily live in. The home of the SLA's brain? It didn't seem possible. It didn't match my mental image.

The young men had moved in only that week. All they could tell me was that a young woman had been the former tenant, and that she had had a roommate called Mizmoon Soltysik. But perhaps a woman who lived above, up the winding steps, would be able to help; she had been there longer.

The woman was less than hospitable. When I asked her if she knew anything about Patricia Soltysik, she responded, "I wouldn't tell any pig reporter if I did."

I was tired, my head aching from reading the voter registration cards. I was pressed for time and worried now that Chris Thompson might change his mind about the interview. I was in no mood to take any guff from this Berkeley woman, with her stringy hair and unkempt appearance.

"Look, lady," I snapped, "this is what I get paid to do. Maybe I'm not clever, but I don't live off food stamps or welfare, and I sure as hell pay the taxes that let people like you live off them. Now all I want are some simple answers to some straight questions."

My outburst took her by surprise. She lost her belligerence. "Oh, what the hell—okay. The other girl moved out last week. The feds have been around here. They were looking for this Soltysik. I didn't know her myself, but some of the neighbors say she was heavy lesbian."

A few more questions—she even spelled "Mizmoon" for me—and I drove off to the flower shop owned by the landlord of the Parker Street house. He was Asian, with a thick, musical accent that I could hardly comprehend. The only sentence I was able to grasp was the one he repeated several times: "She, that woman, she had colored men there all the time."

Another piece of the puzzle fitted. Black men were in the SLA, and Soltysik had black male acquaintances. She had moved from her last known address in August 1973. She'd been underground since. But where had she been before?

Her previous address had been 2021 Channing Way, also in Berkeley. This one was exactly what I had expected—an old dilapidated building with posters on United Prisoners' Union in the windows and hand-painted clenched fists dappling the grime of the building's front. An apartment turned commune, a typical Berkeley radical haven.

My knocking on more doors resulted in their being slammed in my face. My ego was bruised as people poked their heads out of windows, demanding I "get the shit outta here." But I knew the odds were in my favor. For every one hundred who refused to talk, there was one who would. The odds held on Channing Way.

Slowly, Patricia Soltysik's history came together—her love affairs, her fears, her politics, and her Symbionese involvement. Her portrait was now complete. It had been a good day.

By the time I walked into the law offices of Gordon Reynolds to meet Chris Thompson, the mystery witness of the grand jury, I knew who I would ask him about. Patricia Mizmoon Soltysik, Camilla Hall, Nancy Ling Perry, Emily Harris and her husband Bill, Angela Atwood, and Willie Wolfe; it already appeared, however, that the men were strictly supporting players in the SLA tragicomedy.

If Patricia Soltysik's cottage had been a surprise, Thompson provided an even bigger one. He was no rhetoric-spewing revolutionary. He didn't even fit the stereotyped image of Berkeley.

Thompson is black. He is tall, almost majestic; thin, like a steel rod. His wide eyes peer from behind thick glasses, his hair is

89

clipped almost to the scalp. His walk seems paced to "Pomp and Circumstance." And, sitting erect in a chair facing his attorney, Chris Thompson seemed to be waiting for something. He was most impressive.

His first words were, "I don't think I want to be on camera."

I had hoped to tape up to airtime for "Newsroom." Now my subject was shying away. I pleaded, but Thompson wasn't buying. Each reason I offered for why he should go on camera brought back at least two why he should not. His attorney, a comfortable white man in his middle years, seemed somewhat appalled to find himself even remotely connected with the SLA. He was obviously embarrassed. But they had called me. I argued that a camera crew was cooling its heels in the lawyer's library. "You can't just call out a crew and then refuse to face it," I said. Thompson finally relented.

We started the interview. It was the first time I'd talked to anyone who not only knew the SLA but was also willing to talk about it.

Over weeks of interviews, the birth of the SLA became clear. Chris Thompson had been an unknowing midwife at that birth. He poured out the facts as though they were public knowledge. I didn't take notes. The camera whirled. Videotape could run for hours and be erased and reused if what it taped did not turn out to be gold. There was little of Chris Thompson's interviews that would be erased.

First he talked about his testimony to the grand jury: He had sold Russell Little a Rossi .38 revolver for $65. Of course, he had no receipt. This was the weapon the police believed to be one of those used in the murder of Marcus Foster. That's why Thompson had retained Gordon Reynolds and volunteered to go before the grand jury. The gun was registered in his name and he knew he could be called in. It would be better if he appeared voluntarily.

I met this man day after day; I was his student whom he instructed about the people of the SLA. It had started when Thompson lived at Peking Man House, the commune Russin and I had attempted to infiltrate, where Russin had finally spent hours "rapping politics" and had come away with only misinformation. The place was owned by jazz musician David Gunnell, and named after a street-vendor stand his Asian girlfriend Jean Wa Chan ran on Telegraph Avenue.

Thompson had lived at Peking Man House with Russell Little and Willie Wolfe. Thompson didn't like Wolfe. He thought he was spoiled and "off the wall" in his politics. He told me Wolfe was the son of a doctor in Pennsylvania, and that his divorced mother was wealthy. Wolfe was "playing at revolution," Thompson said. "He'd go up to prisons like Vacaville. He'd sit around and rap with black prisoners, in the thing they had called the Black Cultural Association. It was nothing but tokenism. Blacks don't need whites to talk to, to save themselves. But Wolfe thought he was saving them just because he went inside that prison gate to talk to them.

Little had joined the BCA with Wolfe and they both went to the weekly sessions at Vacaville.

"Was Willie Wolfe a leader? Did Little follow him?" I asked.

"Hell, no, Willie was no leader. Nobody would go anywhere with Willie. People wouldn't follow Willie Wolfe to the bathroom."

"Why not?"

"He was a loser. He was just a rich white kid playing at politics. No one respected him, not even in Peking Man House," Thompson emphasized.

The BCA wasn't unknown in connection with the SLA. We knew Little and Wolfe had been members. We knew that Emily and Bill Harris had been active in it. Prisoners had said even Nancy Ling Perry had been at one or two meetings. Several white women known for membership in other revolutionary groups also went to the BCA prison sessions. It was headed by Colston Westbrook, a fat black man who wore a vest and a fancy knit cap. He seemed more nightclub comic than political activist. Russin told me he had learned that some wanted the BCA to provide white women for the black prisoners. It was all part of the rehabilitation therapy, of course, and a way for the black prisoners to be pacified. The girls themselves, wrapped in political rhetoric, felt they were offering a "meaningful relationship" with "relevant dialogue."

"Give the blacks some white snatch and they're happy" was

what Russin had told me he had been told by BCA sources. "Right under the stage, while the BCA meetings went on over their heads. It was a big thing to recruit young white chicks, get them to attend in miniskirts and bikini panties. And that's how you help a black prisoner."

A pattern was emerging. The SLA women were either lesbian or liked black men.

But as Peking Man House residents went into the BCA, they brought a new kind of "help." They wanted to teach black convicts all about revolution, to bring Maoist lessons inside the prison. Westbrook fought it. "These poor black brothers don't need no Maoist politics when they're locked away inside," Westbrook argued.

But it was too late. Contacts had already been made. Russell Little and Donald De Freeze had become friends. Thero Wheeler knew Wolfe and Little as well. The aid offered these convicts was far beyond the favors of a white woman. Thompson explained, "It was last March when Little came to me and said he had this black dude who needed a place to stay. He didn't have to spell it out. I knew. It was an escaped con. I arranged for him to move in with Mizmoon Soltysik, into her Parker street cottage. I'd been having an affair with her, so I knew she was cool about blacks."

The escaped convict was De Freeze, who had been serving time for an assortment of violent crimes; from March until August 1973, he had lived in the quaint cottage with its cared-for gardens.

Another piece of the puzzle fitted. The comment by Mizmoon's landlord, "She had colored men there all the time." De Freeze and Thompson. It seemed almost unreal to be sitting talking to Thompson, just as the whole SLA game of code names, war councils, and weapons seemed unreal.

But the weapons had been real, Thompson assured me. They held regular gun classes on Sunday mornings, downstairs in Peking Man House. They learned about caring for their weapons and how to use them. Then they'd spend Sunday afternoons target shooting, out at Chabot Range in the Oakland Hills.

"We spent a lot of evenings together, too," Thompson offered.

What was a typical evening like with this strange band? "Oh, I'd go over to Mizmoon's. Her roommate always stayed in another room, so there'd just be me, Mizmoon, and Cinque. That's what De Freeze wanted to be called. It was almost routine. Cinque was around the house all day, so he'd clean it. He liked to cook. He was pretty good at it, too. He'd even worked as a short-order cook once. So he'd cook dinner, we'd eat, Mizmoon and I would talk—maybe about some film I was working on for political causes—Cinque would clean up."

Cinque's only claim to distinction is that he drank plum wine, but as Thompson pointed out, "If there wasn't any of that, he'd drink anything."

The image was in sharp focus. Strong dominant bisexual Mizmoon keeping Thompson interested, even though her lover, Camilla Hall, was back from a trip to Europe. Cinque, little more than a cook and handyman, waiting to please Mizmoon's palate with his latest culinary triumph.

"Mizmoon didn't really drink, so just Cinque would have the wine. Mizmoon, she liked herb teas—peppermint and rose hips. Things that were health foods, organically grown things. Cinque, he fried a lot of stuff. Sometimes it was greasy. But he did ham and black-eyed peas and chili very well. That was good."

It was almost a caricature—a black man stirring the black-eyed peas while a white woman intellectualized in the living room. But where did the articulate, regal Chris Thompson fit into the picture? "Oh, Mizmoon and I had a thing. But when Camilla came back, she didn't like the idea. She was much more rigid in those things than Mizmoon, so we sort of tapered off. Mizmoon was a private sort of person anyway, spent a lot of time alone. Cinque, he was a talker, at least he would if anyone would listen."

Not many bothered to listen, according to Thompson. Cinque was more a handy symbol: the living, breathing proof of the white radical's desire to aid black prisoners. It didn't mean, however, that they had to socialize with him.

While an inmate-member of the Black Cultural Association in Vacaville Prison, Cinque had tried to be elected its leader. But the inmates wanted no snitch for a leader. So a handful of white middle-class radicals got him. And what did Cinque get in return? Thompson thought he knew: "The SLA had to try to pretend they had black-community support. The fact is, they did not. But they put Cinque up front, paraded him like the house nigger. He was their token black. In return, he had a safe house,

food to eat, wine to drink. That's all he really cared about anyway. All this political terrorist stuff was just something he talked
about to try and sound like a man."

Although Cinque's background was cut and dried, Thompson's
was not. Why had Thompson called me to interview him? It was
fairly well known that I was not basically sympathetic to radicals
and certainly not sympathetic to any type of terrorism. I had
publicly labeled the SLA exploiters of the people a week after
Patty Hearst was kidnapped. Surely Thompson couldn't have
expected me to sympathize with him as he sat there calmly
giving me the details of the SLA membership.

He said he had been active in the Black Student Union in New
York City. Other street sources among the radicals told me he
had been involved in a bomb case that had made headlines in
San Francisco the year before. He had the ability to be in dead
center of some activity and then to walk away without a scratch
when it blew up—even away from the SLA.

He was sitting with me at KQED, drinking coffee, when he
heard the news of another SLA tape's being delivered to KPFA
radio. We went downstairs to find a small transistor radio that
we could listen to without the hum of the newsroom around us.
Thompson's attorney, Gordon Reynolds, was with us. The radio
crackled with static, and the poor quality of the original SLA
recording made understanding difficult. But each of us heard,
loud and clear, the announcement of the death warrants issued
against Robyn Steiner, the ex-girlfriend of Russell Little; Colston
Westbrook, the BCA founder who had tried to keep Maoist politics out of the BCA; and Chris Thompson, labeled an FBI and
CIA informer and agent. Each was marked for instant execution
by the SLA.

Reynolds went into a rage. "My God, oh my God, I've got to
get Chris to safety. He's my client. I have to protect him." He ran
off to use the phone.

Thompson was quiet. He paced around the empty studio we'd
been standing in. "What are you going to do?" I asked him.

"I just don't know. I need time to think. Time to evaluate it. I
just don't know," was his answer.

At 6:00 P.M., while I was still sitting with Chris Thompson,
two burly investigators from the district attorney's office in
Oakland, where the grand jury was waiting to indict SLA soldiers

94

Little and Remiro, came to the studio to take Thompson into protective custody. They rushed him down the back stairs to an unmarked car waiting in the alley alongside KQED with its engine running. The tight-lipped efficiency attending his exit had all the earmarks of a scene from "The Untouchables."

By noon the next day, the hot potato was tossed back in my lap. Thompson called. The police had stashed him in the Piedmont jail, a two-cell affair rarely having a tenant, in a small city of good homes and old families high in the hills above Oakland. But jail wasn't Thompson's idea of sanctuary. I agreed to find another place for him to hide.

Whenever I need the impossible, I go to my son Jeff.

Jeff's only income was from the G.I. Bill. It barely covered the rent on his two rooms in a tenement. "Send him on over, I'll cover him," he agreed with resignation in his voice. But even Jeff's devotion has bounds. Within two days he called. "I'd sure like Thompson to find another place, like right now."

I know better than to push Jeff. His instincts are far better than mine. I drove over, told Thompson he'd have to relocate, and he left. Then Jeff filled me in on why he had wanted to be rid of his marked houseguest: "He sat here, telling me how beautiful the Arabs were in Munich when they killed all those people, what a glorious action that was. The only mistake they made—the Arabs didn't get the media on their side so they didn't get public sympathy. That kind of dude I can do without." Jeff had been too long in Vietnam to find beauty or glory in killing.

"We went out to Cal State Hayward University," Jeff said, "and we walked into the cafeteria, and Thompson tells me he's going to talk to a couple of guys there, but don't be surprised because they'll call him by some other name. He said the other name, but I don't remember it. I wondered, why a phony name?"

What Jeff had said only added to my puzzlement concerning Thompson. It had only been a few days before that he had sat and told me he was willing to testify against the SLA because "violence is never the answer." About Marcus Foster's murder, he'd said, "It was the biggest mistake the SLA ever made." Had I misread him? Had he meant killing the Oakland school superintendent was the mistake—or that not winning public support for the killing was the mistake?

Other facts I was able to turn up only clouded the picture of him more.

Each time we talked, his involvement with the cobra cult became more obvious. He had soon dropped the pose that he had not seen any of them since the summer of 1973. He brought me a hand-painted card that Mizmoon had delivered to him in October, just weeks before Foster's murder and the public revelation of the SLA. He told me he had had an affair with Nancy Ling Perry. In his various accounts of his last meeting with her, the time got closer and closer to the Foster murder date. He finally said he had seen her in Berkeley at Christmas, after the Symbionese murder, when she was hiding in the house in Clayton, the house she eventually tried to burn down.

"I've boxes full of things from them," he said.

Would he bring me some of these things? "Oh, sure, that's no problem."

He did. Candid photos he'd snapped of Mizmoon, drinking coffee, walking in the woods, laughing at jokes he told her. A hurried letter from Nancy, penciled on notebook paper, dated May 11, 1973.

Thompson reminisced about Nancy, recalling conversations they had had. He remembered once she had apologized to him for some misunderstanding: "Naturally I love you . . . but too many scary changes this week . . . I'm such a nervous bitch . . . but anyway, that's all periphery . . . but I have this awful problem of being something fucked up which means I don't even stop to say 'hello brother.'" Nancy had told him she was moving. The SLA had already formed. She told him to keep in touch.

The SLA Sunday gun classes had been going on for months by then. Thompson had taken Nancy to Peking Man House to meet the others who would form the hard core of the cobra cult with her. He had taken Mizmoon there, too. But when Russin had tried his sweet-talk approach on those still living at Peking Man House, they had flatly denied ever hearing of Nancy or Mizmoon or the SLA.

The more pieces of the puzzle Thompson gave me, the more puzzled I became. Why would he answer a question directly one time, then become vague and distant when I asked a comparatively simple question? Why was he pulling out these personal treasures for me? Was there a message in them?

I knew Chris Thompson had a message to get across—the message of a Black People's Union. It was his idea, his plan to help his black brothers and sisters. He freely admitted, "I can only deal with the problems of my own people right now. I can't take on the problems of the whites, too." He wanted me to take him to meet Randolph Hearst to talk about his notion of a Black People's Union. To get money from Hearst? "Absolutely not," he said.

Nevertheless, I had no intention of arranging the meeting that Thompson wanted. Randolph Hearst by now had new problems, trying to initiate the People in Need program, a rather innocuous name for what was actually the ransom for his daughter.

Hearst had put up a half-million dollars of his own money, plus another million and a half from the Hearst Foundation. The two million was now supposedly buying food to be handed out to whoever lined up for it at distribution points in the core of the ghettos around the Bay Area: Oakland, Richmond, San Francisco, East Palo Alto.

The SLA had demanded that there be no press coverage of the food handout. And, as with all SLA demands, the news media promptly rolled over and played dead. But word leaked out anyway. A few reporters tucked notebooks inside their jackets and wandered into the maelstrom called People in Need. They brought back the word: It had to be the biggest rip-off in history. Food was being tossed from trucks and used to bash in store windows, which were then promptly looted. Chickens, meant to feed the hungry, were sold from door to door in Hunter's Point, three for $5. Riots broke out. The police were powerless. The SLA had ordered them to stay away. Hearst pleaded that the cops obey the criminals. They did.

Only one photographer, Victor Wong of "Newsroom," managed to photograph the Oakland riot. When he was threatened, he told the black thugs towering over him, "I'm taking these for the Black Panther newspaper," so they left him alone. His camera alone recorded the truth of that food throwaway.

An attempt was made to hand out food in San Francisco's Chinatown, where real hunger exists. Again, the thugs came, most of them blacks. They beat up the priest at the Catholic church that was serving as a distribution center; they battered two old women; they carted off the food.

The Black Muslims sent a bill for $99,080 for fish they claimed they had distributed to the needy. Hearst paid the bill. No one ever found anyone who got any of that fish.

The secretary of state from the state of Washington, Ludlow Kramer, arrived to administer this new People in Need program, now known as PIN. His was just one of many attempts to keep the gun-toting thugs out of the collection center, to stop the hijacking of the food-filled trucks, to bring some semblance of order out of the chaos. It was a battle lost before it began.

Hearst clung to the thread of belief. The SLA had promised him news concerning the return of his daughter if he followed through on the food giveaway plan. Patty's voice itself had held out hope on another of the never-ending tapes found around the city tucked under phone booths, in the backs of toilets, under tables in all-night diners. Patty assured her distraught parents, "Whatever you can do will be okay . . ." But Cinque's voice had quickly followed hers, warning that he and his band of criminals would judge if Hearst's efforts were sincere or not, and that anything less than sincerity meant death for Patty.

The SLA demanded another $4 million. Hearst shrugged dejectedly, "It's out of my hands now," and the Hearst Foundation spokesman took over. The $4 million would be paid only if Patty were released to her parents. That the offer was never even acknowledged was evidence of the fact that the SLA put its own hold on publicity above the needs of any people.

Privately Hearst said, "What can I do? How do you deal with squirrels like these SLA?" No one had the answer.

There was one group that drew Hearst's admiration during the disaster that was the PIN program—the American Indians. The United Bay Council of Indians, representing perhaps the most truly oppressed of all American citizens, issued a statement: "We will not take any of this blood-money food."

Adam Nordwall, an Indian leader, was asked, "Aren't there hungry Indians?"

Nordwall raised his head high and said, "No Indian is ever *that* hungry."

"I just wish I could give all the food to them," Hearst told me one night. He worked to dispel the rumors of violence and rip-off that streaked through PIN. But he couldn't win. The rumors were true. One horror story followed another.

Dick Carlson, investigative reporter from ABC-TV in Los Angeles, stood two blocks from the Oakland giveaway. He stopped a 1974 Chevrolet Malibu, one that he'd seen the young driver load with free food.

"Mind showing me what you got?" Carlson asked while the camera turned.

"'Course not. Here it all is, right in the trunk," the young black in the dapper suit answered, opening the trunk to show bags of various foods.

Carlson paused, then asked. "If you don't mind me saying this, you don't look very poor. Why did you come to take food?"

"Man, it's for whoever can get it and I got it. I'm not poor, but I got it."

"Do you think your folks would approve?"

"Well, you can ask them when they get here. That's my mother and sister waiting in the line for theirs right now."

Carlson's report was cut out of the news program that night. The vague explanation was that blacks did not make up the majority of the food recipients. The observers were obviously color-blind. Blacks outnumbered all others, ten to one. But not the poor blacks, those who struggle to rear children on welfare checks, or the old who eke out their pensions with cornflakes and Jell-O. They were afraid of the food distribution, the Cadillac traffic jams, the shoving pimps and pushers. They stayed home, hungry.

Hearst knew this but was helpless to do anything about it. I had thought about all this when I'd decided he didn't need the added burden of trying to help Chris Thompson start his dream of a Black People's Union. It would have been nothing short of traumatic for the Hearsts to sit and talk to this slim young man who had known and loved some of their daughter's captors.

Thompson showed me other mementos of the SLA. He told me of a poem Mizmoon had recited to him, a simple verse with infinite meaning:

> In love, we struggle
> In struggle, we love.

CHAPTER **8**

CAMILLA HALL WAS the gentle member of the Symbionese Liberation Army. She was the last to join, and she did not go underground until February 19, 1974—two weeks after the Hearst abduction. She was moved more by love than by revolution—a love she found with another woman, SLA leader Patricia Soltysik.

Camilla was born March 24, 1945 in Minnesota, and how different her life and death might have been if she had found a diet that worked. Friends from her University of Minnesota days still talk of "her problem": overweight. Not just the baby flab of a fast-growing girl, but weight bordering on obesity. She had weighed more than two hundred pounds when she attended classes there in the mid-sixties.

"I took her out once. She was nice, but frankly, you just didn't want to date someone that fat," a college classmate recalls. He remembers it was shortly after that date that Camilla started speaking out on campus for Gay Liberation.

Camilla's politics were more that of the flower child than the gun-toter. She told the world of this belief in love in poems she wrote, poems that always ended with love, even when she wrote of revolutionary women. Camilla wanted to give the world her message through these poems. But now her father, The Reverend George Hall, refuses to allow his daughter's poems to be reprinted unless he is paid a substantial sum. Camilla's poetry has now become a commodity in the capitalistic marketplace she hated.

In the summer of 1971 she had met and fallen in love with Patricia Soltysik, and in typical Camilla fashion she had written a love poem to the woman who had won her heart. In the poem she renamed her lover "Mizmoon," and it must have touched her deeply when Patricia adopted Mizmoon as her only true name.

But Camilla's love was not just for Patricia. She seemed to have had enough for everyone and everything. "It was a kind of Peter, Paul, and Mary attitude—just spread some love on the sore places and the hurt will go away," one of Camilla's former professors remembers.

Camilla had tried to spread a little love on the hurts of humanity: She became a social worker, a proper endeavor for a young woman setting out to help mankind. But humanity didn't get better. The poor were still poor, the sick died, and the problems defied solutions. Camilla gave it up after three years.

When she arrived in Berkeley, she didn't even try to put her college training to use. Instead, she turned her love to the care of other living things—plants and trees and animals. She looked for work as a gardener but found the doors closed to a woman attempting to enter a masculine world. She didn't want to live off her family or take charity, so she sold pots and pans, door to door. The humanity she had set out to save slammed doors in her face.

She decided to battle sexual prejudice in hiring practices. Her target, the East Bay Park System. To her it was a logical choice—the park system was part of the state and the state represented the people. And weren't women part of the people? By summer 1973 she had succeeded in being hired as a full-fledged gardener for the East Bay Park System, working in the topmost regions near the quiet lakes that were found only by the hardiest hikers. She had Mizmoon's love; she had her small duplex with its profusion of potted plants flourishing under her care; she had her poetry and her art—oil paintings as well as drawings that were semicartoons, almost Thurberesque. She was happy.

But it was Camilla's fate not to keep such happiness. She already knew the sorrow of helplessly watching her two younger brothers and a sister die, one of a heart condition, the others of congenital kidney disorders. The tragedies haunted Camilla. She worried that she too had been marked for an early death.

She had been eager to express herself. It hadn't worked through social work. In the fall of 1973, she found it didn't work regarding equality either. The park system laid her off, saying it only hired women as temporary summer replacements. Camilla demonstrated, posing with a rakish grin on her chubby round face, holding a pair of pruning shears as her new badge of belonging. Her protest didn't work. She stayed fired.

She continued to draw, and even had a couple of one-woman shows. People liked her work but not enough to support her by buying it.

Camilla also knew her poems wouldn't sell. But she no longer thought of art in any form as the way to achieve independence. Art was now an outlet, a way of showing the love that overflowed. Her large-boned body, finally down to a reasonable weight, didn't seem to matter anymore. Nothing helped her loneliness, a loneliness that screamed out from the quiet lines of her poems. She wrote stanzas pleading for just one person to love her, one out of the two hundred million.

Camilla found her one in Mizmoon. That was all she needed, one small corner of love to share. She had her oils, her poems, her plants, and, most of all, her cat, a long, svelte Siamese, as independent as Camilla herself had hoped to be. The cat, Keya, let Camilla love it.

Her father, a Lutheran minister in Minnesota, loved his surviving child, but it was more love for her soul. Camilla didn't want the love of childhood anymore, and even considered her nickname—Candy—more a taunt than an endearment. Everyone said she was called that because she was so sweet. She had not used it in her new life in Berkeley.

But by fall of 1973, with her job gone, she was on welfare. Her old terror of not surviving took over again. She found a lump in her breast and had it removed surgically. She didn't even call the hospital about the biopsy report to learn if it was malignant.

Camilla was able to save some money from her welfare payments and that, added to money she managed to borrow, enabled her to go to Europe for a few weeks. When she returned to Berkeley she found Mizmoon unfaithful—sharing her bed with Chris Thompson. Camilla, who by now had totally rejected men, wrote more poems to the stoic Mizmoon; in them she talked of others who had left her, and warned that she would not be left again. She rhapsodized in rhyme the love she had found, extolling the joys of a woman's caress. For Camilla, that woman was Mizmoon.

Mizmoon's dominance was to be expected. She wanted more from Camilla than Camilla could give. Not just love—but time. Camilla never had enough time. There were pictures to paint, emotions to capture in poems, and plants to grow. To Camilla, their love was shared whether they were together or not. Mizmoon was not that certain of her capacity for love. She needed a physical presence to reassure her. Camilla had to make a choice—lose her love or buy a gun. She bought the gun.

In January, when Mizmoon and the other SLA members were already underground, Camilla went alone to the Chabot range and learned to shoot the weapon. She mastered the finger of death. And on February 19, 1974, she shut her door to the tiny duplex, leaving behind all that she loved, except her cat. She took Keya and her commitment to Mizmoon, and joined the SLA underground. The decision was final. In order to love and be loved, she would give or take life.

Patricia Soltysik was not an easy person to understand. She had become a lesbian and had taken the name Mizmoon because Camilla had written it in a poem. She was the SLA's leader and brain trust. At the root of these mutants was Patricia Monique Soltysik.

Born May 17, 1950, in Goleta, a small town on California's southern coast hidden in the mountains outside Santa Barbara, she was one of seven children—five daughters, two sons. Their mother, Anna Marie, loved her offspring and the Catholic Church. Their father was a druggist who, despite the Church, finally left his family and divorced their mother.

Patricia was popular in high school with both boys and girls. The boys all noticed her centerfold figure, shown to advantage by cashmere sweaters, tight skirts, nylons, and high heels that made the most of her femaleness. The brightest kid in class, she made straight A's and was elected president of the Usherette Club. In Goleta, high-school events were social occasions, and Patricia Soltysik performed her duties as leading hostess with grace and charm.

She easily won a cherished scholarship to the University of California. There was some family talk about utilizing it at the Santa Barbara campus, only a few miles from the Soltysik home. But Patricia wanted to conquer new worlds. She was ready for Berkeley, the fountainhead of all state universities—home of the mid-sixties free-speech movement that ended in riots; center of the Vietnam peace marches; radical stronghold of the world. Patricia Soltysik wanted to take on a challenge worthy of her mettle.

For the first time in her life, Patricia had taken on a battle she could not win. Berkeley was bigger than she was, its students smarter than she. Instead of being a VIP on campus, she was only one of the thousands of unseen faces. She was lost in the flatlands of Berkeley before she finished her first year.

But though she hadn't conquered the academic worlds, she had found love with a young man studying for his degree. They shared a two-room apartment in a building on Channing Way that had degenerated into a commune. The young couple managed to create an air of suburbia even in this small niche of Berkeley's most unstable area. Pat cooked and sewed. She enjoyed sewing so much that she bought an old foot-pedal sewing machine. She tried to stick it out with her studies—French and German—and tutored in French to earn money. But her lover, whom I interviewed while she was being sought by the police, evaluated her ability with the cold analytical eye that afflicts Berkeley dwellers. "She thought she was good at languages. Actually, she was fair, not good."

Once she insisted that her lover hitchhike down to Goleta to be presented to her family, as any proper young man in love with a proper young lady should be. He agreed to do it but, as he told me, Pat's importance of family seemed more gesture than commitment.

What Pat had thought would be a lasting love affair, born in Berkeley's rubbled flatland, tapered off into little more than a sharing of bed and board. She complained, "Why don't you talk to me more? I want someone who will talk to me!"

But the young man was busy. His life was planned, directed toward a good job in computer programming. He told Pat, "I just don't have time to play all these rap-session Berkeley talk-games. I have studying to do."

So, by mid-1970, Pat had found others to talk to. She went outside their two-room apartment, across the street to a more acknowledged commune, complete with a five-foot-high clenched red fist standing guard at the front door. Her lover remembers Pat's new friends: "I didn't really like them. They sat around and talked radical politics most of the time. There was one guy she met named Russ. She talked to him a lot."

That was Russell Little, newly arrived in Berkeley from Florida, having brought with him from there a girl named Robyn Steiner. They lived in the Red Fist Commune and they, like Pat Soltysik, were looking for the Berkeley of the newspaper headlines.

Pat's lover-turned-roommate wasn't jealous of her new friends. "I knew they just talked. In fact, Pat would get turned off. She said the problem was that all they did was talk. No one would take action."

What action did the young woman from Goleta want to take? "Oh, I don't mean violence, not SLA action. Pat meant they wouldn't even take petitions out and gather signatures. All they would do was talk about change."

To a degree he humored her concerns for the people—people who were fast losing individuality in Pat Soltysik's mind and becoming the masses. But her new concern for the masses didn't affect her and her man's home life too much. He said, "We went to some demonstrations, the ones just about everyone living in Berkeley went to. The peace marches, a few boycotts of lettuce, that kind of thing."

He and Pat spent more time walking to the nearest ice-cream parlor and buying their favorite food, ice cream. "We'd do that several times a week," he said. They listened to music, primarily blues and rock, on stations KPFA and KSAN, required listening for Berkeley's "real scene."

"Why don't you pay more attention to me?" she'd ask. It became a refrain to every evening's meal.

He remembers, "We'd end up in a big battle, and she'd start crying. Damn, it was hard. I couldn't pay attention to her and study too. She'd gotten active in the Lutheran Youth Center, where I worked part-time. I thought that would help. It didn't."

In the summer of 1969, Pat Soltysik went to Europe—a long step from Goleta. She had saved her tutoring money and earned a little extra at odd jobs. Her family also helped. But if she expected traveling abroad to make any difference in her life, she was mistaken. She came home to the same things—KPFA on the radio, dinner on the stove, her man on the sofa studying.

"I guess that's when she really started to change. She'd expected so much. She got so little. I'd hear the whispers. Pat was having affairs with people on the block. We all knew each other; it was sort of one gigantic commune. I tried not to hear, but it hurt. Finally I faced her and asked her flat out 'Are you having affairs?'

"She just looked at me, straight at me, and said, 'Yes.' We both knew it was over then, but we went on living together, more out of convenience than anything else."

Pat had made friends with a girl across the hall—a huge, silent girl who was into a dozen different causes. Pat liked that.

"I'll never forget the final day. I kept remembering the times she'd cried about us, cried because she wanted more attention. But not that last day. She told me there was no place in life for emotion—it got in the way of helping the masses—and she actually flipped a coin to see which one of us would keep the apartment and which one would move out. She lost. She moved out, across the hall, in with this other woman. I even tried dating that woman a few times, but it hurt too much to see Pat there. Funny about that—it hurt me, but Pat didn't seem to mind at all. I don't even know if she noticed."

Perhaps she didn't. There was a new love in her life, a love for "the masses." She quit school entirely, and since, if she was to be the lover of the masses, she had to be close to them, she repackaged herself: mattress-ticking overalls, heavy boots. She went to work as a handyman, first at the YMCA.

But she found the masses cold. By 1972, she'd found a real flesh-and-blood love, one enhanced because it would have been forbidden back in Goleta. That made it even more proper for Berkeley. She fell in love with Camilla Hall.

At twenty-two years of age, three hundred miles from home, in a universe apart from all she'd known before, Pat Soltysik became Mizmoon. She and Camilla were devoted, seeing each other almost daily, and Camilla quickly drew Mizmoon into the life of art that she had fashioned for herself.

Camilla was already active in Gay Liberation when she and Mizmoon met, and Mizmoon went along, though without commitment. They also went to the Lutheran Youth Center. For Mizmoon, it was the lone continuation of her first years in Berkeley. For Camilla, it was the logical extension for the daughter of a Lutheran minister. All this soon paled for Mizmoon. She took another job, this time as a janitor for the Berkeley Public Library. Her janitorial duties became secondary to her efforts to organize a union for the library employees.

Mizmoon moved out of the apartment house where she'd lived for two years with her male lover and later shared an apartment with the activist girl across the hall. She rented the yellow cottage at the rear of 2135 Parker Street, about ten blocks from the communes. It was also about six blocks from where Patty Hearst was settling in with her lover, Steve Weed.

Mizmoon had the lower floor, which she shared with still another woman. But the rent was all they shared. Mizmoon had her own life; it was full. She was bursting with plans for the union that would free the masses of the Berkeley Public Library system.

Though she still loved Camilla, who had gone abroad, Mizmoon began an affair with Chris Thompson. He suited her perfectly. Whereas her life had been on the fringes of the radical movement, confined to an occasional puff of pot around a floor-and-pillow discussion group, Thompson had lived in Peking Man House, a radical stronghold. He was at the center of the circle that Mizmoon hadn't found a way to enter. He quickly took her inside. At Peking Man House she met his friends and fellow radicals. There was Russell Little, from the old days on Channing Way, whom Mizmoon told of her new name and her new life. She met others, too: Willie Wolfe, a towering, dark-haired young man, who didn't seem to work for his money but who nonetheless talked of the same love for the masses that Mizmoon found so comforting. Joe Remiro came by, and there was other talk about the Vietnam Veterans Against the War. But the war was over. What could they be against now? Then there was Nancy Ling Perry—another woman in Chris Thompson's life. She and Mizmoon met, without either hostility or affection.

By March 1973, Mizmoon's life had settled into an almost comfortable routine. She spent a little time dusting the library shelves and the rest urging the workers to unite and throw off their chains. While she waited for Camilla to come back from Europe, she had Chris Thompson to fulfill her physical needs. They took long walks in the woods. Thompson always had his camera with him and he snapped Mizmoon laughing under an elm, sipping coffee across the dining-room table, and striding, arms akimbo, across the top of a hill.

Her brother came from Goleta to visit. He was shocked at her appearance. She greeted him in drooping Turkish pants, with "tons of room in the crotch," he later told his mother. She wore peasant blouses. The clothes of the masses. He suggested she leave Berkeley—since she wasn't attending the university, why live on its fringes? "She claimed it gave her the support she needed," her brother recalled.

It was after this that Russell Little asked Chris Thompson to find a "place that's cool for a friend."

"That's all he needed to say. I knew what it meant—an escaped prisoner," Thompson told me. "I sent the guy to Mizmoon. Funny, I did it because she wasn't a leader of anything, she wasn't even well enough known in the radical movement to be suspected of hiding an escaped con."

And so Mizmoon took Donald De Freeze into her cottage and her routine was even more pleasant for the next six months. De Freeze stayed home and cleaned while Mizmoon went off to spend her eight hours of work trying to organize the library workers. She was impatient. Many of them kept saying, "What do we need a union for? We like our work; we're happy with our pay." Mizmoon told them they were exploited, used, slaves of the capitalist masters. They told her to go back to her dustbins and brooms.

She went home each night to find a hot dinner waiting on the table. De Freeze loved to cook and was good at it. Evenings were pleasant. She told him of her frustration in organizing a library union. He gave her copies of the Latin American terrorist tracts he had read in prison; she would read them while he washed the evening dishes. Once Chris Thompson brought to the cottage a film he had put together with Remiro, Little, and others who studied audiovisual arts at a nearby city college. He, De Freeze, and Mizmoon looked at it and agreed that it needed stronger words, a harder message for the masses.

De Freeze was content. He had a home, a woman when he wanted one, and he could cook. Life was good. Mizmoon was the impatient member of the group. There had to be more, just as there had to be more when she shared the life of the young man studying computers, or when she had gone to Europe, or when she had left Goleta for Berkeley. She had to help people en masse, since she had failed to reach them as individuals. This was why, all through the spring of 1973, she and a select few worked to form the Symbionese Liberation Federation. The overall setup proved boring. A branch of it, however, the Symbionese Liberation Army, attracted and held the attention of this small band of rejects from Berkeley's radical movements: Russell Little, Joe Remiro, Nancy Ling Perry, Emily and Bill Harris and their roommate and fellow traveler from Indiana, Angela Atwood, who was drawn in more by her attraction to Remiro than by her interest in politics.

They all adopted code names. Mizmoon was now Zoya—twice removed from the Patricia Soltysik who had arrived in Berkeley four years earlier, once removed from Mizmoon, the contented lover of Camilla Hall. Zoya was a revolutionary, a leader.

The small ring of middle-class, white young people decided De Freeze was to be their leader under the title, General Field Marshal Cinque. After all, what good was a revolution to free the oppressed if you didn't have a black or a brown or a red man to lead it? De Freeze was all they had, the only color among their white faces. His color was his sole qualification for the leadership that he readily accepted. The title alone sounded more important than he had ever been.

Spring and early summer blended together. Each weekday Mizmoon went off to the library to try and rally her fellow workers around the revolution of unionizing. Each night she went home to De Freeze's cooking and more talk of the new Symbionese. On weekends, the group members held their gun classes, trained their soldiers, practiced dismantling the weapons, and spent countless hours on the firing range.

By high summer the springlike fantasy of the Symbionese Liberation Army was replaced by reality. Mizmoon's fellow workers at the Berkeley Public Library had rejected her by voting down the union she had worked to organize. She was so embittered that she refused to scrub their floors or empty their trash. By late summer, she was fired. Fair enough. Fired by the capitalist system, she decided to fire back as the Symbionese.

She and De Freeze left the cottage and went underground, cutting off the world, except for their fellow Symbionese. For Mizmoon, it had to be a total break. She wrote her family: "Burn all my letters and pictures. You will not see me again."

Nancy Ling was born September 19, 1947, a Virgo. It was an appropriate sign for the beautiful child.

Her early life was very much like Patty Hearst's. Her father owned a quality furniture store and was as important in the quiet town of Santa Rosa, California, as Hearst was in cosmopolitan San Francisco. She attended the proper schools, received good grades. Like Patricia Soltysik, she was an important member of the student body. She was also a cheerleader, a leader of yelling students. Nancy loved every minute of it.

She hadn't been too interested in politics. She quietly accepted the conservative politics of her parents, and in 1964 thought the thing that would help the world most would be the election of Barry Goldwater as president of the United States. At that time, she was enrolled in Whittier College in Orange County, the heartland of California's conservatives. The college is the alma mater of Richard Nixon. Again, she was a leader on the campus. She followed the same paths as the other SLA women, paths that could not cross in a place like Whittier.

By 1966 Nancy wanted to transfer to Berkeley. That's where it was at—excitement, headlines, happenings. To be a leader in the backwater of Whittier was one thing; to stand out in the mob that is Berkeley was another. Hadn't she led the cheers in Santa Rosa? Worked for Goldwater? Stood up for many causes? Going to Berkeley seemed the logical move. It needed saving from those shaggy-haired, bearded, foul-mouthed radicals.

Childhood friends of Nancy's recall, "She was always so suscep-tible, so easy to use. She believed people, everyone. She'd give so much more than she'd get. Berkeley is a hard place, and she was a soft girl."

In 1966 she enrolled at Berkeley as an English literature major and became a full-fledged member of the Berkeley cesspool. She was swallowed up in it, lost in its seething thousands. Later, nobody could remember her name or recall her face. But Nancy had looked around and seen that there were certain "in" groups on the campus. Some were only self-important, one being the salt-and-pepper group—the black and white couples. The mix-ture was the student status symbol of the late sixties.

Since Nancy wanted status, it was the logical progression from "take a black to lunch." She took him home. Her parents were horrified. She refused to listen to their objections. But she did cling to some of their teachings, such as, "You don't live with a man before you marry him."

The man was Gilbert Perry. He is tall, with an angular face, black eyes, and an Afro. He quickly corrected me when I called him a "music teacher."

"I am a composer, not a music teacher."

When I had first heard that Nancy's married name was Perry, I'd thought it was the typical Berkeley-style marriage, one of shared living without the vows. Gilbert quickly put me straight.

"No way. She wouldn't even stay with me till we did the whole thing, I mean the whole thing, right up to the minister. So I went along. I married her."

When did he agree to favor her with his vows? "Let's see, that was December, back in 1967. Right after Christmas. We were married right here in Berkeley, at the First Unitarian Church."

What kind of wife was Nancy?

"A good wife, a good woman," said Gilbert without pause. "We loved each other. We still do. We always will."

He spoke with almost a dramatic flair, as if he were reading a well-rehearsed script. Maybe he was. After all, he had known Nancy was being sought for questioning as a suspect in the arson attempt on the SLA hideout in Clayton. He probably had expected the news media to pound a path to his door. I was a little surprised when I found I was the only one who had found this link to Nancy and her past.

His living quarters were a dilapidated, one-room apartment above a grocery store around the corner from the Berkeley police station. There was one big armchair in the room. Boxes littered the entire floor. He was just moving in. I knew that—his mother had told me, after I'd first learned from the San Francisco Conservatory of Music that a musician named Gilbert Perry did exist, just as a childhood friend of Nancy's had said.

Gilbert leaned back in the chair while I squatted on a box. His eyes were half closed; he said all the right things:

"We lived a good life—quiet. Nancy went back to school in 1972 to study chemistry. She got her B.A. in English lit in 1970. But she only stayed one semester. Then she left. She cooked and kept house; she was a good, loving wife. She didn't have any hangup about this women's lib thing. She took my name. She was Mrs. Gilbert Perry."

Was Nancy involved in any political activity? He grinned broadly. Politics? His little doll, Nancy? "No, she wasn't into any of the stuff." He almost laughed at the idea.

What about drugs? Many of Nancy's friends had said she was a heavy user of LSD and popped various pills. Again the grin, this time more knowing than deriding. "Man, we didn't do any of that stuff."

Did Nancy hate cops?

"Hell, no. Why, I remember one time we were driving along and this police officer starts to pull me over for something. I don't remember what. I hadn't done anything wrong. Nancy saw him first, looking out of the rear window, and she said, very calmly, quietly, 'There's an officer about to pull you over.'"

Yes, that was a perfect recital of what a loving wife should say to her adoring husband. He was determined to play out his role. I decided to ask the obvious. "If you and Nancy had such a perfect marriage, why did she leave you?"

He didn't like the question. He wouldn't deal with it. A string of disjointed words flared back, ". . . didn't leave me . . . we would get back together soon . . . just took different paths. . . . Why, I saw Nancy just last fall, we stopped and talked awhile. She told me she still loved me."

What did he think about this loving wife now being sought as a Symbionese leader? He didn't even bother to mask his reaction. He laughed. "Ridiculous. Those SLA people are crazy. Nancy would have no part of them. She may be in trouble, because of knowing someone or something, but if she is, she'll call me. She'll come to me if she needs help."

I asked a standard question. "Do you have a message for Nancy?"

"Yes, tell her I love her," he recited.

Okay, we'd deliver that message if we found her. But what would he do in the meantime? Try to locate his missing wife? Would he talk to her parents?

"No, I doubt it."

Did they approve of Nancy's marrying a black man? "Of course, they approved."

How often did he and Nancy visit her family in Santa Rosa during their four years together? It's less than a hundred miles away. "Oh, yes, it's near, but we just never got time. They did drop down here, maybe once, maybe twice. We got along."

Others disagree. Friends paint an altogether different canvas of Nancy as Mrs. Gilbert Perry. They claim that it was after her marriage that she got involved with heavy drugs. They say that she adored Gilbert, all right, but that he was something of a ladies' man and Nancy spent many nights alone, crying. But Gilbert Perry would have no talk of such things. He simply said they never happened.

In the year before her involvement in the SLA, Nancy was one of Berkeley's street people, one of the thousands of youngsters who come as students, then hang on, as though proximity to the campus will somehow reinforce their youth, their aims. Nancy held on. She got a job selling fresh fruit juice at Fruity Rudy's, a stand on Telegraph Avenue. She told co-workers that she was getting off drugs—and into revolution. She also told of working in a topless joint in San Francisco.

Nancy dated only black men. It was part of her effort to bring about freedom for the oppressed. It was typical of her middle-class heritage to think that giving herself to a black man was the ultimate gift of freedom. She dated Chris Thompson, who had had a fresh-produce stand near hers which he called Harlem on My Mind or Black Market. They had an affair. He says of her:

"She was a little wild, but nice. She liked opium and she'd pay one hundred dollars to get this tiny little vial of opium, liquid kind. You dip marijuana into it for a special kind of high. Nancy liked those highs."

Thompson took Nancy to Peking Man House, where he introduced her to Mizmoon, Joe Remiro, and Russell Little. She found a new way of belonging. She became part of the SLA, one of its soldiers, a leader. She moved in with Russell Little, replacing quiet Robyn Steiner. Nancy could now have a white man— she would help the oppressed by terror. She joined the gun classes. She went to the target range. She was a good shot, indeed an excellent shot. She seldom missed the bull's-eye.

Whatever Nancy did, she did thoroughly. Dealing in terrorism was no exception. And Nancy would lead, whether it was a high-school cheer or the Symbionese. She worked harder than the others, became more adept at setting down codes; she also set the standards for renting safe houses, their hideouts. She could twist her thick brown hair into a neat chignon and pass as middle America. She was the eyes of the SLA; Mizmoon, the brain.

Nancy was also the SLA mouth, writing long, laborious letters to the media, telling and retelling the goals of the group. She never got her message across.

Angela Atwood, who became General Gelina among the Symbionese, had enjoyed changing her name. Born on February 6, 1949, she was Angela De Angelis when she enrolled at the University of Indiana, the favored daughter of an Italian family in New Jersey, a girl so used to compliments about her looks that admiration became a tribulation. She was a high-school prom queen with security as strongly etched on her as it had been on Patty Hearst. She loved parties and pretty clothes, and was invited to all the social events on campus. And she had a reputation for being kind to animals. "She wouldn't hurt a flea," says one of her university friends. "She used to take in stray cats and puppies."

Angela's father had neatly mapped out her life. His plan included marriage to a young attorney, the son of a neighboring Italian family, and her father never doubted that she would fulfill his wishes.

Her father didn't send Angela to Berkeley, the hotbed of

radicals. Instead he sent her to safe, sane Bloomington, where the University of Indiana sits frozen out of the fifties—home of sock hops and weekend beer busts, a relic of gentler days. He indulged her love of clothes, and she was tagged a campus fashion plate—fringed shoulder bags, angora sweaters, pleated skirts that snapped in Bloomington's brisk winds. Angela even chose a new name to go with her collegiate image: Angel. She drew a small halo right in the center, above the g. But she looked for more than a hallowed name to insure her immortality by posing for photographer friends—languid poses, long looks cast over bare shoulders.

There were so few radicals on the quiet Indiana campus that each was well known. One was Gary Atwood, an idealist studying radical theory, a man who had refused to serve in Vietnam, a registered conscientious objector. The military finally assigned him to hospital work near San Francisco, but before he left he married the pride and joy of the De Angelis family.

According to friends, Angela's family "just about disowned her." Gary Atwood stood for everything they hated. Yet that was the big attraction he held for the beautiful, spoiled girl. She adored her family, but to fulfill the ultimate demands of being Miss Coed, she had to revolt from the binding family ties.

Angela and Gary left for the west, where they moved into a pleasant apartment in Berkeley. Angela worked as a waitress right in the bosom of capitalism—in San Francisco, the Bank of America's world headquarters—at a restaurant called The Great Electric Underground. She tried to radicalize the waitresses in the city's topless joints, but they laughed at her. Then she ran into a classmate from her Bloomington days—Emily Harris. Emily had changed. She was no longer the sweet girl with a dimpled smile; she was strange, exciting, and somehow dangerous. Angela was intrigued. Emily wasn't faceless or lost; she was important in this place that was a hodgepodge of ideas.

When Atwood's military obligation was completed and he was ready to return to Bloomington, Angela told him she had decided to stay in Berkeley. She moved in with Emily and Bill Harris.

Before she had been largely apolitical. Perhaps she still was; but now she met Joe Remiro and fell in love with him. And so she joined the SLA. And she went to the firing range to stand alongside Joe Remiro and Russell Little and Mizmoon and Nancy and Emily and Bill: sighting along the barrel, squeezing the trigger, learning to hit the target. The pretty twenty-five-year-old hit the target dead center.

Emily Harris was delighted with Angela's eagerness. It was good to have a friend from home, from the quiet University of Indiana days. Emily, too, had met her husband on the Bloomington campus. Initially, she had been unimpressed with the nice guy so committed to getting black and white radicals to work together. Emily was not like that at all. A slim, lively blonde, she was more interested in sorority activities than in the problems of the world.

But Emily's and Bill's backgrounds were similar. Both came from upper-middle-class families and were reared in expensive suburbs of large cities. Emily was brought up with three brothers at the edge of a golf course in Clarendon Hills, near Chicago. Her father, Frederick Schwartz, is a consulting engineer and serves on the local school board. As the only daughter, Emily was pampered. She was the smartest kid in class and a teacher's pet. She earned straight A's in high school and joined an organization which collected money for the poor.

Bill grew up with two younger sisters in Carmel, Indiana. His father, a commercial building-equipment salesman, had died when Bill was twenty, and his mother later married an air force lieutenant colonel. Bill was the classroom comic in high school, with a sharp, irreverent wit he was quick to use at the expense of his teachers, the establishment, or whatever target took his fancy.

During her freshman year, Emily had pledged Chi Omega. Such an action would be archaic at Berkeley, but it was appropriate for Bloomington, where even an antiwar protest failed to outdraw the Saturday football game. She was everything a sorority sister should be.

In the summer of 1967, the Chi Omega sisters went west to work in Disneyland during their vacation. Emily took a job at a clothing store in the Disneyland Hotel and fell in love with another summer employee, Tim Casey, an anthropology major. They joined the Disneyland social whirl, made up of long hot weekend afternoons on the beach and nightly parties.

Throughout the next school year Emily and Tim wrote long,

loving letters to each other and continued their romance the following June when Emily again returned to California and got a job in a Newport Beach restaurant. But the romance went stale that summer, and Emily returned to Bloomington that fall, unattached. For a while she and Tim kept in touch with letters that gradually stopped. He remembers her fondly as a nice, sensitive, gentle girl, witty and full of fun.

Bill Harris, meanwhile, had joined the Marine Corps and served in Vietnam. When he returned to Bloomington, he joined the VVAW. He told his friends war had changed him, that he now hated guns. His landlady recalls that he would no longer even go hunting. He began to get "involved." He spent the night with a black family that had received racial threats and gave his wardrobe to a destitute family. He joined a political-prisoners committee and worked on one of Bloomington's newspapers, *Common Sense.*

It was a mysterious new world for twenty-year-old Emily, who up till now had been quite happy dating different boys, socializing, working toward her teaching credentials. She was intrigued by the moody radical who was involved in many different causes and crusades. All races must work together, Bill explained to her —there must be black leaders, and brown leaders, and women, too, must take leadership roles. Emily listened, wide-eyed, and was soon converted.

Her Chi Omega sisters were appalled. Why was their sister dating a hippie, a campus radical? But Emily soon discarded her pretty feminine dresses in favor of hippie gear: mismatched clothes, uneven hems, jeans with messages sewn on the seats, hair ungroomed and flying in the wind. And she no longer wore lipstick to accent the dimple near her chin.

But Emily's was a commitment of the heart. She hovered near Bill as he worked, churning out posters and messages, trying to share his beliefs with the media. She studied his passions and made them her own. She loved him and was prepared to pay the price—to merge her identity with his, to lead his life, to follow his star. They were married in Bloomington in chic hippie fashion, to the sounds of a rock 'n' roll band.

Like the good wife she intended to be, Emily went to work so that Bill could continue his studies and get a master's degree. She taught elementary school in Bloomington while Bill continued his radicalism on the university campus. Emily didn't worry about Bill's being snared by another coed—few girls wanted him; Bill had never really dated until he met Emily.

Once Bill had the master's degree, the couple headed west, where causes change with the seasons. They moved into a railroad apartment, the upper-west unit of a four-unit building in West Oakland, and filled it with expensive clutter. They lived comfortably among their elegant china and potted plants, posters of Marx and Lenin in the hallway and books on revolution and the class struggle in the living room. Their closets were filled with stylish clothes, the kitchen with labor-saving devices. They had color television, a king-sized waterbed, and a set of the best French knives.

They ignored their college degrees and took working-class jobs, Bill as a part-time truck driver and Emily as a clerk-typist on the Berkeley campus. Between them, they made $1,200 a month, but it was Emily who was the main support of her husband and marriage.

She began to meet the brilliant young people who make up Berkeley's student body, whose radical ideas sounded commonplace in their conversations. At first Emily lived on the fringe of two worlds: the campus by day, with its blend of intellectualism and radicalism; her neat apartment by night, with its well-scoured coffee pot and sparkling silverware. Her home could have been in Kansas or Nebraska or Indiana. Instead, it was six blocks from the heart of Oakland's black ghetto, twelve blocks from Berkeley—almost at the hub of the East Bay activists.

It was not long before Emily was swept into the activist stream. She joined Venceremos and began visiting state prisons, playing her part in rehabilitating black prisoners—another white girl liberating the oppressed. She and Bill joined the hard-core SLA and started attending the weekly gun classes.

But now Emily had found a new love. And like any good midwestern girl, she wrote to her father in Indiana about him: "I am in love with a beautiful black man who's conveyed to me the torture of being black in this country." She added, "Bill and I have changed our relationship so it no longer confines us, and I am enjoying relationships with other men."

Her new lover was Donald De Freeze, the symbol of the oppressed. He was a man Emily could never have known at Chi

Marcus Foster, Oakland
superintendent of schools.

Russell Little

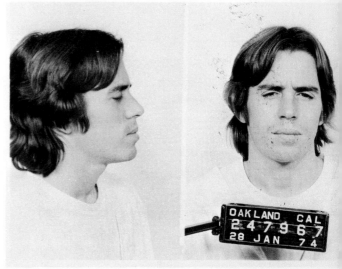

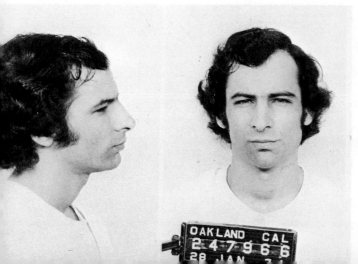

Joseph Remiro

The "safe house" at 1560 Sutherland Court in Clayton, which the SLA torched when they abandoned it. (*Courtesy of the* San Francisco Examiner)

The interior of the Clayton house. (*Courtesy of the* San Francisco Examiner)

Patty Hearst

The 2603 Benevenue fourplex from which Patty Hearst was kidnapped. (*Courtesy of* Jeff Baker)

Catherine and Randolph Hearst outside their Hillsborough home.

TV cameras outside the Hearst home. (*Courtesy of Rick Beban, The Pacific Sun*)

Marilyn Baker interviewing Steven Weed.

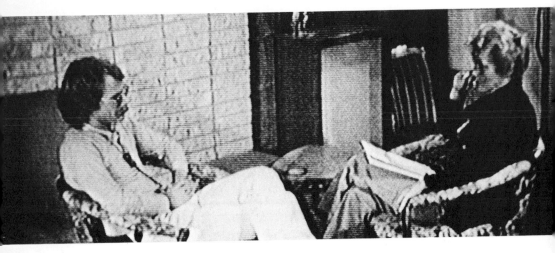

LEFT: "We won't endanger Patty's life," Charles Bates (*right*), agent in charge of the FBI in San Francisco, assures the press. James Browning (*left*), U. S. Attorney General for Northern California, would later charge Patty with bank robbery. RIGHT: Thero Wheeler

Patricia Soltysik

Donald De Freeze lived at
2135 Parker Street after his
escape from Soledad.

Patricia Soltysik's house at 2135 Parker Street, Berkeley.

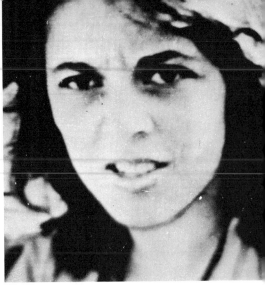

Willie Wolfe   Nancy Ling Perry

The Peking Man House at 5939 Chabot Road, West Oakland, where
Nancy Ling Perry and Willie Wolfe lived.

The 434 41st Street house in West Oakland, where (*left, top to bottom*) Emily and Bill Harris and Angela Atwood lived.

Camilla Hall's house at 1353 Francisco Street, Berkeley.

Camilla Hall

Marilyn Baker interviewing Chris Thompson.

Three faces of Mizmoon (Patricia Soltysik), the "brains" of the SLA.

1827 Golden Gate Avenue, where the SLA hid Patty Hearst from about March 1 to May 1, 1974. (*Courtesy of Rick Beban*, The Pacific Sun)

LEFT: Hallway outside the SLA hideout. KQED cameraman Bob Huestis is at far left; Marilyn Baker (*back to camera*) is seated on floor. (*Courtesy of Rick Beban*, The Pacific Sun). RIGHT: Inside the SLA hideout, Marilyn Baker stands in front of the cobra symbol that the SLA had painted on the wall. (*Courtesy of Rick Beban*, The Pacific Sun)

Tania makes her debut. This photograph accompanied the taped message from Patty Hearst on April 3, 1974, announcing that she had decided to join her captors.

Patty inside the Hibernia Bank. Rifle seen in upper left-hand corner is held by Cinque.

Patty with carbine during bank holdup.

Marilyn Baker interviews Police Officer Rodney Williams after he had received the April 24th tape from the SLA in which Patty announced she had willingly participated in the San Francisco bank robbery.

Mel's Sporting Goods store, where Bill Harris was caught shoplifting.

Police rescuing children from house near scene of the Los Angeles shootout. (*Courtesy of* UPI)

It was inside this roaring inferno at 1466 54th Street in Los Angeles that the six SLA members met their death. (*Courtesy of* UPI)

SLA family group picture. In back (*left to right*): Emily Harris, Willie Wolfe, Donald De Freeze, Bill Harris, Camilla Hall. In front (*left to right*): Patricia Hearst, Angela Atwood, Nancy Ling Perry.

Marilyn Baker and her "secret weapons"—
sons Chris (*left*) and Jeff.

Left to right: Jeff Baker, Marilyn Baker, and Steven Weed (June 19, 1974).

Marilyn Baker and her co-author Sally Brompton. (*Courtesy of* Jeff Baker)

WANTED BY THE FBI

NATIONAL FIREARMS ACT; MATERIAL WITNESS

William Taylor Harris

FBI No. 308,668 L5

Date photographs taken unknown

Aliases: Richard Frank Dennis, William Kinder, Jonathan Maris, Jonathan Mark Salamone

Age: 29, born January 22, 1945, Fort Sill, Oklahoma (not supported by birth records)

Height: 5'7"
Weight: 145 pounds
Build: Medium
Hair: Brown, short
Occupation: Postal clerk
Eyes: Hazel
Complexion: Medium
Race: White
Nationality: American

Remarks: Reportedly wears Fu Manchu type mustache, may wear glasses, upper right center tooth may be chipped, reportedly jogs, swims and rides bicycle for exercise, was last seen wearing army type boots and dark jacket

Social Security Numbers Used: 315-46-2467; 553-27-8400; 359-48-5467

Fingerprint Classification: 20 L 1 At 12
  S 1 Ut

Emily Montague Harris

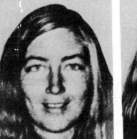 

FBI No. 325,804 L2

Date photographs taken unknown

Aliases: Mrs. William Taylor Harris, Anna Lindenberg, Cynthia Sue Mankins, Emily Montague Schwartz

Age: 27, born February 11, 1947, Baltimore, Maryland (not supported by birth records)

Height: 5'3"
Weight: 115 pounds
Build: Small
Hair: Blonde
Eyes: Blue
Complexion: Fair
Race: White
Nationality: American

Occupations: Secretary, teacher

Remarks: Hair may be worn one inch below ear level, may wear glasses or contact lenses; reportedly has partial upper plate, pierced ears, is a natural food fadist, exercises by jogging, swimming and bicycle riding, usually wears slacks or street length dresses, was last seen wearing jeans and waist length shiny black leather coat

Social Security Numbers Used: 327-42-2356; 429-42-8003

Patricia Campbell Hearst

FBI No. 325,805 L10

Date photograph taken unknown

Alias: Tania

Age: 20, born February 20, 1954, San Francisco, California

Height: 5'3"
Weight: 110 pounds
Build: Small
Hair: Light brown
Eyes: Brown
Complexion: Fair
Race: White
Nationality: American

Scars and Marks: Mole on lower right corner of mouth, scar near right ankle

Remarks: Hair naturally light brown, straight and worn about three inches below shoulders in length, however, may wear wigs, including Afro style, dark brown of medium length; was last seen wearing black sweater, plaid slacks, brown hiking boots and carrying a knife in her belt

CAUTION

THE ABOVE INDIVIDUALS ARE SELF-PROCLAIMED MEMBERS OF THE SYMBIONESE LIBERATION ARMY AND REPORTEDLY HAVE BEEN IN POSSESSION OF NUMEROUS FIREARMS INCLUDING AUTOMATIC WEAPONS. WILLIAM HARRIS AND PATRICIA HEARST ALLEGEDLY HAVE RECENTLY USED GUNS TO AVOID ARREST. ALL THREE SHOULD BE CONSIDERED ARMED AND VERY DANGEROUS.

Federal warrants were issued on May 20, 1974, at Los Angeles, California, charging the Harris' and Hearst with violation of the National Firearms Act. Hearst was also charged in a Federal complaint on April 15, 1974, at San Francisco, California, as a material witness to a bank robbery which occurred April 15, 1974.

IF YOU HAVE ANY INFORMATION CONCERNING THESE PERSONS, PLEASE NOTIFY ME OR CONTACT YOUR LOCAL FBI OFFICE. TELEPHONE NUMBERS AND ADDRESSES OF ALL FBI OFFICES LISTED ON BACK.

C m Kelley

DIRECTOR
FEDERAL BUREAU OF INVESTIGATION
UNITED STATES DEPARTMENT OF JUSTICE
WASHINGTON, D. C. 20535
TELEPHONE, NATIONAL 8-7117

Omega; a man who said things she had never heard, could barely imagine, but longed to share; a man who lived from day to day, haunted by the constant threat of recapture by the authorities.

On January 10, 1974, Emily telephoned her office to say she was sick. It was almost the first time in more than a year that she had missed a day. Later she rang again to say she was resigning for "personal reasons."

The mail began to pile up at the Harris apartment. On January 25, the landlord received a call from Emily explaining that Bill's father had died and they had had to rush back to Indiana. But the landlord had also heard the operator ask her to deposit fifty cents for the first three minutes and knew from this that she was in the Bay Area.

He was sorry to see them go. They had been outstanding tenants; he agreed to sell their possessions and to mail the money minus his costs to Emily's mother. They had left everything—toothbrushes, underwear, even a pot of drip-through coffee standing on the stove waiting to be brewed.

The Harrises had followed their comrades and gone underground, vanishing into the shadows of the metropolis. They had learned their lessons well—to shoot and fight and to keep one step ahead of the enemy. Mild Emily and boyish Bill had joined the ranks of terror a million miles from Chi Omega.

Their war was about to begin.

PART THREE

THE CHASE

CHAPTER **9**

THE HUNT WAS ON, one that took us into areas we had never known. It was a hunt almost as strange as the hunted, an orchestration of co-workers and friends, cops and FBI, Jeff and me.

Sometimes it was muddled—who was parent and who was child in our tight-knit family: twenty-five-year-old Jeff, college student, Vietnam vet, long-haired radical; and twenty-three-year-old Chris, City Hall executive, married, the all-American image that parents dream about.

My sons constantly worry about me, dreading what weird place I'll be plodding into next. My own image of myself as a nice, middle-aged lady is hardly the image my sons hold. They see Mom more as a "wild woman, out there where she shouldn't be." Their conversations about me are laced with the protective "We've got to take care of her." They do their best to keep an eye on me, trudging around beside me on stories, invaluable on those that are really tough to break. We had worked together a lot—Chris and I when we went after the topless joints of San Francisco that paid substandard wages to their women workers;

Jeff and I when we tramped through California's coastal mountains looking for a murderer who had beheaded and mutilated eight victims. My sons are my good right arm, my extra effort, my secret weapon, but most of all my constant, unfailing support in spirit and stories.

But this time Chris couldn't get off work. He couldn't risk the job he'd wanted so much and won so recently, as executive assistant to San Francisco County Supervisor, Peter Tamaras.

So Jeff took up the role again, with no paycheck, not even expense money. KQED is public television; there is no budget. They wouldn't have paid him anyway—"company policy" is: no blood relatives may work together. Jeff could have used some extra money. He was in his last year of college, a year heavy with studies. He had spent the last four years living on the G.I. Bill, restricting his food to one Big Mac per day. His total income— thanks to Uncle Sam and a tour in Vietnam—$200 per month. Rent: $115, for a hole-in-the-wall where the shower barely dribbled and the toilet overflowed—outrageous, but it was the price he paid for being a student and long-haired one at that. That left $85 a month for food, books, transportation, and clothes. I wondered why he was struggling so, since at the end of four years, he wouldn't even have a degree because he wasn't taking anything that added up to that prized piece of paper that gets one jobs and earns one more money.

"But I took what I wanted to learn," Jeff constantly reminded me—paleontology, black history, English literature, biology. He didn't worry about using knowledge to make a good living. "So I'll deliver mail or drive a cab," he shrugged whenever I prodded him toward the work-ethic I endorsed. It would be no disgrace for Jeff to drive a cab after four years of college. There was a time when I would have thought it all a pitiful waste, but my sons teach me a lot. Knowledge isn't wasted, even when it doesn't add to a paycheck.

Jeff was active in a dozen campus causes and marched against the Vietnam war he'd fought in, chanting the slogans of peace while he remembered the bloody battles of the Tet offensive. So now he took the low road, into the communes, back to the campuses, talking with contacts, other radicals, people he knew from the antiwar marches, the lettuce boycotts, the women's liberation movement.

But that wasn't all he did. There were other trails we tracked—like the bird at the San Francisco zoo.

It all started with the taped communiqués from the SLA. Joe Russin and I had listened to them inch by inch until we heard them sing in our heads. We had used up the goodwill of tape experts by going over the same ground again and again, listening for any background sound, any faint noise, that might give us a clue. Russin and I had caught music playing behind Patty's voice on one. I knew the tune, one from the forties called "Till"; I had identified it for the FBI and the police.

But our ad hoc experts had come up with an even more tantalizing clue—a bird call, more squawk than song. They said it might be a peacock, not a domestic, caged-in-a-house bird. Not that kind of call. Jeff and I quickly narrowed the bird search to the zoo. That's where peacocks live, so that's where we went one crisp, early spring day. We learned some nature lore that day: Peacocks tend to favor the elephant compound—they hang out there, necks stretched to the ground, tails spread in the wind. We found the peacocks. Where was the SLA? Not that we actually expected them to be sitting there, waiting for us. But we did expect some lead, some faint clue, something other than the stench of elephant manure.

There is a dirt road behind the elephant compound. It is outside the zoo grounds proper, easily reached by anyone driving along the southern side of the zoo, with trees hanging over it—an ideal place to stop and tape a terrorist communiqué.

An hour later we left. Maybe we had found a taping site, but it didn't tell us anything we didn't already know. We knew that sections of the taped communiqués had been made in different places. Patty's voice, on all those first tapes, was not recorded in the same place as General Field Marshal Cinque's. Differences in echo and tone added up to different locales. The road behind the elephants was probably one locale, but the SLA wasn't there now.

We also checked other tape clues, strange fleeting sounds that escaped one's first hearing of the SLA communiqués. A water drip, every twenty-three seconds. We called the water companies, but it was an impossible lead.

But no lead, no matter where or whom it came from, could be ignored. After all, the SLA was not the average next-door neighbor, so tips that would normally be downgraded as coming from crackpots suddenly took on a semblance of validity. We checked them all.

One was a telephone call to Joe Russin at nine one night, a voice claiming its owner had just escaped from the SLA: "I'll tell you where they are. I promised Patty I'd help get her out. I have a taped message from her; it tells where she is."

The mystery caller demanded that $300 in cash be left at the back of a deserted parking lot in West Oakland in two hours. The tape would be lying there, in brown wrapping, with a phone number to call for further information. It was an off-the-wall call that would have been ignored any other time, following any other story. But the tip could be for real.

When Russin had called me at home to tell me about it, I'd said, "Call the cops. This is their bag, not ours."

Russin wouldn't hear of such a thing. It might ruin the contact, if it *was* a contact. So, following a block behind Russin, I drove to West Oakland, a sleazy part of the black ghetto. Only a hamburger stand on one corner offered any light on this dark rainy night. While I waited in my car across the street, Russin walked to the parking lot to make the drop. He paused momentarily, holding the brown bag, then stooped to leave the cash—*his* cash. "Newsroom" has no budget for such fancy trimming on stories.

We met two blocks away. I could see at once that Russin was furious. "The goddamned tape is for an eight-track car deck," he stormed.

We had brought only our old Norelco, which wouldn't play the tape. Therefore we couldn't know whether Patty's voice was there in our hands, telling us where she was being held captive. Quickly, we made a new plan. Russin would go back to San Francisco, to KQED, and play the tape. I would call him at midnight. In the meantime, I would stake out the money, see who picked it up, and follow whoever it was to his lair.

I drove back to the scene of the money drop, a lonely corner of a ghetto where even the hardiest criminal stayed inside on such a night. I watched from inside my car; if someone grabbed me, at least he would first have to smash the car window.

As the minutes dragged by, I almost froze. I couldn't use the heater because the engine had to remain silent. The windows quickly frosted over, making them difficult to see through. Then he was there, at my door, his hand on the handle—a towering black man, a deep scowl on his face that was pressed against the window, two inches from my own. I rolled down the window.

"Lady, why are you sitting here all this time?" It was a sharp voice.

The words poured out. I was waiting for my lover—my husband was going to kill him, I was waiting to warn him. It seemed logical at the time, in the middle of that night. Surely he wouldn't kill a woman waiting to warn her lover. My teeth chattered. Rain splattered across my face. He leaned farther inside, his face puffing hot breath on mine.

"Damn, lady, we got tricks waiting to drive in here and you're making them go away. They figure you're a pig."

It took two minutes to sink in. Tricks? Of course, prostitutes' customers. Drive in? Where? The garage behind my car, where this bulk of a man had come from.

"Sorry about that. I'll move now." And I did, almost running over the man as I slammed the gas pedal to the floor and skidded away from the stakeout.

Perhaps the car was too obvious. I decided to stake it out on foot. I parked behind the hamburger stand and sauntered in— a white middle-aged woman among ten black men, most of them half-drunk, playing penny pitch; beer cans and wine bottles, inside brown bags, that were lifted to their mouths with regularity. I was as conspicuous as a nun at a love-in. But it beat big dudes creeping up on my car.

"Hey there—yeah, you! Here's the two bucks, let's go." It was more a slur of words than a sentence. I looked at the form wavering above me, tall, thin, and old, as old as the $2 price he obviously figured I was soliciting. I was forced back to the car. It was better than being mistaken for a two-dollar whore.

It was midnight—time to call Russin to find out if we had Patty neatly tied up in a tapedeck. I parked at the door of a single sidewalk phone booth a block away and had already stepped inside when it hit me: There would be no one to answer if I called; the station's switchboard shuts down at eight every night (another inconvenience brought about by public television's being a no-money operation). Why hadn't we thought of that before Russin rushed off with the tape?

Now we were cut off, Russin in San Francisco, and me standing in the rain on a deserted corner in West Oakland, watching a brown bag with $300 in it getting soaked.

As I had so many times, I turned to San Francisco's street cops. "Go to KQED, give Russin this number, tell him to call." I spat it into the phone at staccato pace, anxious to know if I had to stay on this corner of hell.

They didn't ask why, just a quick, "Sure you're okay?"

Within five minutes came a wonderful sound, a link with civilization, the phone ringing in the booth and Russin growling, "What the hell kind of messenger service do you have? It scared the shit out of me—two cops banging on the door and saying to call you."

I reminded him about our non-working switchboard. Russin took the time to mutter a few well-chosen expletives regarding KQED's no-night-phone policy, then said, "Our machines won't play the tape. Be at this number in thirty minutes. I'm on my way to KSAN to play it."

Thirty minutes? Why hadn't I called Jeff to meet me, to help me watch the brown paper bag with the money in it?

The brown paper bag? Was it still there? It was not.

A tall thin young man who would no doubt call himself a dude was strutting away from the dark parking lot, away from where the money had been a minute ago. He carried the brown paper bag under his arm like a swagger stick. Why not? It was probably the quickest $300 he'd ever made. I walked behind him, one block, two blocks, but he kept walking—no sign of a car. I couldn't follow him all night. Back in my car, I wrote a hurried description of the dude as I waited for the pay phone to ring again.

When it rang, I heard: "KSAN can't play it either. We have to wait till morning."

That's all Russin said. It hit like a rock. Wait all night for nothing? I told him I would head home; the money had been picked up, and I had a description of the pickup man. Russin added, almost as an afterthought, "The phone number written on the tape's bag is a phony."

The next morning we learned that the tape was, too. It had nothing on it but a rock song titled "My Baby's Daddy Is a Millionaire." The pickup man was finally apprehended when he called the Hearsts, saying he wanted eight hundred dollars left on a car seat. He promised, "When you hear a horn honk, look up—and Patty will be sitting there." When he came for the pickup, the cops were waiting for him. The police discovered that he also had a heavy heroin habit and was known to be dangerous, and that the three hundred dollars was a pittance of what he had already collected from almost every television news director and newspaper editor in the Bay Area.

Follow the clues was the game we played twenty-four hours a day. Such as those provided in the maps we found in the scorched Clayton house, maps with neat, red-penciled circles noting deserted mine shafts in the Oakland Hills. It was a job for Jeff. He put on his hiking boots and took off for three days of climbing down holes in the hills, looking for the SLA and its captive. Neither the SLA nor Patty was in any of the old mine shafts, and Jeff wondered aloud afterward, "What the hell would I have done if they *were* there?"

"Wing it," I told him. "Just say, 'You're surrounded.'"

He didn't laugh too long or loud. Neither did I when I realized where I'd sent my son. But there wasn't time for careful planning.

My purchase of a new police radio on which I could tune in on the FBI channels made it possible to continue working around the clock. When I could no longer pound on doors at midnight, I curled up on the sofa with my head by the radio, listening to the crackle of agents talking to each other in code.

Their code wasn't hard to break—exotic names for the various SLA sympathizers they were watching; different names for well-known streets; meeting places at markets that had been closed for hours.

"Call my wife and let her know I won't be home tonight."

"Do you need a ride or is your car pool meeting you?"

"Can I write this report tomorrow? I'm beat."

"My radio's got static. I can't read you."

Human problems came out of the impersonal black box, over the secret channel assigned to the FBI under the blanket heading "Government Agency Use Only."

They didn't know I knew their codes. Nor did I ever use them on the air, despite the temptation.

Another night Jeff and I spent in Haight-Ashbury, the former stomping grounds of flower children, once the turf of the pusher, now a newborn community of cohesive elements, all working toward a better neighborhood, a true symbiosis.

Jeff had contacts in Haight-Ashbury. We had lived there during its worst period, in 1970. He knew some of the area's burglars and pushers. He talked to them about white women living with black men, something that doesn't even draw a second glance in this mixed-bag neighborhood.

I had some contacts too, left over from a battle by the residents to keep the neighborhood police station open. The brass of the police department had closed it, but a coalition had been formed —cops and hippie communes, ministers and hucksters—all working to reopen their own police station. They won, and now remembered that I had kicked off their campaign on "Newsroom" and had spent long hours working to help them win their fight. They talked, but they didn't know much.

Nancy Ling Perry had been seen buying beer at a corner liquor store two weeks earlier. Willie Wolfe had hung out at a nearby market until the week before. A dude in a doughnut shop last weekend had looked just like Bill Harris.

But it was always a week ago. Never today.

I carried the SLA pictures in plastic folders, bringing them out so often that the plastic finally gave way and had to be held together with Scotch tape. "Have you seen any of these people?" We asked the question a thousand times. We wouldn't stop with the first no but went over each picture.

Out of every fifty we asked, there'd be one who had seen one of the SLA. But they had never called the police. Such "sightings" could be verified if the ones seen were Patty or Emily. The confirmation was made by two dogs. One dog slept each night with Patty's clothing, taken from her and Steven Weed's place on Benvenue Avenue; the other, with the clothes Emily had left behind when she, Bill, and Angela went underground from their Oakland apartment. Each dog would react only to the scent of the woman it had been trained to search out.

They reacted. It had been Emily in Dolores Park, talking to several long-haired young women standing near a park bench.

The two German Shepherds were the only edge the FBI had. They were the top-guarded secret of their hunt for the SLA. They are still the sole keys for distinguishing true sightings from phony leads.

But the dogs could not confirm every sighting. There were too many. So there was no confirmation that it was Emily Harris and Willie Wolfe who shopped at a market across the street from the Black Muslim Mosque each Thursday night. Only the store's employees were certain of it. They studied the well-thumbed photos, each dimple and freckle, and finally said, "Definitely, it's them."

Russin, Jeff, and I began staking out the market, one of the few all-night markets in the city. Primarily night people shop there—workers on the midnight shift, pimps and their girls, cops getting off duty, doctors returning home from emergency calls. The market is well known. Only a few weeks before, the dreaded Zebra killer had murdered a young Salvation Army worker a block away.

We were certain our first actual sighting was Willie Wolfe. I was driving—Russin was still at KQED—and Jeff sat at my side. He kept cautioning, "Stay back, don't follow too close. You'll burn him off." I tried not to tailgate the rusty old truck the SLA suspect had driven out of the market parking lot. We tailed it in and out of blocks, wondering if he was using evasive action. When he drove toward the old car barn, up the hill which dips down into San Francisco's Richmond district, he swung the truck a tight right, and I missed his turn and sped by. We lost him.

I couldn't stop cursing. Jeff kept trying to talk, but I didn't want to hear him. I'd had Willie Wolfe right in front of me—another blowup, another mistake.

"Goddamnit, Mother, shut up!"

Jeff cursing and shouting at me? It had never happened before. It was the one thing that could have shut me up. I swung around, facing him, my foot still on the gas pedal.

"Hit the brake, Goddamnit! You just passed the truck!"

He was right. There it sat, right at my rear fender—the truck I'd lost ten blocks back, parked in front of a look-alike Richmond district apartment. We backed off, took up a stakeout, and called Russin. He immediately joined us and we spelled each other for hours, huddled in our cars sipping cold coffee, Jeff with me, Russin alone.

Russin left to drive two blocks to an all-night diner. He hadn't eaten all day, and it was getting close to midnight. While he was gone, the truck took off, with us on its tail, determined this time not to lose it. But we did. It slowed to three miles an hour, then accelerated to sixty. I couldn't catch it. When we returned to the corner, Russin was pulling in. "What the hell happened?" he asked.

I looked at Russin's face and was more concerned about losing a news director than a truck. He looked awful. He finally admitted that he'd passed out in the restaurant, the victim of too little sleep, too little food, and too much tension. We quit for the night. Not even the SLA was worth a nervous breakdown.

A week later, another Thursday night, two of my best friends, Johnny and Jack, joined me for some excellent French-Russian cuisine at a small restaurant tucked away from tourists. The conversation, food, and wine relaxed us, and we left in a mellow mood. Driving back toward the city, past the same all-night market Russin, Jeff, and I had previously staked out, I asked, "Would you mind if I just drive through and check?"

A two-voiced chorus answered, "Of course not, go ahead."

We hadn't yet reached the parking lot when Johnny, next to me in the front seat, suddenly sat up. So did I. There was Emily Harris! She was paying for two bags of groceries. A white man was at her side. We grabbed Emily's picture from the plastic folder and held it up as we studied each of the features against those of the woman at the check-out counter.

"Hang on—this time I won't lose them," I warned, as the couple got into a new compact car and drove off.

It started just like the truck chase. They circled blocks; I stayed behind, but only a few feet behind. Wherever the small car in front of me went, my larger car went. We followed them past the dark spires of St. Ignatius Church and across the hills of San Francisco in huge sweeping circles.

Johnny was copilot on the chase. "Turn left . . . you're clear on the right . . . run the light, there's no car there." I obeyed more with instinct than mind. The two cars, practically locked bumper to bumper, drove up hills, through valleys, around San Francisco, for ten, fifteen, twenty minutes. Our speed increased. The small car rolled onto Geary Boulevard, a long wide path across San Francisco from the Bay to the ocean. I rolled right in behind it.

Every intersection had a traffic light. They all looked red, but the small car in front of me didn't stop. Neither did I. We'd started out driving forty miles an hour, then fifty. Now we began pushing sixty. Other cars' brakes squealed in their efforts to dodge our wild chase. Horns blasted along our path, but they didn't stop us. We barely noticed the open-mouthed pedestrians who scattered like chickens in front of us.

Johnny's voice shouted, "He's going to hang a U—get ready."

I didn't stop to wonder if my long, chromed car could take the tight U-turn the compact had deftly executed. I grabbed the wheel and pulled all the way to the left, as hard as my hands and arms allowed. The tires screamed but somehow made it around the intersection. Continuing after our prey, we now barreled through the same obstacle course of cars, traffic lights, and people as before. We were heading back toward the city, away from the beach. The speedometer peaked at seventy.

"Where in hell are the cops?" I screamed. Why didn't they see this chase? They always see an expired parking meter.

"Stay on them, they're pulling away," Johnny shouted. I obeyed.

"I'm staying down on the seat. I don't want them to know there are three of us here," Jack yelled from the back. We didn't ask why.

The small car in front turned sharply right into a dark residential street off busy Geary Boulevard.

It suddenly hit me. "They've turned toward the Richmond district police station!" I shouted at my companions who had become part of the obsession that had taken hold of my life since February 4. "We can get help! Be ready; I'll stay on the horn as we go by!"

But the car in front of us stopped. It swung right into the curb, smack in front of the door of the police station. The driver jumped out and we could hear him screaming, "Help! Police! Help!" As I pulled in behind them, a police car appeared at our side. I rolled down the window, ready to flash my press card and explain my pursuit. I didn't have to. One of the cops asked, "What's up, Marilyn?"

"That may be Emily Harris—the SLA—in that car! Check them."

It wasn't a request. It was a demand. We didn't stop to question my right to issue it. The police pounced on the hapless man screaming for help. They ordered his female companion out of the car, spread-eagled both of them, and had them and their car thoroughly searched. Their I.D.'s were checked over the police radio.

Jack, Johnny, and I waited. Strange to think this small police station, covering the city's quiet Richmond district, would be the scene of the capture of Emily Harris of the SLA. I, of course, was already writing the lead of my exclusive. Johnny and Jack were laughing. One of them said, "When you take guests to dinner, you certainly provide a great floor show."

But something was wrong. The two cops walked over to my car as the suspects got back into theirs and prepared to drive away.

"It's not Emily Harris," one of the cops said. "It's a couple who live out here. They check out completely."

I listened to the words he said but couldn't believe them. He must have sensed what I was thinking, for he quickly added, "She is a dead ringer, though, Marilyn. Don't feel bad."

Don't feel bad? We could have been killed chasing this couple all over the city, and she wasn't even Emily Harris! Now the couple stopped their car alongside ours. "Would you mind telling me which one I look like?" the woman asked through her open window. I couldn't even talk, my throat was too thick.

The one cop seemed as disappointed as I. He turned and brusquely said, "Well, it sure as hell isn't Donald De Freeze."

After they drove away, the cop explained further. The couple had thought I was one of the still-on-the-loose black killers known collectively as "the Zebra," who shot only white victims on San Francisco's streets. They thought I was following them to add two more whites to my list of murders.

The night was still young and I wasn't about to go home without getting something on the SLA. I asked Johnny and Jack, "Do you mind if we go check out a parking lot where we saw a 1962 white Chevy wagon with a luggage rack?"

Russin, Huestis, and I had made this find weeks before. The Chevy wagon had been driven by a woman who looked like Emily Harris. She'd met a man in an old Chevy Nova who looked like Bill Harris. Employees of stores around the parking lot had identified both. It was one of our numerous hot leads that never lead anywhere. Tonight it seemed hotter than ever.

Jack and Johnny said all right to my request that we head

there now; they couldn't say much else. I was already driving off toward Haight-Ashbury and the parking lot. We found the station wagon in front of a nearby apartment building. Johnny checked it, but the license plate was gone. And there was no new paper plate inside.

We had just pulled away and gone one block—starting a run through the empty parking lot down by the small alley that joined it to the street—when a huge black Buick swung across the alley. I hit the brakes and stopped inches from it. Two black men had already leaped out and were running toward our car.

"Oh, my God, we've found the Zebra," was all I could stammer.

As I was rolling down the window, my companions warned me, "Keep the damned window up."

It was too late. One of the black men leaned inside; the other had his hand in his jacket, no doubt holding the .38 used in the Zebra kills. Their conversation, however, wasn't at all Zebra-like. They screamed at me, ". . . jiving around our station wagon, you honkie mother-fucker . . ."

I screamed back, with more bravado than bravery. 'If you own that wagon, why in hell didn't you call me? I left my business card on it the other night." And I had, although Russin thought it foolish at the time. It had made sense to me. If the wagon belonged to the SLA, they would make some move to scare me off. If it didn't, the owner would be curious enough to call me to find out what Marilyn Baker of KQED's "Newsroom" wanted.

"You the damned pigs?" they kept asking. I kept denying it. Johnny and Jack kept quiet. The black men got across the fact they didn't intend to kill us. I got across the fact I wanted to talk to the woman who had been driving the wagon the other night.

"Why do you want her?"

"She may have murdered and kidnapped."

"Yes, she sure as shit would do all that, but what's in it for us?"

I promised them money if they promised to help find the SLA.

They were as good as their word. Days later one of these midnight parking-lot friends called and said if I'd come to his house, he'd give me "what you want."

I asked Russin to come along with me. "Okay," he agreed, "but I'll drive my car."

When I reached the address I'd been given, I got out of my car and went inside. I knocked on the door of the apartment and a voice called from upstairs, "Come on up, lady."

What was keeping Russin? I wondered. But this was no time for hesitancy, so I climbed the stairs, and at the top, stepped through an open door into a world I'd never before seen or even imagined. Light shows flickered on every wall and ceiling, drum music beat out of the stereo speakers that towered above me on all walls. The windows were covered with weighty draperies, and the heady smell of hash was thick in the heavy air.

The same deep voice that had summoned me up here called out again, "Come right on into the front room, lady."

I walked in and stopped in my tracks. The black man from the other night was stretched out full-length on a sofa. All he wore was a paisley turban wound around his head—nothing else.

"Come to me, little mother," he mumbled.

"Go get some clothes on," I shot back.

He obeyed. He stood up, staggered out to another room, and returned quickly, wearing sheer black boxer shorts and knee-length black sheer hose. He still wore the turban.

I started questioning him. He gave me book, chapter, and verse—every detail. *But* nothing he told me was about the SLA! It was about the ring of white prostitutes he runs, their tricks, their motels, their payoffs. He was still talking when Russin arrived thirty minutes late. We both listened as politely as possible. It would be one hell of a good story, some other time. But we couldn't take on prostitution and the life and loves of a pimp in the middle of the hunt for the SLA. We finally excused ourselves, and left our friend in his turban and boxer shorts stretched out on the sofa, smoking a pipe.

If there is any consolation for all the dead ends I've run into while tracking the SLA, it is the company I met in those same dead ends—the police and the FBI. It was almost as if the FBI didn't believe the Hearst kidnapping had ever happened. From February 4 until February 20, Charles Bates, the FBI agent in charge of the San Francisco office, made an almost nightly visit to the Hearst home and daily statements to the press, all encouraging, all stiff-upper lip. "It's just a matter of time," he kept repeating.

Would he move in on their hideout and risk Patty's life? he was asked at the daily sessions.

"Absolutely not. We will not do that," he reassured everyone.

Some didn't believe him. I did. I knew he could not move in even if he wanted to. He hadn't the foggiest notion where Patty Hearst or any of the SLA might be.

On February 19, Bates made the statement that became the classic of the SLA case. The next day would be Patty's twentieth birthday and her parents hoped that the SLA might become sentimental and send her home for cake and presents. I had no such delusions, nor did any working cop or any field agent of the FBI. Charles Bates, however, went along with the theory to the extent, in fact, of announcing, "I believe Patty will be released."

"How do you know that, Mr. Bates? What do you know that leads you to say that?" the press corps asked.

"Oh, I've just got a seat-of-the-pants feeling," came Bates's classic reply.

Bates's statement made headlines but no sense. The FBI had brought in two out-of-town sharpshooter teams, and the news media had a field day speculating on the location of the trigger agents. Was the SLA hideout under their surveillance? The truth was mundane. The sharpshooters had arrived for nothing more than a prescheduled routine training mission. But no one in the upper echelons of the FBI seemed to realize how it would ignite rumors if it went ahead as scheduled, in the middle of the Hearst case.

Although no one wanted to talk about it, at least not out loud, there were hints that the federal government had sent U-2 spy planes that could fly over Berkeley, or any other areas where Patty might be held captive, in order to take infrared photos that might reveal who was underneath suspected rooftops.

There were other whispers about a tiny sensor that could be put under the skin of someone to send out a beam that could be tracked a half-mile away. But who would wear such a skin sensor into the cobra camp? Randolph Hearst was offering himself as an exchange hostage for his daughter Patty, but he flatly refused to make such a bargain unless there was some show of good faith. He was still abiding by the gentlemen's code of honor as he tried to deal with the hoods of the seven-headed cobra.

All that we knew for sure was that the FBI had set up "towers," their name for locations from which agents watched possible SLA friends. Scarlet Tower, Yellow Tower, Blue Tower, each color a different address, a different city. None brought results. I knew that from monitoring the police radio. They checked out a thousand leads and ran down a hundred phony SLA contacts—all calling the Hearst home and demanding money, either for Patty or for information.

The FBI twice dropped strips of paper cut and bundled to resemble a package of $25,000 along a freeway in San Jose, in answer to the demands of an anonymous voice. Twice the same voice called back and offered a blow-by-blow description of how the agents had muffed the drop. Was this promise to tell more after a $25,000 drop a real SLA linkup? No one yet knows.

In Los Angeles a man was arrested for picking up $10,000 in a trash can. He had allegedly called and demanded a ransom for Patty. And in Florida, a call demanding one billion dollars sounded too phony. It was never followed up.

Even San Francisco's mayor, Joseph Alioto, running for governor, got into the act. Emily Harris had supposedly been spotted staking out his daughter's home. The story made headlines, but even the police discounted it. The sighting dogs didn't verify Emily's presence.

Psychics came from around the world, some directly to the Hearst home in Hillsborough, where they set up makeshift altars on a dining-room table and tried to communicate with the missing Patty. Others called, almost daily. I got a number of the calls. "She's in an abandoned winery in Napa." . . . "You'll find her tied up in a shack at a deserted airfield in the Santa Cruz Mountains." Others suggested streets she was on: "Serenity"; or "Find a street that starts with *K*." One sent a sealed letter, not to be opened until March 1. Inside was a single typed sentence: "Patty Hearst is dead."

Shoes and blouses and pieces of furniture that Patty had touched were doled out to the most promising psychics, each sure he could "see" where the Hearst daughter was being held. Each saw a different place. Each was wrong.

A whole gaggle of left-movement leaders rushed into the SLA circus. Each was convinced, and gaining headlines with his convictions, that he alone could act as the linkup with the SLA.

For instance, Paul Jacobs bobbed his shaved head and announced he was in consultation with Randolph Hearst. Jacobs's left-wing credentials were based primarily on his candidacy for the U.S. Senate on the Peace and Freedom ticket in 1968, the year Eldridge Cleaver was the party's presidential nominee.

The Reverend Cecil Williams arrived at KQED in a Rolls-Royce, to go on camera and say he would act as intermediary for the Hearsts and the SLA, as head of a coalition to work out "terms." The SLA was being accorded the ceremony befitting a respectable political party. Somewhere along the line everyone had forgotten or overlooked the murdered Marcus Foster.

Even Russell Little and Joe Remiro got into the act from their cells, where they awaited trial as the alleged SLA murderers of Marcus Foster. They wanted a nationwide television press conference, not too different from those held by politicians, where they would only read their own statements, and would allow no questions to be asked.

At Vacaville State Prison, a man known as Death Row Jeff joined two other prisoners in urging the SLA to release Patty, adding that the SLA were "beautiful." Randolph Hearst had driven to Vacaville and pleaded with him to intervene. Death Row Jeff—actually Clifford Jefferson—serving a life sentence for the murder of a fellow prisoner, is known to have had an active dislike for Donald De Freeze when they were in Vacaville together. In fact, he had labeled De Freeze a prison stoolie and a snitch, and had opposed everything he did. Why the turnabout?

Steve Weed went to Mexico to get a personal letter from Regis Debray, an acknowledged political revolutionary who served a prison term for his part in Che Guevara's aborted attempts to take over Latin America. The letter was read on "Newsroom" as an appeal to the SLA.

Vincent Hallinan, the grand old man of the left, used his law offices to stage press conferences to plead for Patty's release, believing his activist role over the past thirty years could get recognition from the SLA.

It was all in vain.

The Reverend Mr. Williams had had two of the taped communiqués delivered to him, but the SLA appeared to be more interested in the use they could make of the minister's ability to get press attention than in his role as mediator.

Even a plea from the American Indian Movement at Wounded Knee went unanswered.

The underground media were in the worst bind. They didn't quite want to come on with public appeals to the SLA to stop its terrorism, but neither did they want to take stands that favored the crimes the SLA bragged about. Thus many of them remained little more than channels for the SLA to use in sending their communiqués, demanding that they be read. KSAN and KPFA radio stations received some, as did *The Berkeley Barb,* an underground newspaper. But that was the only recognition the SLA accorded them. They were delivery boys, nothing else.

CHAPTER **10**

AT NOON ON APRIL 2, Russin shouted across the desks of the news-room: "Bake, get rolling out to John Bryan's. He claims he's got an SLA communiqué."

John Bryan's publication, *The Phoenix,* is more throwaway than newspaper, and its readership is confined primarily to his family and friends. Though I figured it would probably be a wild-goose chase, I pulled on my shoulder bag with its cargo of pens, pads, and cigarettes, and headed for the van. Huestis was off, so Raeside was on camera, and an engineer was doubling as sound man of the crew.

Within ten minutes we rolled out of the KQED garage, and drove toward the Fillmore district where Bryan operates his newspaper from his home, a small Victorian house lost in a sea of similar structures. Bryan was waiting at the front door.

"Please show identification," he was asking the arriving media personnel.

I started to show mine. "Oh, you don't need to, Marilyn. I've watched you a long time." He quickly stopped my struggle to find the press pass in my shoulder bag.

"Why are you even asking for I.D.?" I asked.

"We want to make sure the FBI doesn't infiltrate this meeting."

We didn't have to wait long to find out why he had called this conference. Bryan pointed to a small vase on the mantel, filled with rather withered short-stemmed roses, and said, "These were delivered just an hour ago, with an SLA communiqué inside."

A chorus from the newspeople demanded, "How do you know it's authentic?" It appeared that some of my colleagues shared my doubts about Bryan's reliability as a source of information.

We had good reason to doubt him. Two weeks earlier Bryan's newspaper had carried a boxed ad, asking the SLA to contact him. The following week he had printed what he claimed was the SLA's answer, a long, rambling letter so pat in its rhetoric that no one had believed it to be the real thing.

We were again being told by him that the SLA had sent another communiqué, this one consisting of four typed pages. We demanded to know why we should believe him.

"I have proof, believe me, proof! This time it's real!" he shouted, waving a small slip of paper. "Here's half of Patty Hearst's driver's license."

The piece of license was quickly deemed authentic. We stopped challenging and sat down to listen to Bryan's strange scenario of events.

"Today I heard a gentle knock on my door and there were the roses. Inside the roses was this card." He held it up. On the outside was a picture of a stork, carrying a traditional bundle of joy. The message inside read, "Happy Birthday—scared the hell out of you, didn't I?"

It was pure Nancy—her brand of humor, harking back to her comment to the neighbors, before she torched the SLA hideout in Clayton, that her husband was "in the army."

Bryan showed the four sheets of paper, claiming they had been tucked inside the envelope with the birthday card. Two were titled "Codes of War of the Symbionese Liberation Army." But the other two drew the most interest. One was simply a short paragraph, all typed in capital letters, setting out just how the communiqué should be released and to what news outlets.

The second was a letter:

SYMBIONESE LIBERATION ARMY
INFORMATION INTELLIGENCE UNIT 4

Communiqué No. 7 March 29, 1974   Court Order: Release of
Subject: Negotiations and   Codes of War of the SLA
      Release of Prisoner   Court Order Issued by: The
                                  Court of the People

Herein enclosed are the Codes of War of the Symbionese Liberation Army, these documents as all SLA documents are to be printed in full and omitting nothing by order of this court in all forms of the media.

Further communications regarding the subject prisoner will follow in the following 72 hours, communications will state the state, city and time of release of the prisoner.

I.I. Unit 4
Gen. Field Marshal
Cin. SLA

Patty would be freed. The realization ran around the room like an electric shock. Reporters raced for the only phone in the house. They started shoving, each wanting to be sure his or her editor got the word first, the word we had all been waiting for since February 4. Thank God. She'd be home; it would be over.

I was intrigued, however, by the Codes of War, which obviously had been carefully drawn up:

CODES OF WAR OF THE UNITED SYMBIONESE LIBERATION ARMY

Penalty by Death

All charges that face a death penalty shall be presented to a jury trial made up of the members of the guerrilla forces. The jury shall be selected by the charged also. The charged shall select his or her defense, and the trial judge shall select the prosecutor. The jury shall number at least ¾ of the remaining members of the cell, and the verdict must be unanimous.

1. The surrender to the enemy.
2. The killing of a comrade or disobeying orders that result in the death of a comrade.
3. The deserting of a comrade on the field of war:
   a. Leaving a team position, thereby not covering a comrade.
   b. Leaving a wounded comrade.

4. The informing to the enemy or spying against the people or guerrillas.
5. Leaving a cell unit or base camp without orders:
   Any comrade may leave the guerrilla forces if she or he feels that they no longer feel the courage or faith in the people and the struggle that we wage. A comrade, however, must follow the CODES OF WAR in doing this: that is, he or she must inform the commanding guerrilla of their wish to go from the guerrilla force. Thereupon, the guerrilla in command will release them in a safe area. This ex-combatant may only leave with his or her personal side-arm. REMEMBER, this is the ONLY way a comrade may leave the SLA; any other way is deserting, punishable by death.
6. All paid or unpaid informants operating within the community against the people and the guerrilla forces are sentenced without trial to immediate death.

Penalty by Disciplinary Action

Disciplinary action should be primarily to aid the collective growth of the cell, so that through positive action the mistake is understood. All charges that face disciplinary action shall be under the full control of the guerrilla in command, and she or he shall weigh all evidence and shall decide the verdict, and if needed, direct the disciplinary action to be taken by the charged comrade necessary to correct him or her. Examples of disciplinary action are: The cleaning and maintenance of all cell arms, ammunition, and explosives for one week, the upkeep of outhouses, the full suspension of wine or cigarettes, and extra duties such as additional watches, practice and study periods, correspondence, filing, typing, washing, cleaning, cooking and physical exercises.
1. Lack of responsibility and determined decisiveness in following orders.
2. Non-vigilance or the leaving of an assigned post without orders.
3. Lack of responsibility in maintaining equipment or in maintaining proficiency in all guerrilla skills, especially shooting.
4. The use of any unmedically prescribed drugs:
   This rule relates to the use of such drugs as heroin, speed, peyote, mescaline, reds, pep pills, whites, yellow jackets, bennies, dexies, goof balls, LSD and any other type of hallucinatory drugs. However permission is granted for the use of only two types of relaxing drugs: those are marijuana and/or beer or wines or other alcohols. This

permission is only granted when approved by the guerrilla in command, and with very restraining use only. No officer may grant the use of any of these said drugs to the full number of forces under his or her command; if this permission is granted, only half the force will be allowed to take part, while the other half will stand post and guard duty. The past has shown once true revolutionaries have seriously undertaken revolutionary armed struggle, marijuana and alcohol are not used for recreational purposes or to dilute or blur their consciousness of reality, but rather in very small amounts for medicinal purposes only to calm nerves under times of tension, not to distort reality.

5. The failure to sever all past contacts or failing to destroy all evidence of identification or associations.

6. Killing of an unarmed enemy; in this instance the *enemy refers to members of the U.S.A. military rank and file only and not* to any members of the CIA, FBI, or special agents or any city political police state agents; members of the U.S.A. military rank and file are to be accorded this distinction because we recognize that many of them have been forced into membership either directly, through the draft, or indirectly due to economic pressures.

7. Tortures or sexual assaults on either a comrade or the people or the enemy.

8. Criminal acts against the poor or comrades or guerrilla forces.

9. Malicious cursing or any kind of disrespect to those in command, a comrade, or the people.

10. Deceiving or lying to fellow comrades or the people.

If any of these acts are committed on a continuous basis, the charged shall become a prisoner of the cell and shall remain in this prisoner status until such time as she or he is able to prove their renewed commitment to revolutionary discipline and principles or the charged may request to be dishonorably discharged.

Conduct of Guerrilla Forces Toward the Enemy Soldier and Prisoners

1. Prisoners of war shall be held under the terms of the international Codes of War, they shall be provided with adequate food, medical aid, and exercises.

2. All U.S.A. military rank and file forces shall be allowed to surrender, upon our conditions of surrender, and thereupon they shall be carefully and fully searched and interrogated. All prisoners are to receive instruction on the goals of the Sym-

bionese Liberation Army, and then released in a safe area.

3. All weapons, medical and food supplies, maps, military equipment and money are to be confiscated and turned in to the guerrilla in charge.

4. Under no conditions shall any rank and file enemy soldier be relieved of his or her personal property.

Conduct of Guerrilla Forces Toward the People

All guerrilla forces shall conduct themselves in a manner of respect towards the people, and shall when able and safe to do so, provide food and other aids to the people. They shall when possible inform the people of the goals of the United Symbionese Federation and encourage other women and men to join our forces, and to serve the people and the fight for freedom.

All comrades have one main responsibility, that is to struggle to win and to stand together, so no comrade stands alone, all must look out for each other, all must aid the other, black, brown, red, yellow, white, man or woman, all or none.

This document may change from time to time, so officers are requested to follow the changes with discipline.

To those who would bear the hopes and future of the people let the voice of their guns express the words of freedom.

GEN. FIELD MARSHAL
SLA
Cin.

We started to videotape the materials but Bryan rushed forward, shouting, "You can't do that! I can't let any pictures of any of this communiqué be taken."

Yet the release letter had specifically said that all the media must reprint it or carry the message. I asked him why the contradiction? He became hostile and grabbed at the letters Raeside was videotaping, repeating, "I can't let any pictures be taken."

Suddenly the style of the letters became as important to me as their content. Why no pictures? Why the ban when Bryan was allowing everyone to read them? There was no time to look for the answers.

We inquired about the roses. Where had they been purchased? Bryan said a shop called Crete had delivered them. We left in the van for the nearest phone booth, and Raeside quickly found it listed: Crete Florists, at the corner of Polk and Sutter streets.

The SLA was back in the same area where it had delivered

tapes during the past two months. The florist is across the street from Foster's Cafeteria, where SLA tapes had been left in the men's room. We drove there and parked on the narrow street. Raeside strapped on the camera and we walked to Crete Florists, a name promising more than it offers. It is more a stand than a shop, just large enough for two people and the short, stocky woman who runs it. The flowers are simple bouquets, and there are identical bunches of roses, red and yellow and white, pre-wrapped in tight cones of waxed paper: $2.99 the dozen.

The saleswoman remembered the girl who had bought the roses to be delivered to John Bryan. She had come in the day before, April 1. She had paid for the flowers as well as an extra $1.50 for delivery, asking that a sealed card be enclosed. She had handed it to the saleswoman; it was the size of most birthday or greeting cards. The woman said, "I never even thought about it. I just stuck it inside the roses."

What did the purchaser look like? "Well, she was small, about your size," she said, looking closely at my frame. "She had long brown hair and big eyes and she was sort of pretty. She wore a nice neat skirt and sweater. She was no hippie." It had to be Nancy.

We walked outside the four-by-four shop and looked down the street. "Get that shot, Raeside, pan right down this street," I said. The shop is in the shadow of the Federal Building, within sight of the sixth floor, where the FBI is headquartered.

Charles Bates would have had good news to take on his daily trek to the Hearst Hillsborough home that day, except the news media got the message to the Hearsts before Bates had a chance to do so. Randolph Hearst was elated. He made one of his familiar appearances on the front steps, faced the battery of cameras, and said he was very pleased his daughter would be released.

Did he believe the SLA would keep its word?

"I'm sure they will, if they say they will," he answered.

Catherine Hearst smiled for the first time in sixty days. "It comes as a tremendous relief to me." She sighed, smiled again, and added, "I'm so happy to see one-half of Patty's drivers license. I hope to see the other half—and Patty along with it."

It seemed there was now no need for the letters from Patty's sisters. Seventeen-year-old Vicki and eighteen-year-old Ann had given written statements to the media, pleading that Patty be allowed to come home. Vicki's had a flare of indignation in it. She referred to the SLA claims of serving the needs of the people, and wrote, "Well, I'm people too and I have needs. I need my sister."

Reporters chuckled. It was the first time good humor hadn't seemed out of place at the Hearst mini-press city. There was some shouting of "It's almost over" among the trailer camp of reporters, some jokes about what had gone on, even a few black-humor comments—"Maybe it's all a joke"—but those were quickly ignored. The day was too bright and the news too good for even the most cynical newsperson.

That night I was careful in my "Newsroom" report. I emphasized the Codes of War rather than the release letter. The only solid fact I had was that the pages had been typed differently. Russin agreed. It was a slim thread at best, but it was something. We decided to go slow, not to start hanging out the Welcome-home-Patty banner just yet.

There was also a suspicion that I felt too foolish even to admit —the woman in the flower shop had said that the young lady had insisted that the roses and message be delivered the day she bought them. But the delivery truck had broken down and Crete Florists didn't get the roses to Bryan that day. If they had, the communiqué would have arrived on April Fool's Day.

By late afternoon of April 3, the momentary elation that the SLA ordeal was over had ended. KSAN received a taped communiqué. They slapped it onto their tape deck, expecting to hear details of Patty's release. Instead, they heard Patty's voice in a cold monotone, devoid of emotion. She said:

"I would like to begin this statement by informing the public that I wrote what I am about to say. It's what I feel. I have never been forced to say anything on any tape. Nor have I been brainwashed, drugged, tortured, hypnotized, or in any way confused. As George Jackson wrote 'It's me, the way I want it, the way I see it.'

"Mom, Dad. I would like to comment on your efforts to supposedly secure my safety. The PIN giveaway was a sham. You attempted to deceive the people, the SLA, and me with statements about your concern for myself and the people. You were playing games—stalling for time—which the FBI was using in their attempts to assassinate me and the SLA elements which guarded me. You continued to report that you did everything in your power to pay the way for negotiations for my release. I hate to believe that you could have been so unimaginative as to not even have considered getting Little and Remiro released on bail. While it was repeatedly stated that my conditions would at all times correspond with those of the captured soldiers, when your own lawyer went to inspect the 'hole' in San Quentin, he approved the deplorable conditions there—another move which potentially jeopardized my safety. My mother's acceptance of the appointment to a second term as a U.C. regent, as you well know, would have caused my immediate execution had the SLA been less 'together' about their political goals. Your actions have taught me a great lesson, and in a strange kind of way I'm grateful to you.

"Steven, I know that you are beginning to realize that there is no such thing as neutrality in time of war. There can be no compromise, as your experiences with the FBI must have shown you. You have been harassed by the FBI because of your supposed connections with so-called radicals, and some people have gone so far as to suggest that I arranged my arrest. We both know what really came down that Monday night, but you don't know what's happened since then. I have changed—grown. I've become conscious and can never go back to the life we led before. What I'm saying may seem cold to you and to my old friends, but love doesn't mean the same thing to me anymore.

"My love has expanded as a result of my experiences to embrace all people. It's grown into an unselfish love for my comrades here, in prison, and on the streets. A love that comes from the knowledge that 'no one is free until we are all free.' While I wish that you could be a comrade, I don't expect it. All I expect is that you try to understand the changes I've gone through.

"I have been given a choice of 1) being released in a safe area, or 2) joining the forces of the Symbionese Liberation Army and fighting for my freedom and the freedom of all oppressed people. I have chosen to stay and fight. One thing which I learned is that the corporate ruling class will do anything in their power in order to maintain their position of control over the masses, even if this means the sacrifice of one of their own. It should be obvious that people who don't even care about their own children couldn't possibly care about anyone else's children. The things which are precious to these people are their money and power—and they will never willingly surrender either.

"People should not have to humiliate themselves by standing in lines in order to be fed, nor should they have to live in fear for their lives and the lives of their children, as Tyrone Guyton's mother will sadly attest to.

"Dad, you said that you were concerned with my life, and you also said that you were concerned with the life and interests of all oppressed people in this country. But you are a liar in both areas and, as a member of the ruling class, I know for sure that yours and Mom's interests are never the interests of the people. Dad, you said you would see about getting more job opportunities for the people, but why haven't you warned the people what is to happen to them?—that actually the few jobs they still have will be taken away.

You, a corporate liar, of course, will say that you don't know what I am talking about, but I ask you then to prove it, tell the poor and oppressed people of this nation what the corporate state is about to do, warn black and poor people that they are about to be murdered down to the last man, woman, and child. If you're so interested in the people, why don't you tell them what the energy crisis is really about? Tell them how it is nothing more than a means to get public approval for a massive program to build nuclear power plants all over this nation.

"Tell the people that the entire corporate state is, with the aid of this massive power supply, about to totally automate that entire industrial state to the point that in the next five years all that will be needed will be a small class of button-pushers. Tell the people, Dad, that all the lower class and at least half of the middle class will be unemployed in the next three years, and that the removal of expendable excess, the removal of unneeded people, has already started. I want you to tell the people the truth. Tell them how the law-and-order programs are just a means to remove so-called violent (meaning aware) individuals from the community in order to facilitate the controlled removal of unneeded labor forces from this country, in the same way that Hitler controlled the removal of the Jews from Germany.

"I should have known that if you and the rest of the corporate state were willing to do this to millions of people to maintain power and to serve your needs, you would also kill me if necessary to serve those same needs. How long will it take before white people in this country understand that we must fight for our freedom?

"I have been given the name Tania after a comrade who fought alongside Che in Bolivia for the people of Bolivia. I embrace the name with the determination to continue fighting with her spirit. There is no victory in the half-assed attempts at revolution. I know Tania dedicated her life to the people, fighting with total dedication and an intense desire to learn which I will continue in the oppressed American people's revolution. All colors of string in the web of humanity yearn for freedom.

"Osceola and Bo [Little and Remiro], even though we have never met, I feel like I know you. Timing brought me to you and I'm fighting with your freedom and the freedom of all prisoners in mind. In the strenuous jogs that life takes, you are pillars of strength to me. If I'm feeling down, I think of you, of where you are and why you are there, and my determination grows stronger. It's good to see that your spirits are so high in spite of the terrible conditions. Even though you aren't here, you are with other strong comrades, and the three of us are learning together—I in an environment of love, and you in one of hate, in the belly of the fascist beast. We have grown closer to the people and become stronger through our experiences. I have learned how vicious the pig really is, and our comrades are teaching me to attack with even greater viciousness in the knowledge that the people will win. I send greetings to Death Row Jeff, Al Taylor, and Raymond Scott. Your concern for my safety is matched by my concern for yours. We share a common goal as revolutionaries knowing that Comrade George lives.

"It is in the spirit of Tania that I say:
'PATRIA O MUERTE. VENCEREMOS.'"

With the tape had come a color snapshot of Patty posed defiantly in an army-style shirt, jeans, a beret, firmly grasping a weapon with what appeared to be a starscope—an attachment enabling the user to see in the dark—on top of it. Behind her hung a red flag with the seven-headed cobra of the Symbionese Liberation Army.

Patty Hearst had embraced the SLA. She was now Tania the

Terrorist. The captive had become the captor. We studied every word, every inflection, of Tania's voice for some clue that would tell us why. It was still the flat monotone of the pouting child, the same voice that, on every tape, had only talked of herself.

The pose of Tania was ludicrous. Her feet were spread apart, with the gun jutting out from her hip. News reports called the gun everything from a submachine gun to a sophisticated Russian automatic rifle. I figured that any woman who would pose in front of that flag with its seven-headed cobra symbol, adopt a guerrilla name, and slant a black beret over one eye would also try to make her weapon into something it wasn't. I went to ballistics experts in the San Francisco, Oakland, and Berkeley police departments, driving from one to the other all day, watching careful men behind locked doors study the picture under microscopes. They all agreed. Patty's gun was a plain over-the-counter M-1 carbine.

What about the bulge along the top of the barrel, the bulge everyone thought was a starscope, the secret night-sighting device that had turned Vietnam's darkness into daylight for jungle fighters?

"No, that's no starscope at all," they told me. "That's just an old four-cell police flashlight, taped to the barrel with friction tape."

I decided to check out the two kinds of typing in the four-page communiqué that John Bryan claimed he had received with the roses. I called Charles Bates at the FBI. "Are they all authentic?"

"Well, Marilyn, we really can't say. The SLA switches typewriters sometimes. But let's put it this way: we asked John Bryan to let us take some samples of typing off the typewriters in his office, so we could see if any of those four pages were written there. He flatly refused."

Then I heard from another underground news reporter—but one with top credentials of reliability. He spoke quickly: "John Bryan's here with me now. That whole interview he ran last week—the one he claimed was from the SLA and contained their philosophy—well, it's totally phony. He's admitted it. In his latest edition, he's telling about the hoax."

I asked if he could get Bryan to come to KQED for a "Newsroom" interview with me. "Yeah, I'll tell him to get over to you now. Wait there. He should be there in fifteen minutes."

While I waited, I sent out for and read Bryan's confession in *The Phoenix*. It was there. He had printed a long tirade in his weekly edition at the end of March.

Everyone—reporters, police, and even the Hearst family—had thought there was something phony about the first "communiqué" Bryan released, but when he got the roses, with half of Patty's driver's license, the previous communiqué took on the cloak of authenticity.

It was now stripped away. Bryan had committed an unpardonable offense. He had used journalism to print a phony story—one he had written himself and had signed "The SLA."

I was so furious that Russin was afraid to let me interview Bryan when he arrived. Finally he agreed that instead of a live interview during the "Newsroom" show, I should do a pretape with him in the afternoon. Then we would have time to edit it for that night's airing. "Don't hit him till you finish the interview," Russin warned.

By the time Bryan arrived, I knew even more about him. I had called the *Los Angeles Examiner*. They had fired him ten years earlier, and because of that, he was bitter toward the Hearst family. He had fallen out with several other underground newspapers, and had reached a point where he couldn't get on the staff of any of the better-known underground sheets, such as the *Los Angeles Free Press* or *Berkeley Barb*. He had to print his own.

Bryan walked in and we went to the set, waiting for lights to be put in position and tape to be loaded in a camera—delays that take the fine edge off reporting. He knew I was angry, and he was whining, "Don't be too hard on me. After all, I admitted it was all a hoax this week—and I did get another communiqué from the SLA and the one with the roses was real."

I tried to keep my temper, asking him where he had worked before. He named a list of major newspapers, including one that had gone out of business. "When did you work on that one?" I asked, more to pass time than to gain information.

He took another drink of Coke from the bottle in his hand and said, "Oh, I was there in 1965."

It was more than I could resist: "That's a neat trick, since it closed in '61."

The bottle flew toward me, splattering cola as it went past.

He jumped up, screamed a string of expletives, and ran out the door.

"Did you get that? Is it on tape?" I yelled at the cameraman.

"We didn't have it rolling. Sorry."

So John Bryan's interview was never on "Newsroom." And there is still no proof that all four pages supposedly tucked into the dozen roses are any more authentic than the dozen-paged communiqué John Bryan wrote himself and passed off as an SLA letter. Some of it—one, two, three, or four pages—is real. After all, there had been half of Patty Hearst's driver's license inside the envelope.

CHAPTER **11**

THE SLA, STILL playing their grandiose game of titles, rank, and
war, had declared they were holding Patty as a prisoner under all
the rules of the Geneva Convention. Those rules included the
right of observers to inspect the prisoner's compound. I asked
Hearst's permission to volunteer to make an inspection. He
agreed. Huestis and I got an okay from Russin and that night, on
"Newsroom," I suggested the SLA live up to their Geneva Convention claim and permit us in to observe. They ignored the
suggestion.

Under the Geneva Convention, prisoners can receive letters
from home. I asked, via television, that the SLA permit this, if
they were sincere about their Geneva Convention claim. They
ignored this as well. Now, Patty was no longer a prisoner.

On Monday, April 15, I was at a press conference called by California's Attorney General Evelle J. Younger for 9:30 A.M. The
A.G.'s press people had hot coffee and doughnuts waiting for the
ragtag crew of journalists wending their way to the long press
conference table. The KQED camera crew was late, so I sat up

front in one of the chairs set up for a camera, not for a reporter. Cameramen from other stations looked over, annoyed that a reporter would take one of the seats reserved for the magic lens. I assured them, "Just a holding action—my crew is late." They relaxed and I continued sipping coffee. It had become the mainstay of my diet.

We were handed a prepared statement. It was what we expected, all about the problems of dealing with terrorists such as the SLA. Younger was going to get tough. He arrived by 9:45 A.M., flanked by his usual deputies, each in a neat gray suit, a spotless white shirt, and a narrow tie. Younger lowered his ample body into the swivel chair at the head of the table, flashed a few smiles as lights were adjusted and cameramen thrust light meters in his face. Then he started reading from a four-page statement.

He spoke about the extra $4 million the Hearst Foundation had agreed to put into the People in Need program, provided Patty was returned unharmed. The $4 million was sitting in a bank escrow, waiting until Patty came home before it would be handed over to PIN, which had already proved a miserable failure. It was a desperate act by desperate parents. Randolph and Catherine Hearst had flown to New York to plead with the corporate officials, some of whom weren't eager to hand over the $4 million. They reminded Hearst that the foundation set up by his father was marked for charitable donations.

Younger hammered at this point himself. "To what extent should the trustees of a charitable trust use trust funds to meet extortion demands? To what extent should a corporation's directors use corporation assets to ransom an officer's loved one?" he asked, as the cameras whirled. Younger then did what few had dared—he publicly labeled the PIN food giveaway a farce, adding, "We need to ask ourselves whether the food reached the people in greatest need. Should we allow a small band of extortionists to dictate our welfare policies?"

It was all good stuff, things that needed saying, but the news people were listless. Too much of Younger's statement was couched as questions. We were there for answers. But Younger got our full attention with his next statement:

"It is a fair question to ask whether a free press can responsibly comply with extortionist demands that it publish political rhetoric designed to influence public opinion in favor of the kidnappers."

156

Now he locked eyes with the reporters. He didn't pull back, but went on: ". . . the SLA manipulation of the media . . . a free press compromises its own freedom when it permits itself to be abused in this manner."

We squirmed in our chairs. How many of us had had the same dark thoughts? How many other reporters had worried about running the SLA's taped messages in full on prime-time television and radio, and on the front pages of newspapers? A number of us had worried, but few had spoken out. Younger had the press now and he wasn't going to let it get away with just a few swift jabs at its soft midriff. He turned to law enforcement itself, a subject on which his opinions carry some weight, since he is California's senior law-enforcement officer.

He said political kidnapping could not be tolerated. We had all heard that, but what would he do to stop it? He was oblique, but he said it—" . . . we cannot in good conscience place the safety of one citizen above all others." Did that mean a shoot-on-sight order against the SLA, including Patty Hearst? Younger dodged the question. He wasn't saying that, but he repeated his claim, ". . . no one above all others."

Evelle Younger is an inveterate politician. Yet that day he came perilously close to putting law enforcement ahead of his elective position. He chided: ". . . the timidity of police response." And when asked if the FBI was holding back, he hedged, "I can't speak for them."

He said he would ask for a new state law that would make it unlawful to accept the fruits of extortion. One of us pointed out that there already is such a law. It hadn't been enforced when people took the food distributed on orders issued by the SLA. He did a swift duck again: "That was different."

I asked, "Will you prosecute radio and television stations that, because of extortion demands, turn over time, as we all have done for the SLA?" I'd forgotten just how evasive the man could be; the question elicited an answer that said little. But by now it was after ten, and we reporters were getting restless, wondering what we would use for the nightly lead in our SLA stories. No one discussed using Younger's statements about the media's paying extortion in the form of time and space.

When the conference officially ended, a few of us hung back, asking Younger specific questions.

Would he release the pictures of the SLA suspects?

"Aren't those already in your hands, Marilyn?"

"No, sir. I've been trying to get them for more than a month. I named them on the air on March 22, but I still can't get their pictures."

"You should have all of them. I'll get on it today. Call me in the morning."

At 9:40 A.M., while we reporters were closeted with Evelle Younger, a rented car was parked in the lot of a closed gas station on the southeast corner of Noriega Street and Twenty-second Avenue in the heart of San Francisco's Sunset district. Four people sat in the red Hornet sports car—Emily and Bill Harris, Willie Wolfe, and Angela Atwood. A rented green station wagon pulled into the bus zone across the street, on the northeast corner. No one noticed.

The intersection at Noriega and Twenty-second is a small hub of shops, with a branch of the Hibernia Bank on the northeast corner. The bank had recently started a new early-opening policy, 9:30 A.M.

At 9:44 A.M., four white women and one black man slid out of the station wagon parked in the bus zone next to the bank. All wore knee-length dark coats which they clutched around them, and dark leather gloves, even though it was a mild April morning. They glanced once at their comrades parked across the street.

Two of the women separated from the other three persons and entered the bank. The first wore an obvious wig of heavy dark curls that flopped about in a way that had little relationship to her head. She squinted—new contact lenses were bothering her eyes—and held a carbine under her coat. She was Camilla Hall.

The woman next to her wore a long dark wig with lacquered layers of waves. Legs of baggy jeans were visible below her coat. A bulge gave her the appearance of being pregnant. The bulge was caused by a carbine. This was Patty Hearst.

Camilla walked to the rear of the bank, turned, and looked toward Patty as if awaiting instructions. Patty walked to the center of the floor, tripping once as she bumped into a chrome-plated pole holding the velvet rope behind which customers wait their turns to be served. Today there was no waiting. A few customers were transacting business at the four tellers' windows that were the only ones open at the time. Now in position, Patty turned, facing the desks of the junior bank officers; her back was to the tellers' cages.

A man walked in behind Camilla and Patty and went swiftly to the wall that jutted out from the tellers' cages. He wore an old gray felt hat, its wide brim hanging down over the stubble on his face. He slouched low, looking shorter and fatter than he was. His dark coat also concealed a carbine. He was Donald De Freeze.

Behind him came a small woman, her hair in a pixie cut. She wore tennis shoes instead of combat boots, and her dark double-breasted coat seemed three sizes too large for her petite frame. She was grinning. This was Nancy Ling Perry. She also carried a carbine under her coat.

Suddenly, shouts erupted from the mouths of the four robbers: "It's a holdup! Down on the floor! On your faces, you mother-fuckers!"

Customers screamed and fell to the floor, secretaries crawled under desks, the two bank guards stood staring. They couldn't believe it was happening, not in Sunset. One guard quickly tossed his gun toward the man who was now pointing his carbine at him. The other put his hands in the air.

"You, goddamn you, toss that gun over and get on your face!" De Freeze barked at the still-armed guard. The guard obeyed. By now he could see the carbines that all were carrying. They had every corner of the bank covered: Camilla, at the far-east wall, her rifle scanning the tellers along the north wall; Patty, in the center, her gun making sweeping arcs across the bodies prone on the carpeted floor along the south wall; De Freeze, standing by the end of the north wall, backed into a niche where the west wall jutted out and ran along to the double glass front doors; Nancy, just inside the doors, her gun ready to cover not only the bank, but anyone outside.

A fifth person ran forward. She wore baggy pants tucked into combat boots; a light-gray knit cap covered her hair and was pulled low over her forehead. In her left hand, she carried a canvas bag; in her right, a revolver. It was Mizmoon. Within seconds, she was at the tellers' cages, and with one hand on the counter, she hoisted herself in a graceful leap and cleared the four-foot obstacle as if it hadn't existed.

"Give me the keys!" she shouted. A teller handed them over, staring at the blue-black metal of the revolver thrust in her face. Mizmoon unlocked two of the four cash drawers and began slipping bills into the canvas bag as though she had rehearsed the movements a million times.

Outside the bank, a fifty-nine-year-old man was walking along Noriega toward the front door. He had gotten an early start to do some bank business. It was 9:46 A.M. He pushed the swinging glass door and started inside. He saw the girl with the long dark hair in the middle of the bank, near the roped line where he would have to wait for a teller. She lunged at him, screaming. He doesn't remember what she said, he didn't hear the words. He was too busy looking at the barrel of the rifle she jabbed toward him.

Nor did he see the smaller girl. She just swung around from the doors and he felt a bullet bite into him. He fell to the carpet, the sting of the shot blanking out the voices and commands shouted over his head.

With her same earlier grace, Mizmoon vaulted back over the counter. Carrying the stuffed canvas bag, she ran toward the door without looking to the right or left. She knew her role. Her comrades knew theirs. She didn't even glance at the man lying on the floor by the entrance. She pushed the door open and ran outside.

Nancy swung in after her, as though taking part in a precision drill; she held the gun high across her breast, ready to use it again if necessary. She glanced once at De Freeze. He was sidestepping toward the doors. Nancy also ignored the wounded man as she ran out to the waiting car.

De Freeze reached the doors, yelling. "Stay down or we'll kill you!" He looked back at Patty and Camilla. Camilla seemed confused. She ran toward the door, then turned and looked back. Patty was impatient. She took her left hand off the rifle, where it had held the barrel pointed at her victims, swung her arm in an arc toward Camilla in a clear signal; "Get going, get out!" Patty's right hand was shoved through the cutout pocket of her coat, holding the trigger of the carbine. Camilla obeyed. She followed Mizmoon and Nancy out the front doors.

Patty danced toward the doors, one step in one direction, two steps in another, high excitement in her movements. She and

De Freeze, now standing at the entrance, were the only two of the holdup gang still in the bank. Patty turned her back on their hostages, grinned at De Freeze, and ran out the door. De Freeze turned on his heels and followed.

Outside, an elderly man, his seventieth birthday just weeks away, was taking a morning stroll along the quiet street. He reached the bank doors just as Patty and De Freeze were leaving. De Freeze wheeled around and fired once. The bullet sent the man sprawling across the sidewalk.

The holdup had been carefully planned. Within four minutes, they had taken the bank at gunpoint, robbed it of more than $10,000, shot two innocent bystanders, and roared off in a getaway car.

It wasn't yet 10:00 A.M. Evelle Younger's press statement to "toughen up on terrorists," was still being heard by news personnel from all over the city.

Both carloads of the cobra kill-cult members sped down Twenty-second Avenue and took a fast left onto Lawton, a street similar to Noriega, with quiet homes and small shops. They drove another eight blocks, to the corner of Thirtieth Avenue and Lawton, where two dark green sedans were waiting—a Maverick and a Ford Ltd. One was parked next to a schoolyard, the other by a home. Children played on the school grounds. The SLA had carefully selected this corner to switch from the holdup cars to the two other cars they had rented three days earlier. They changed cars, dragging with them the large canvas bag and their rifles, after having made certain nothing was left behind. The two green sedans then drove off toward Golden Gate Park.

It was noon before the news media knew that the Hibernia Bank robbery was the work of the SLA cobra. Attorney General Younger had not realized when he spoke to us that his "get tough" policy was an hour too late. After the press conference, the camera crew had left for KQED, and I'd walked to City Hall to meet my son Chris for lunch. By the time we had finished eating, the news was out: the SLA had robbed a bank—the cobra had struck again. And Patty Hearst was identified as a part of the seven-headed monster.

Randolph and Catherine Hearst were in Mexico the day of the holdup; they'd managed to slip by the reporters and to fly across the border with two of their daughters, Virginia and Ann, whom they were afraid to let out of their sight. It wasn't an unusual trip. Hearst often stays at a cottage in La Paz owned by Desi Arnaz. He enjoys it because little can intrude in that isolated place. It was what the Hearsts needed now, a place where they could shut out reality. They were on the edge of exhaustion.

When officials telephoned the Hearsts in Mexico to report that Patty was one of five who had robbed a bank in San Francisco, Catherine and Randolph Hearst refused to believe the accusation. Could the FBI prove Patty had been a willing participant? Not yet. In fact, the law-enforcement officials held out some small hope to the Hearsts—a study of the pictures taken by the bank's automatic cameras might show that Patty's right hand had been tied down inside the black knee-length coat.

It was false hope. They had already seen the pictures, had seen Patty use her left hand to give Camilla directions. But they were loath to destroy the Hearsts' final hope. Perhaps she had been coerced into acting as she did, they offered.

By four that afternoon cameras, lights, and reporters spilled out of the staid FBI reception room on the sixth floor of the Federal Building, awaiting a statement. I prepared to join the mob, but took one last phone call before I left the newsroom from a friend at ABC-TV in New York, who said, "We're worried. Our man in San Francisco is saying Patty Hearst was in on the bank job. We don't want to use that unless you confirm it."

I had already talked to witnesses and had combed through my police sources. "Yes, she was there. That's all I'm sure of," I said.

"Thanks, we'll use it then," came his reply.

I was exhausted but went to the FBI office and took up my square foot of space, waiting for some official word. The receptionist ordered everyone out at the regular five-o'clock closing time of the office, so we went out in the hall to wait. At six, we were still waiting, sandwiched together between two banks of elevators, sitting or squatting on the cold marble floor.

I tried a bluff. I wrote a note to Charles Bates: "Dear Charlie —I'm going on the air tonight with the fact that Camilla Hall was in on the robbery. Will you confirm? Marilyn."

No one had paid much attention to Camilla Hall. I had done a story weeks earlier, saying she had vanished, that she was

Mizmoon's lover. I seemed to be the only reporter concerned with Camilla.

Would Bates take the bait and come out? He did. "Marilyn, it will be about an hour, then I'll have a statement."

That's all. He gave a quick smile and disappeared again behind the locked door. The other reporters looked at me. What had I sent in on the slip of paper that elicited such a fast response?

It was almost seven when the door opened again. We all jumped up, lights flashed on, and cameras rolled. An agent, in wing-tipped shoes and a gray suit, rolled out a chair. "This is for you, Marilyn," he said and disappeared behind the locked door.

I wasn't pleased by this show of courtesy. The one thing I didn't need was to be singled out by the FBI in front of my peers. I didn't even know the agent. I could have ignored this special treatment and remained on the floor; or I could have sat on the chair in comfort. I chose comfort.

At seven-thirty "Newsroom" had been on the air for half an hour. It would be over in another thirty minutes. Still we waited. A agent emerged from behind the closed door and suggested that we go to the press room on the twentieth floor.

At seven-fifty, Bates joined us. With him was James Browning, U.S. Attorney General for Northern California. They had a fistful of pictures, still smelling of the hypo they had been pulled from. There were pictures of Patty with the gun, standing in the center of the bank; pictures of the five in various candid poses: guns raised, mouths open, feet moving. There was just the one set of photographs. Bates said the rest would not be ready for another half-hour.

I called Bates aside and reminded him of favors two of his assistants had asked of me, assistants whom the news media had nicknamed Frick and Frack after a comedy team with the Ice Follies. Bates agreed to let me accompany him back to his office. As we stepped out into the small hallway where I had previously camped with the others for two hours, the elevator door opposite us was closing. Only a slice of a man was still visible, and he had a handful of pictures.

Bates reacted instinctively. He flung himself between the narrowing aperture, stopped the doors from closing, and grabbed the wet prints from the astonished agent's hands. He tossed a set of them to me. "Okay? Now we're even."

I didn't answer. I was jamming my thumb against the down button. Outside I ran down the block to the car and took off across the busy city to KQED. The speedometer never dropped below sixty. I rushed directly onto the "Newsroom" set, where Russin was stalling for time, promising that "Marilyn Baker will be here any minute with the full story of the bank robbery."

I wasn't even settled in my chair when he introduced me and I broke the story. There was no time to pin the pictures on easels or to do any of the fancy production work that is the hallmark of our big-sister commercial television news shows. I held the pictures up, using a pencil as a pointer. "This is Camilla, here's Nancy, that's Mizmoon, this is De Freeze. And this one is Patty Hearst, holding a carbine on the bank employees."

Russin was grinning. We had beaten all other news media, including TV, whose next shows were at 11:00 P.M. We had had the photographs on the air by 7:55 P.M.

Randolph and Catherine Hearst flew back to Hillsborough, to the home that had become their prison. Randolph again faced a barrage of cameras and notepads. His words were slow, spoken almost in a whisper. "This is the most vicious thing I've ever seen. Sixty days ago a lovely child; sixty days later there's a picture of her in a bank with a gun in her hand. . . . It's terrible."

I talked to him on the phone that night. It was hard to ask him questions. He was despondent, his voice was without hope. But he still clung to whatever thread dangled. "If somebody stepped on my instep, I guess I'd pose for a picture with a gun in my hand," he murmured. I had the feeling he meant it.

By 5:30 the morning of April 16, I was out in the Sunset district, still pounding the sidewalks, door to door, with the worn mug shots of the robbery suspects. By that time they had been seen on television and in newspapers as well. The Sunset district had never seen so much traffic along its residential streets. FBI cars, unmarked except for their short, rigids aerials, circled around each block. San Francisco police in their black-and-white patrol cars, and the unmarked cars of the elite Bureau of Inspectors, were tailgating each other.

Residents grew tired of answering their doors, hearing the same routine questions: "Have you seen any of these people? If so, where and when?" Although the questions were routine, the answers varied. Shopkeepers admitted they knew the suspects. Camilla had bounced a couple of checks at a nearby market; they wouldn't forget her. Regular gas-station attendants could give us no information, but a relief attendant could: Camilla, again—she had bought gas and had complained about having to wear glasses all the time. Nice girl, clean-cut. A drugstore clerk shuddered when she saw pictures of Camilla and Mizmoon. "Why, they were in here just last week." She thought they had bought makeup.

At one point a reporter from the *Chronicle* approached me, asking, "Where are you looking, Marilyn? I was told to follow you." I drove into Golden Gate Park, which borders Sunset's north end, and quickly lost him. Only then was I able to return to the pavement, the stores, and the doors.

As a woman, I had a decided edge—housewives related to me. Also, I had no time schedule, other than going on the air at seven each evening. I took the time to chat with the housewives about their petunias and children.

In one such idle conversation I hit paydirt. A woman was watering her flowers as her two sons played around the garden. I mentioned that my two are now adults. She said hers were only ten and twelve. I asked her if either of them had a paper route.

"Why, yes, one does."

"Could he look at these pictures and see if he knows any of the people?"

"Of course," she replied, immediately calling the older one. He glanced at the photos, uninterested in this grown-up cops-and-robbers game. None looked familiar, he said. He turned to walk toward his bike, then looked back and said, "But I still think those bullet boxes and gun stuff in the park yesterday were important."

What bullets and guns? He poured out the story. At ten-thirty the morning before, he and a friend had been playing in Golden Gate Park, near the Forty-eighth Avenue entrance, sliding down a grassy slope on cardboard boxes. "Then my friend went by this trash barrel, and he saw this stuff," the boy said.

"What stuff? Can you describe it for me?" I asked.

"Sure, lady. There were about fifteen or twenty boxes, ammunition boxes, but they were all empty. There was a part of a rifle.

I know it was a carbine—I know about guns. It was wrapped up in a woman's blouse, white with some sort of flowers on it. There were two empty boxes that were for handcuffs, too. It was all in the trash barrel."

"Did you do anything with all this stuff?"

"Sure," he replied. "We walked over to a gun store right near the park and we had the man there call the police. They came out and got it all. The gun-store man said the rifle piece was the bolt action out of an M-1 carbine. The cops took it all, even the boxes my buddy and I were going to bring home to keep."

I hastily said good-bye and went to the nearest pay phone. When I inquired, the police were polite but emphatic. No report had been made about articles found along the escape route of the SLA within an hour after the bank holdup. I asked where these things would be if they *had* been found.

"Oh, they'd be turned over to the property department, lost property, so the owner can reclaim them."

I didn't bother to check further. It seemed less than likely that the SLA would trot into the Hall of Justice to reclaim discarded property. So by 6:00 P.M. I was back at KQED, with blisters on my feet and a grin on my face. Russin agreed we had a good story—the ammunition boxes, part of a rifle, and handcuff boxes —but suggested, "Let the feds know. Don't embarrass them too much."

I called Charles Bates and told him. He swore softly, then said, "The San Francisco police never tell us a thing."

I called a friend at the Hall of Justice to alert him about the find, so he wouldn't be caught short if questioned about it. He swore more openly than Bates. "I'll try to find out what those idiots have done," he said and hung up.

At 7:00 P.M. I broke the story on the air.

Thirty days after I had named the SLA members on "Newsroom," the district attorney of Alameda County (an area known as East Bay) announced that formal complaints had been issued against Emily and Bill Harris, Angela Atwood, and Willie Wolfe. They had all applied for, and received, drivers' licenses under aliases.

In September 1973, Bill and Emily Harris had received their

phony licenses under the names of Anna Lindenberg and Richard Frank Dennis. Willie Wolfe had taken out a driver's license on November 5, 1973, under the name Charles Morgan. On December 20, Angela Atwood had gotten one under the name Deborah K. Cruse. The day after Christmas 1973, Bill Harris had gotten a second license, this time using the name of Jonathan Mark Salamone.

While I checked and rechecked every conceivable source, a special federal grand jury was trying to get witnesses to explain what was behind the SLA. A Janet Cooper was subpoenaed. It was her driver's license that had been used to rent the four getaway cars used by the SLA. She stated that her wallet had been stolen last fall. She lived on Hearst Avenue, in Berkeley, only a block and a half from Camilla Hall. She admitted that she knew some of the suspects, but refused to answer any further questions.

Cynthia Garvey was subpoenaed but provided no real news. She had lived with Joe Remiro until the fall of 1973. Could a woman live with a man and not know he was in the SLA? She refused to answer. Two other witnesses, Paul and Joyce Halverson, were called. They lived in San Francisco and were a complete mystery to me.

I went back to more tangible clues, such as the ammunition. The SLA had had to buy it somewhere. I began calling gun shops, starting with the largest. The owner is a "Newsroom" fan, and we chatted about news and television and women reporters. He finally said, "Look, I know why you're calling. It's about all the ammunition the Halversons purchased around the first of April. But I don't know if I can talk to you. I'd better check with the FBI."

He checked and the FBI said, "Don't talk." But a clerk had already told me about the newest twist in the strange SLA tale: Not only had the Halversons allegedly purchased a thousand rounds of .30-caliber ammunition, the proper size for M-1 carbines, they had returned the unused portion on April 16, the day after the bank holdup. In inquiring about the ammunition, I had found the reason why the two mystery witnesses had been called before the grand jury.

A check of the Halversons' home and a long talk with neighbors and friends provided the information that Paul Halverson had driven a cab. I wanted a copy of Halverson's cab permit, so I called the permit bureau of the police; I was told that in five minutes the office would close for the day.

Victor Wong of KQED grabbed his camera and ran. But once there he was blocked. "Why," the police brass demanded, "do you want Halverson's picture?" Victor retreated behind his Asian smile and nods of "No English." Then he called me from their phone. I demanded that the police obey the law and permit public records to be seen by the public. It worked. Victor snapped the picture of Halverson. There was only an hour left before "Newsroom" would go on the air.

As Victor left the bureau, he heard one official shout to another, "Notify the Zebra hunt—Baker has a lead on a guy named Halverson." They obviously didn't know Halverson was a secret witness before the SLA grand jury.

We could find the ammunition, but why couldn't we find the cars? That was a stumper. Cars aren't easy to hide. We had every detail, right down to the license plate numbers. Russin and I prowled, trying to find some lonely alley they could have been dumped in. We thought about checking garages, but when I called the police and the feds about following up that possibility, they told me, "We've had men check out every major garage in the city." Russin and I agreed that there was no need to backtrack on that.

On April 22, one week after the bank holdup, Badge called. It was almost 10:00 A.M. "We've got the cars—they were in the Japan Center Theatre."

Huestis and I raced to the van and drove out to the hotel-and-shop complex that borders on the Fillmore district. We were the only press people there, but the FBI was everywhere. Both cars were neatly parked in stalls. How could they have been there and not been found sooner? Both cars had been checked in at 10:14 A.M. on April 15, less than thirty minutes after the SLA had held up the bank and shot two men. They had been sitting there since.

No one knew if the garage had been searched. The FBI said they had no way of knowing which agent should have done it, so they had no way to check. The cops said the same thing. The final irony was sounded when I found that the Japan

Center Theatre has its own private security officer, Rodney Williams, who, when he isn't moonlighting, is an assistant inspector on the San Francisco police force.

Forty-eight hours later I received another call from Badge: "Rodney Williams is on his way to the Hall of Justice. He just got an SLA communiqué."

A policeman receiving an SLA communiqué? Yet, Rodney Williams is not a run-of-the-mill cop. First of all, he is black; second, he's a radical; third, he is in community relations, a unit that permits him to decide his own work and his own hours.

Huestis and I drove to the Hall of Justice, waiting for Williams to make his message public. It was a strange performance, even for the SLA. First, Williams flatly refused to say how he had received the newest tape of Patty's voice and the poster that accompanied it. The poster was soggy with rainwater. Its hand-drawn message was smeared but still readable: "Change is the law of nature; we are either in the process of dying or being born." It ended: "Death to the fascist insect"—not adding, as previously, "that preys upon the lives of the people."

Officer Williams made a statement, declaring he must protect his sources; therefore he could not reveal where or how he found the latest communiqué. Police brass stood helplessly by in the face of this new tack by one of their own. Charles Bates fumed. If only the cops had called the FBI first, they could have kept the tape secret and forced the SLA to deliver another. Two of Bates's agents rushed into the police room where Williams was holding forth. When they saw the crowd and the confusion, they looked at each other in dismay and left, realizing they would be unable to question Williams until he decided to meet them.

If the mode of the tape's delivery was bizarre, the message was more so. For the first time there was emotion in Patty's voice as she declared again that she was Tania. There was defiance in her words as she said:

"Greetings to the people. This is Tania. On April 15 my comrades and I expropriated $10,660.02 from the Sunset Branch of the Hibernia Bank. Casualties could have been avoided had the persons involved cooperated with the people's forces and kept out of the way until after our departure. I was positioned so that I could hold customers and bank personnel who were on the floor. My gun was loaded and at no time did any of my comrades intentionally point their guns at me. Careful examination of the photographs which were published clearly shows this to be true.

"Our action of April 15 forced the corporate state to help finance the revolution. In the case of expropriation, the difference between a criminal act and a revolutionary act is shown by what the money is used for, as with the money involved in my parents' bad-faith gesture to aid the people and to insure the survival of the people's forces in their struggle with and for the people.

"To those clowns who want a personal interview with me, Vincent Hallinan, Steven Weed, and the pig Hearsts, I prefer giving it to the people in the bank. It's absurd to think that I could surface to say what I'm saying now and be allowed to freely return to my comrades. The enemy still wants me dead. I am obviously alive and well. As for being brainwashed, the idea is ridiculous to the point of being beyond belief. It's interesting the way early reports characterize me as a beautiful, intelligent liberal, while the more recent report I'm a comely girl who has been brainwashed. The contradictions are obvious.

"Consciousness is terrifying to the ruling class, and they would do anything to discredit people who have realized that the only alternative to freedom is death and that the only way we can free ourselves of this fascist dictatorship is by fighting—not with words, but with guns.

"As for my ex-fiancé, I'm amazed that he thinks that the first thing I would want to do once freed would be to rush and see him. The fact is I don't care if I ever see him again. During the last few months Steven has shown himself to be a sexist, agist pig, not that this is a sudden change from the way he always was. It merely became blatant during the period when I was still a hostage. Frankly, Steven is the one who sounds brainwashed. I can't believe those weary words he uttered were from his heart. They were a mixture of FBI rhetoric and Randy's simplicity.

"I have no proof that Mr. Debray's letter is authentic. The date and location it gives are confusing in terms of when the letter was published in the papers. How could it have been written in Paris and published in your newspaper on the same day, Adolph?

"In any case, I hope that the last action has put his mind at ease. If it didn't, further actions will.

"To those people who still believe that I'm brainwashed or dead, I see no reason to further defend my position. I am a soldier of the people's army.

"*Patria o muerte, venceremos.*"

Huestis and I drove back to KQED, with only minutes to prepare the airing of the latest SLA turn. I stared ahead, trying to place the fury in Patty's voice. It had a familiar ring to it. It was the voice of a woman furious over wasted years.

CHAPTER **12**

IT WAS THE lowly cockroach that uncovered the seven-headed cobra. Once again the SLA had hidden itself beneath a layer of filth which, in this instance, attracted the crawling insects from all around the block. Cockroaches invaded the hideout, covered the walls, and scrambled over each other until they spilled down into the apartment below.

Everyone knows cockroaches breed in old buildings, but not like this—in a solid swarm. A tenant downstairs called the manager, who quickly followed the trail of the creatures back upstairs to Apartment 6, at 1827 Golden Gate Avenue, a one-room apartment with a wall-bed unit, its single large bay window fronting on the street that runs down the hill to the headquarters of the FBI. Besides roaches, the manager found enough evidence of the SLA to prompt him to call the authorities.

Bob Huestis and I took up our routine positions of waiting outside doors until the FBI opened them. We watched silent agents haul away two truckloads of possessions, small pieces that should tell them something of the SLA life-style—a new blender, still in its box; a tank vacuum cleaner, still in its box; green plastic waste-baskets, some decorated with fluorescent purple decals; a woman's bicycle, rusty, but with new hand brakes wired on. There were also old clothes, dark knee-length jackets, the same as those worn in the bank holdup; wigs. We heard bandsaws buzzing inside the apartment, then saw a piece of the kitchen wall being carted off for special fingerprinting treatment.

We knocked on doors and spoke to neighbors, people who had lived beside the cobra. Across the hall, a man who was in the military police, stationed with the U.S. Army at the Presidio, was too scared to talk. A blind woman downstairs recalled that some-one from Apartment 6 had come to her door, asking to use her phone. Since she didn't trust anyone in the neighborhood, she hadn't let the person in. The manager was unsure of what he should say, and when he did talk, he had nothing of any signifi-cance to tell us.

A call to the tax assessor's office produced the name of the owner of the property at 1827 Golden Gate. A subsequent call to the owner resulted in further information. It was believed that a black man had rented Apartment 6 around March 10. I remem-bered the taped communiqué of March 9, in which Patty said she had been moved "to a safe house." The reporters speculated about the number of tenants who had actually occupied the one-room hideout. Had all nine of the SLA lived there?

Eventually the FBI carried off its final boxload of evidence, and the manager agreed to permit the media to see the place. We pushed madly through the narrow front door, which had six new heavy-duty locks on it, into a three-by-three front hall in which there was nothing except cords dangling where a phone had once been. The stench inside was overwhelming.

Three doors opened off the hall: the one in front led to the bathroom; the one to the left, to the living room; the one to the right, the kitchen. We walked into the bathroom first. A huge black spray-painted, seven-headed cobra covered one wall. It towered over us. On the wall behind the toilet was a message from the SLA, scrawled by a felt-tipped pen; it read: "There are a few clues in this bathroom—however, you will have to wait until they are dry . . . an additional caution, ½ pound of cyanide, po-tassium cyanide crystals, has been added to this home brew—so, pig, drink at your own risk. There are also many additional juicy clues throughout the safe house. However, remember that you are not bulletproof either. Happy hunting, Charles." We knew the taunt was intended for Charles Bates.

The FBI men had carefully drained the "home brew" from the bathtub, which had been filled to overflowing with water turned dank by cyanide, with thousands of small strips of paper floating in its mess—road maps, maps of St. Paul, and classified ads from local newspapers, everything shredded up and soggy in the cyanide mixture.

The SLA had left this safe house only twenty-four hours earlier. They hadn't planned on its being discovered so soon, and thought that the scraps of paper would be nothing but pulp by the time the FBI found them. A small spray-painted cobra coiled at one end of the tub, as though standing guard over the floating debris in the water. But the cobra hadn't counted on the cockroaches.

We walked into the living room and saw the lone double bed, its mattress caked with grime; three metal folding chairs, like the one found at the Clayton safe house; one lawn chair, its webbing sagging. Nine people had lived here—who slept where, and with whom? These were the overriding questions, but there were no answers. The living room walls were garlanded with graffiti. Across the longest one was a poem dated "January 1, 1974." The date the SLA moved in is obscure; but had some of them actually lived there since January?

Under the date was a poem that read:

RESOLUTION

Is it real to load a magazine of dreams?
no!
We say fire power to the people
Against the hire power of the ruling class
Who chained our hired hands, feet and genitals
Our grip on the gun grows stronger
And they will no longer see day
they'll feel what's real
from a magazine of steel.

Reporters speculated about which SLA member had written the poem. Some thought it must have been Camilla. Wasn't she the house-poet of the cobra clan? I didn't agree. Camilla's work had never been so stilted, so labored, as these scrawls. Near the door to the hallway was another message in pencil: "Freedom is the will of life." It was signed "Cinque." And on another wall was written "Patria o Muerte, Venceremos"; this was signed "Tania." Huestis and I compared the writing with the signature on Patty Hearst's driver's license; it appeared to be similar. Next to the big front window was another scrawl: "Books, once read, make good bullet-proofing." That smacked of Nancy's brand of humor.

Had all nine members of the SLA simply sat around looking at each other in this small room with its one window? Neighbors said the occupants had had a stereo, which they'd played long and loud—not revolutionary music as might be expected, however; they had favored cowboy songs and western ballads.

Huestis pulled the camera cable toward the kitchen. If the living room couldn't reveal how the SLA had lived, perhaps the kitchen would show us what they had lived on. It was as filthy as the rest of the apartment. The stove was covered with a heavy coat of grease, as were the walls behind it. The refrigerator stank from the odor of decaying food. Inside, three small plastic cups that had once held corn-oil margarine cradled the molding remains of canned vegetable soup. A dozen cloves of garlic were tossed across a countertop—heavy seasoning for nine persons living in one room.

It was easy to see why the cockroaches had found the apartment a special feast. Bits of food and grime were everywhere; the floor was sticky, the walls dripping, the sink stained. We looked at the two-by-three-foot hole in the kitchen's wall made by the FBI when they had sawed out a message scrawled there, and wondered why they had taken that particular message and none of the others.

By seven that evening we had the story on "Newsroom." Russin insisted that I read the SLA poem, as well as report on what we had found in the hideout.

I reported that the SLA had paid $125 a month for one room with bath and kitchen, that the man renting the place had tried to pay four months' rent in advance but had been told he could not do so.

We now knew the path of the cobra on the day of the bank robbery. The Japan Center Theatre garage is less than a dozen blocks from the Golden Gate Avenue apartment. The SLA had returned there to hole up, to hide. And they had been there until May 1, the day before.

I had driven down the street a dozen times, passing under the window they may have watched from. Patty's favorite relative, her cousin Willie Hearst III, lived two blocks away on Golden Gate. They had been under our noses all the time. Only the cockroaches found them.

CHAPTER **13**

SHORTLY BEFORE THE SLA's hideout on Golden Gate Avenue had been discovered, I had received two telephone calls, one from an underground source once close to the SLA, the other from the cops. Both calls brought the same message on the SLA's next move: Tania would kill me, in living color, on "Newsroom."

The SLA was planning to rush the studio while we were on the air and hold everyone at gunpoint. Then Tania would fulfill her threat about "further actions," made in the April 24 taped message. Only she would fire the bullets that would kill me. Both sources reported, "It will be on May Day, the SLA May Day action."

Russin asked, "How seriously do you take it?"

I answered, "Frankly, it shows more style and imagination than the SLA has shown before. To kill on camera would be a riveting action, but I doubt that they have the guts to do it."

After all, we had recent history to prove the SLA's cowardice. They had not shot down Foster in front of the school board. They had waited, skulking behind trees, until they found him in a dark alley. They had not robbed the main branch of a bank. Instead, they had sought out one that would only have a few people in it, guarded only by a couple of men.

In the past I had reported on such gangs as Hell's Angels, Gypsy Jokers, and others. None of the members of any of them had shown individual courage. They seemed to have it only in numbers; they took action only when the odds were in their favor. The SLA didn't strike me as being any bolder.

Joe Russin wasn't so sure. He referred to some of my recent on-the-air comments about the SLA, comments I had made to sting the cobra. "After all, you did say they were nothing but a bunch of middle-class whites, with a token black," he reminded me. "We know they hate you. They put your name as the return address on one communiqué. They've made a point of answering your charges. You claimed they wore black makeup to murder Foster. They answered that. You claimed they couldn't attract Third World followers. They've said that's a lie. Bake, you aren't the SLA's favorite reporter."

I knew Joe was thinking of incidents he wasn't mentioning—other phone calls voicing threats to kill me. Once there had been three in a single day. The KQED switchboard operator was nearing a nervous breakdown. Russin also remembered the attempt to put a bomb in my car.

We were in a dilemma. Neither of us wanted to be shot, even on camera. At the same time, neither the ham nor the reporter in us would allow us to lose such a story if there was an ounce of truth to it. There had to be some way to leave the "Newsroom" set vulnerable but still have adequate firepower ready to handle any SLA attack that might occur.

The decision was soon out of our hands. The San Francisco police phoned and said they would ring the station with patrol cars that evening. I was annoyed; if the SLA came near us, the black-and-white police cars would scare them away, and Russin and I felt we had to flush the SLA out, to make them come to us.

I phoned friends at the police department. "Why not stake it out in plain clothes? Then, if this rumor you've heard is true, you have a crack at catching the SLA?"

My officer friend wasn't even polite. "My job is to keep people alive, not use them as bait, goddamnit!"

"But if I volunteer? I have faith your men will be there, and act fast enough so that I'll be okay. This may be your only chance."

After five phone calls, they finally gave in. They would send their special sniper squad, all in plain clothes, armed to the teeth. And by 6:00 P.M. unmarked cars blocked the alley next to KQED, parked across the street, waited at nearby intersections. Even in traffic-jammed San Francisco, it seemed as if our small corner at Fourth and Bryant had suddenly become a rush-hour freeway. The sedans with short rigid aerials were as subtle as a sledge-hammer.

The men poured out, carrying pump-action shotguns, a stream of stern-faced men in business suits, holding the huge guns across their chests. Every person within five blocks knew "something's going on at KQED." By the time we went on the air, I was convinced the SLA wouldn't come near the place. Every window had a barrel pointing out of it; crossfire positions were set up at the front entrance. KQED was a veritable arsenal, a fortress.

I had taken my own precautions. Jeff was there, his rifle in hand. He roamed the building, watching the back doors where the police weren't stationed. Chris, a .38 revolver pressed against his side, sat in the "Newsroom" studio hidden from the camera— just another member of the audience.

Before "Newsroom" went on the air, Russin gave a final order: "Make sure the door to the studio is locked."

"No!" I shouted back. "For God's sake, if we've gone to this much trouble, let them get on camera at least."

Russin quickly vetoed my idea. "Bake, I'm not exactly planning on letting them right in here. I don't really want their guns shoved down our throats on the air."

I knew the SLA would never make it through the front door, let alone down the hall and into the studio. Yet I wanted them to. I thought the SLA was on such a media trip to spew out their message that they would grab any chance at all to talk before live cameras—talk long enough, in fact, to be apprehended.

"Newsroom" went on the air with its usual report of the events of the day. Russin and I sat through that hour almost hopefully. Some of the other reporters simply shrugged the whole notion aside; others sweated more than usual under the hot television lights. The cobra never struck. The trap was never sprung.

Now, of course, we know that the SLA had been preoccupied

on May 1. That was the day they had moved from the Golden Gate apartment into, as we later learned, a small three-room apartment in Hunter's Point, the hard-core black ghetto of San Francisco, scene of the mid-1960 riots, where no one strolls after dark. It was a dumpy place, but the rent was only $150 a month. The landlady demanded two months' rent in advance. The SLA handed over $300 to a black woman who had befriended them in their Golden Gate hideout. She would be the go-between, the one to rent their new hideout.

She had met them in a very strange way. She lived in Fillmore, not far from 1827 Golden Gate Avenue. One day there had been a rap at her door, and she opened it to find a black man with a beard stubble standing there. He introduced himself. "I'm Cinque, and I'd like to tell you about the revolution."

The way he spoke, he could have been selling brooms door to door. She had listened, intrigued by his won't-you-buy-my-revolution? approach, then politely told him she wasn't having any that day and shut the door. Her door was not the only one where Cinque tried his salesmanship.

Cinque may have been getting desperate. After all, he was General Field Marshal of the ragtag band. He had to show his comrades that he could enlist the support of the Third World people whom they were so intent on saving. He didn't give up because the woman had said, "No, thanks."

Two days later two young white women came to the same door. Again the black woman opened it to a sales pitch. This time it was "Do you want to buy some towels?" and one girl shoved forward an armload of neatly stacked towels, not new but clean. Again, the woman declined. "No, no towels today." It was then that she saw the envelope dart out from one of the towels. It fell into her hand. The young women said "Thanks," and left. When the black woman opened the envelope, she found an invitation to join the SLA for dinner at their hideout.

She went, taking along her brother. They ate the piping-hot chili Cinque took such pride in preparing. They sat on the bed and floor, and listened to the white children of the privileged class tell them how they must rise up in revolution. They agreed, for a small monetary consideration, to help the group rent a new hideout. They liked the SLA. They were interesting. It was particularly fascinating to hear them justify the murder of Marcus Foster.

The woman took the $100 they offered in appreciation for her promise to make arrangements for them to rent the small apartment at 1808 Oakdale in Hunter's Point. And her brother took the $200 they paid him for his agreement to buy them a red and white Volkswagen van. So while the police were guarding KQED, the cobra had moved across town into their new hideout.

Cinque again tried his door-to-door want-to-join-a-revolution? approach. The blacks of Hunter's Point had been through one already. They had seen the burning and killing of the sixties' riot. They didn't need a black dude and his eight white friends to lead them into another volley of bullets.

Another woman, however, agreed to buy a second car for them for a price. She lived near their Oakdale hideout. They gave her $1,500 for the car and $200 for doing the job. She never came back. She had ripped off the SLA.

The SLA had a final dinner for friends from their Fillmore recruiting days, inviting them to break bread at the Oakdale hideout on May 4. Not all the invited guests showed up; it was a dismal dinner. The SLA were having poor luck recruiting soldiers. If the San Francisco Bay Area wouldn't accept them as the prophets of revolution they claimed to be, then they would simply move to more receptive ground. They packed up and prepared to move south, to Los Angeles, mecca for crackpot religions, get-rich-quick schemes, slick sales pitches.

Cinque was elated. If he had failed in the Bay Area, surely success was four hundred miles south, back in Watts where he'd come from, the scene of his past successes as a two-bit crook. Those who knew the SLA members well said, "He never told the others about turning in a black brother down there. He never told them anything about his past, how he'd snitch on anyone to save his own skin, how all his victims in crimes had been black. He never told those radical women—Mizmoon and Camilla, and Nancy and Emily and Angela—how he'd beaten the hell out of a black prostitute and robbed her at gunpoint. They didn't know that was what they were going back to. Cinque sure as hell didn't tell them that."

The SLA were lost in Los Angeles. Cinque hadn't been there

since 1970. The horizon was new to him. Even known streets had vanished beneath shopping centers. Watts was no longer the seething hotbed he'd known, the place where a black man could hide from the white police all his life. To the other SLA cobra-cultists, it was mayhem. A city they had never known, names they could not pronounce, people they had never seen. They arrived in the three-van caravan and clung to each other like lost children, caught in the maw of Los Angeles. But they couldn't live in the vans forever; that in itself would excite suspicion. Besides, such a way of life was unthinkable to the SLA. They lived in houses, not in cars.

They drove to Watts, confident they would find followers in the black ghetto. All they found was a burned-out fourplex, one upper unit intact enough to shelter them. They slept fitfully, taking turns guarding each other.

They scanned the classified ads, looking for an apartment or duplex or house that could be their hideout. They finally found what they wanted—a small shack, falling apart but standing alone, without prying neighbors. It was at 833 West 84th Street, near the campus of Pepperdine College, near Inglewood with its racetracks, and Gardena with its gambling parlors. It was in the workingman's south end of Los Angeles, low-blue-collar class. The rent was only $70 a month. The landlord was glad anyone would pay even that much for the place—it was such a dump. But two young white girls said they wanted it. They offered him half a month's rent, with the promise to pay the balance before the month was out. He wondered why the two attractive white women wanted to live in the heart of this rough black land. He thought they might be undercover cops. They were Emily Harris and Patty Hearst.

As Tania was counting out the $35 rent on the house in Los Angeles, Randolph Hearst was offering a $50,000 reward at a press conference in front of the family's Hillsborough home "for the safe return of Patty to her parents." Hearst explained why, after ninety days, he had finally decided to offer a reward for his kidnapped daughter: "The SLA have turned out to be a bunch of criminals," he said bitterly. "And I want my daughter away from them if I can get her. At this point we're going to try and get her back any way we can."

William Saxbe, Attorney General of the United States, had

already branded Patty a "common criminal" along with the rest of the SLA. But Hearst didn't see it that way. He told me, "We still don't know what really went on all those days she was captive. We'll never know until she's home, where she can talk without fear. Until then, I just can't believe Patty would do these things, Marilyn. I just can't believe it."

Catherine Hearst missed attending Sunday Mass for the first time since the terror had taken over her life. Her voice was weary. She talked to me quietly on the phone, concurring with her husband's words and adding, "I'll never believe it."

Reporters outside the Hearst home snorted at this profusion of faith in Patty. I understood it. How could any parents admit, even to themselves, that a child they reared and loved had turned into a vile-mouthed creature who carried a carbine on her hip and branded her family "pigs"?

Charles Bates could no longer carry his shield emblazoned, "We won't endanger Patty's life." Now everyone knew the FBI had never known where the SLA cobra hid. Bates hadn't been protecting Patty. He and Frick and Frack had been hiding the fact that they had no idea where to look.

The San Francisco police were even more embarrassed. One of their own had received an SLA communiqué, the last on April 24, and they still had no inkling about where to look for the seven-headed snake. The Berkeley and Oakland police were quietly relieved. The SLA had been in San Francisco all along, not in their area. But they went on checking every possible lead.

The federal grand jury subpoenaed more witnesses, but it was less than an all-out push; and even the U.S. attorney general's staff seemed bogged down in inertia.

In Washington, D.C., Clarence Kelley, director of the FBI, publicly admitted, "In a city the size of San Francisco and the Bay Area generally, they [the SLA] have found the key to eluding the FBI up to this point."

Kelley didn't add that San Francisco is one of the nation's smallest cities, geographically. Nor did he say that his elite bureau had been helpless, with little to do but wait for the one slip that every criminal makes that leads to arrest.

PART FOUR

THE KILL

CHAPTER **14**

I HAD LIVED in Los Angeles for years, first as a schoolgirl, then as a fledgling reporter, then as editor of *The Spectator,* a Beverly Hills weekly newspaper. The disconnected cities and disjointed life-style had disoriented me. They did the same to the SLA.

After renting their shack at 833 West 84th Street, the SLA set about trying to make itself safe. A "watch roster" was posted, each member reduced to a number. They stood sentry over their sleeping comrades in pairs, never fewer than four eyes guarding at any time, not trusting those outside, watching those inside. Their furnishings were what they had brought in their vans: sleeping bags, old blankets, jackets, wigs and makeup for disguises, and a litter of guitar cases. But the cases held no music. They held the guns that played the song of the SLA.

Thursday, May 16, was a day of decision for both the SLA and me.

It had been 101 days since Patty Hearst had been kidnapped, more than three weeks since the SLA's last tape. It was time my life took on some semblance of normality again. I had lived in the shadow of the cobra all those days and nights.

That morning I returned to teaching a class of federal executives. It was another "how to" session, the subject dealing with ways of getting along with the news media. It was a challenge. Watergate headlines were pouring down on both the media and the federal government. We had to make sure the torrent did not gouge out a chasm between us.

My decision to return to normal living was put into action with a vengeance. At noon I returned to the Woman's Round Table, an exclusive monthly luncheon group headed by Pat Montadon that met in her penthouse atop San Francisco's hills. Here I was as far as I could get from stalking the cobra. Gourmet food was served on the finest china, heavy crystal goblets were filled with vintage wines, maids served in black voile uniforms and starched white caps. Our hostess is the epitome of the good life attained. So were the other women around the ornate table. I sat next to Merla Zellerbach, a friend I hadn't seen since the SLA had first struck. We tried to catch up on the months in between when our only contact had been that I read her column in the morning newspaper and she watched me on "Newsroom" at night.

I relaxed, forgot about Patty and Mizmoon and Cinque and all their brood. It was after 2:00 P.M. when I finally and reluctantly departed, and drove back down the hill, into the grime that is "south of Market," homeland of KQED.

By the time I returned to my desk, I was silently praying: "Let tomorrow be like today." I was tired of the chase.

Four hundred miles south, in their hideout in Los Angeles, the SLA grew tired of being chased. They were tired of living nine together in a two-room shack. It was time to move out, perhaps to the mountains or desert, away from the cities that had rejected their revolution. They made a decision. Three would go to buy heavy socks, sweat shirts, and jackets they would all need for a cold climate. Chosen for the mission were Emily, Bill, and Patty.

At 3:30 P.M. the trio drove off in the red-and-white van, carrying automatic weapons and small hand-drawn maps to show them how to find their way back to the safe house. As were any tourists, the SLA were easily lost in Los Angeles.

In true urban-guerrilla fashion, they had tried to prepare themselves by memorizing code names, secret words, streets they didn't know, routes they couldn't find, all the predetermined meeting places they had agreed upon for their survival. It was a lot to remember. By 4:00 P.M. they had found the huge Crenshaw Shopping Center. Their objective was across the street, across the four lanes of Crenshaw Boulevard traffic: Mel's Sporting Goods, a small one-story shop, with windows across the front, easy to watch. The store's double front doors were propped open because of the late afternoon heat, and browsing shoppers strolled in and out, eyeing bargains.

The van parked in the shopping-center lot, directly across from Mel's. Emily slid out from behind the wheel and Patty took her place. Bill jumped out from the other side and joined his wife, and the two crossed the busy boulevard, walking toward the store. Patty sat quietly, a carbine her companion.

Inside, Emily, with Bill at her side, quickly selected nine pairs of heavy socks and nine sweat shirts. Neither of the Harrises was aware that they were being watched by Anthony Shepard, the clerk, who had seen Bill wad up a white-webbing ammunition belt, turn it into a tight roll, and stuff it up the sleeve of his jacket. It didn't faze the clerk to see crime in action; shoplifting is almost a daily occurrence at the store. That's why Mel's had hired a uniformed guard to stand by the front doors, more to discourage would-be thieves than to apprehend them.

Shepard allowed the couple to pay $31.65 for the merchandise Emily had gathered. Nor did he say anything to the Harrises as they started to walk toward the door, since he knew, that for a shoplifting arrest to hold up in court, they actually had to leave the premises. But, after motioning to the guard to join him, he followed closely behind the pair as they proceeded outside. William Huett, owner of the store, had seen Shepard signal the guard; he came out, too. The three grabbed Bill by the arm and demanded, "Are you going to pay for what you stole? What's in your sleeve?"

No one—Shepard, Huett, the guard, or a fourth man who stopped to help—is sure what Bill Harris answered. They think he said, "It'd be too obvious," but none of them had time to ask him to repeat it. Harris whipped out a revolver from under his jacket; Emily lunged at one of the men, and the gun clattered out of Harris's hand and skidded across the sidewalk. The two SLA members and the four men became a tangled mass as they scrambled for the weapon.

A high voice screeched from across the street, "Let them go, you mother-fuckers, or you're all dead!"

The warning was punctuated by the crack of bullets smashing into the storefront window inches from the guard. The clerk dived behind a concrete light pole, as pockmarks of dust were sent flying around him by the bullets. Customers and other employees screamed and crouched behind counters. They had all seen the woman with the automatic rifle firing from the window of the red-and-white van across the street. Only the violent recoil of the rifle, which jumped higher into the air with each split-second bullet fired, saved the four men who were the intended targets. Patty, her finger tight on the trigger, could not hold the rifle on dead aim. As the weapon in her hands continued climbing skyward, bullets traced their stitching across the front of the store, into the lettering that spelled "Mel's," and then into the sky above.

Emily and Bill ran. Dangling from Bill's left wrist was the one handcuff the guard had been able to lock on him. The clerk saw Emily jump behind the wheel of the van as Patty moved into the back of the vehicle. Bill slid in on the passenger side, and the tires squealed as the van raced away. Shepard ran to his car and followed them. He didn't dare get close enough to be within range of their bullets, yet he was afraid if he hung too far back, he'd lose the van in the growing rush-hour traffic.

Nine blocks to the southeast of Mel's Sporting Goods, the van pulled sharply up to the curb. Shepard, in turn, braked to a stop. He saw Bill Harris jump out with what looked like a machine gun in his hands.

The time was now 4:35 P.M. Kenneth Pierre and Marva Davis were sitting in the 1970 Pontiac, talking. Shepard watched as Bill Harris walked up to the couple in the black-and-yellow car. The couple spun around at the sound of Bill's voice. They couldn't believe the words they heard: "We are the SLA. We need your car. I have to kill someone, and I don't want to kill you."

The pair jumped out of the car and ran to Marva Davis's house, three doors away, without once turning around; therefore they didn't see Emily and Patty rush from the van, jump into the Pontiac with Bill, and speed off.

Four blocks farther, the same routine was repeated. Emily drove the Pontiac up to the curb in the 2000 block of West 115th Street, where Thomas Patin, Sr. and his son Tom were standing next to a Chevy Nova station wagon. The three SLA comrades leaped from the Pontiac with guns pointed at father and son. Bill Harris issued the demand, "We're from the SLA. We need your car." The terrified Patin tossed him the keys. He and his son stood paralyzed with fright as Emily, Bill, and Patty commandeered the station wagon and roared away, heading south.

At seven that night, three hours after Patty had fired the shots among the people at Mel's Sporting Goods store, Emily Harris rang the front doorbell at the Matthews home in Lynwood, a few miles from where she had driven off in the station wagon. "I'd like to test-drive the van you have for sale," she said, nodding toward the dark blue Econovan parked in the driveway, with its For Sale sign slanted under the windshield.

Eighteen-year-old Tom Matthews got the keys and climbed in next to the young woman, who expertly started up the van and swung it around the first corner, stopping alongside the station wagon. "I'd like these two friends of mine to come along," Emily said rather than asked. Tom Matthews agreed and opened the door to the SLA members.

Once inside, Bill pulled open his jacket and showed Matthews the revolver in his belt. Again came the litany: "We're from the SLA. We need to borrow your car. Do what you're told and you won't get hurt." Matthews was forced to lie on the floor of the van; then Bill asked him, "Don't you know who this is? This is Tania." Harris displayed the SLA recruit once known as Patty Hearst.

Tom Matthews started on a drive that seemed to go in ever-widening circles, leading nowhere. Stops were made. At one, Bill got out and returned carrying carbines and more automatic rifles. Matthews doesn't know where the van stopped for Harris to get this cargo.

Emily wanted to buy a hacksaw, to free her husband of the handcuff on his left wrist. She tried several stores before finally getting one at Zody's, a huge discount store. Tom Matthews was ordered to help rid his kidnapper of the handcuff; he did so, afraid he would be killed if he refused.

The radio in the van blared the news of the shootout at Mel's Sporting Goods store; this first report stated that a pair of socks had been stolen.

Bill Harris laughed. "It wasn't socks—it was a bandolier," he informed his captive.

Patty squatted beside Matthews, who again lay shivering on the floor of the van, and talked about her role as a revolutionary. She spoke of her part in the San Francisco bank robbery and of how she had fired the shots into Mel's Sporting Goods store. As she deftly slipped a new full clip of bullets into her carbine, she said, "I'd do it again. I'll die before I go back to the pig Hearsts." Matthews did not doubt her.

Patty was incensed that people thought she was less than willing to pull the trigger of her rifle. "It's ridiculous to say my hand wasn't on the trigger in the bank holdup," she told Matthews. "I always carry my rifle slung low on my hip."

Emily steered the van toward a drive-in movie. The three talked openly of meeting their comrades there. Rags and jackets were tossed over the prone Matthews as the van drove through the pay gate and parked, facing the screen. Matthews was conscious of time slipping away; the first complete show ended, and the second screening started. Then it was midnight; then 1:00 A.M. Cars began leaving the drive-in. No one had met Patty, Emily, and Bill. Something was wrong.

Again, with Emily at the wheel and Bill and Patty standing guard over Matthews, the van circled Los Angeles streets for five hours, until 6:30 A.M. Matthews, his body aching from rolling in the back of the van, knew they were parked on a hill. He figured they were in the Hollywood Hills.

Emily and Patty announced their next move to Bill. "We'll go out and pretend we're hitchhiking. We'll take a car by force." Bill quietly accepted their decision.

The two young women left the van, and within minutes Matthews heard a car pull alongside his vehicular prison and stop. Harris grabbed all the guns—three rifles and the automatics —and wrapped them in a blanket. Then he bent over Matthews: "Stay face down, right here for ten minutes! Remember, we know where you live!" With that he was gone, and his guns with him.

A tan Lincoln Continental, with Emily at the wheel, was parked beside the van. Its owner, Frank Sutton, was in the back seat next to Patty, who moved up front when Bill came. Bill slipped in beside Sutton, shoved the barrel of the automatic close to the frightened man's heart, and said. "We need your car for a couple of hours. You won't get hurt if you do exactly what I tell you. We will hurt you if you don't."

Sutton was forced down on the floorboard, with the blanket that had hidden the rifles tossed over him. Again—nomadic travels, driving down streets to no destination, turning corners for no reason—two hours of suspense.

Sutton felt Harris's hand push into his pocket and pull out his wallet. He heard Harris laugh as he said, "I counted the money. There's two hundred and fifty dollars cash. You can figure this is a loan, but you won't get it back. All I took was the money."

Finally the car stopped—again on an incline, as Sutton could tell from the slant of the car under his body. He heard the two women get out, one saying they would get another car and be back. A few minutes later Bill pulled back the blanket and said to Sutton, "We'll let you out at the top of the hill. Then walk back down the hill a half mile. Don't hitch a ride. Just take your time, because if we see you come down too soon, we'll shoot you."

At the top of the hill, Sutton was shoved from his car and Harris drove off, down the hill Sutton had been ordered to descend slowly. Sutton looked around. He was in Griffith Park, near Vermont Avenue, above Hollywood in the hills that hedge it from Glendale and Pasadena. He walked down the hill very slowly. He found his car with the keys in it, parked alongside the curb on Vermont Avenue.

By noon of Friday, May 17, Patty and the Harrises had slipped over the Hollywood Hills and down into North Hollywood, which is no longer the suburban dream, but more a middle-class ghetto, snared between hills to the south and subdivisions to the north.

Patty and the Harrises slid beneath the surface of the San Fernando Valley's sprawl of cities as easily as they had gone underground in San Francisco. They melted into the white-middle class neighborhood. Three average faces among millions.

CHAPTER **15**

IT WAS SEVEN O'CLOCK in the morning, on May 17, when the assignment editor phoned me. "The cops are staking out a house in Los Angeles—they think it's the SLA. Get to the airport and go down there," he announced crisply.

"With Huestis?" I mumbled.

"No, we can't afford to send a camera crew. Go by yourself."

I exploded. "What the hell use is it for me to go alone? Television's supposed to be visual. What am I supposed to do, call you up on the phone and say, 'Sorry you can't see it, folks?' "

He was adamant. No Huestis, no camera crew. I was equally adamant. "Then no me."

I barely had time to slam down the receiver when Russin called with the same old KQED lament—there was no money to send a camera crew. I told him, "Then I can get as much as I need from a telephone. There's no point in my going down there alone."

He agreed and hung up. I got dressed and went down the hill to the newsroom, where I stacked the Los Angeles area phone

194

directories on my desk and prepared to "mother hen" the story from four hundred miles away.

I started phoning every policeman I had ever known in Los Angeles and a few I didn't know. I called other reporters and talk-show hosts who had interviewed me as the "reporter who revealed the SLA." Russin ripped off each new report coming in on the wire machine that clatters away near his desk and rushed it to me. By noon we were putting the pieces of the story together. The Los Angeles police already knew the gun dropped by Bill Harris at Mel's Sporting Goods store had been purchased by Emily months before. The shoplifters were, indeed, the SLA. The cobra was coiled in Los Angeles.

Fast-acting cops had found an abandoned red-and-white van late Thursday night, May 16. Inside it, parking tickets were scattered on the floor. The tickets had been issued for parking in front of 833 West 84th Street between 6:00 and 9:00 A.M. on a weekday the street sweeper had come by.

In the predawn hours of Friday, the police moved in on the shack at 833 West 84th Street. A hundred policemen and FBI agents, prepared for a shootout, swarmed over a four-block radius, routing residents from their beds and cautioning them to stay out of the line of possible gunfire. Los Angeles lawmen did not intend to make the same mistake the San Francisco police had made. The cobra would not slither through their fingers. They shot tear gas through the small frame windows that were already cracked, the searing-hot cannisters tearing apart the old blankets that had been stretched across the windows. The white smoke stung the early morning air and wafted into the nostrils and eyes of onlookers curious to see the war that seemed about to start in their backyards.

But there was no answering fire. No sound came from within. Crawling on their stomachs, the police edged toward the house, with each move expecting a hail of bullets to rain down on them. Still there was no sound. The first cluster of cops in gas masks and flak vests reached the front door. A foot slammed into it, sending the door splintering back. They rushed in. The house was empty—the cobra had slid away, unseen. Relief and disappointment mingled on the lawmen's faces.

Now that any danger was past, reporters shoved forward.

Police restrained them. There might be evidence, though they did not have much hope of that. The SLA had abandoned safe houses before, without leaving a lead for the police to follow. Officers swarmed through the two rooms, appalled at the filth, unsure what might be a link to the trail of the SLA. They found three suitcases, three women's handbags, a brown paper bag of medical supplies, shotgun ammunition, and two women's wigs, one black, one auburn. There were notebooks with scribbled codes, words that had no meaning strung together in sentences without purpose. A message, left for anyone who might see it to read: ". . . Frank Lloyd cooked William's pot roast."

They questioned Mrs. Velma Davis, the owner of the house, who explained how she had gotten the Symbionese for tenants. She had run an ad in the Los Angeles *Sentinel,* a newspaper for the black community, offering a one-family home for $75 a month, unfurnished. Someone had called to express interest and she had turned the prospect over to her manager, Kyle Jones. When the police asked Jones who had actually rented the SLA hideout, he told them it had been two white women who "looked as if they'd be good tenants." One called herself Ms. Rivera and persuaded Jones to cut the rent to $70 a month, then talked him into letting her pay only half a month's rent in advance. She had refused to sign a receipt when she counted out the cash. Jones told police, "I figured they were undercover cops. Why else would two white women want to live in this place?"

Police verified that the two women were Emily Harris and Patty Hearst.

Finally, a Los Angeles policeman who had been in one of my classes at San Luis Obispo agreed to talk to me off the record. "Yes, we figure all nine of the SLA lived there. We found them all listed on the watch routine; they all took turns standing watch, even Patty. We found something else in there, some more parking tickets, same offense—parking overnight on a street designated for street cleaning at six A.M. This time, the address on the ticket is an old burned-out fourplex on Fifty-third Street, the edge of Watts.

"Before you bother to ask—we've checked the fourplex. There's one unit, upstairs it is, that's still semi-together. We figure they were hiding out there before they rented that place on West Eighty-fourth. We have cars on the way to Fifty-third Street right now. We've had a couple of phone calls. They may be tips. They may be nothing. Keep in touch."

I wanted to know what the police would find in the burned-out building in the 1400 block of 53rd Street. I grabbed a cross-index directory and started looking up phone numbers in the area.

Meanwhile, behind the burned building, in a dirty, squat frame house at 1466 54th Street, six members of the SLA huddled in a rear bedroom. It was cramped and stuffy, and they did not talk above whispers. It had cost them $100 to sleep there for the night.

Cinque had been trying to find followers for days—ever since the three vans first pulled in at the burned-out hulk behind the house. He had talked to young blacks on street corners and even knocked on some doors, but the results had been as negative as they'd been in San Francisco. No one wanted to join his army. It had not been brotherhood or the freeing of the oppressed that had bought the small room they rested in. Hard cash had turned the trick. When the SLA had fled the 84th Street house after learning of the incident at Mel's Sporting Goods store, they were sure Patty and the Harrises had been apprehended. Their safe house might become unsafe at any second. They hadn't even bothered to pack, but had grabbed their guns, satchels with pipe bombs and Molotov cocktails, a brown zipper bag with nine Polaroid pictures. Each of the group had taken a turn snapping the camera as the other eight posed in front of the flag Mizmoon had made—a black seven-headed cobra on a red field.

The night before they had tried to follow the emergency plans. They had gone to a drive-in movie where they were to have made contact if any unit of the SLA were, for any reason, cut off while on a mission. The six had sat through the program twice, until the screen went dark. They had not thought that the maze of Los Angeles could have confused their comrades and that they might have gone to the wrong drive-in.

At two in the morning, they had come back to the charred hulk where they had been camping the first few days in Los Angeles. But they didn't want to stay there all night. They needed walls around them for safety, especially if three of their army might now be captives.

Cinque had volunteered to see about getting other accommodations—he had to. After all, he was General Field Marshal. He had walked to the house behind the burned building, knocked on the door, and told a woman named Minnie Lewis that he needed a room for himself and three whites. "They'll be no damned whites in my house. They bring trouble," she stated and started to slam the door in his face. He persisted, almost desperately. He hadn't been able to find followers, but he wanted at least to be able to find lodgings. But Minnie was adamant. "No whites—they is plain trouble."

Another woman, Christine Johnson, walked to the door to see what was happening. She listened and agreed with Minnie, but when she saw the $100 the black dude was sliding toward her hand, she took it, shrugged, and said, "Three's not so much trouble. Go get them." Cinque rushed back to his waiting army to tell them he had succeeded at last.

The group trooped to the front porch, only to have Minnie again slam the door in the revolution's face. "You said three, that's bad enough. Now you want to walk in five. No way!" But again, after sleight of hand between Christine and Cinque, Minnie was pacified, at least enough to let the six strangers into a rear bedroom.

As the hours passed and Minnie and Christine talked about the money, they heard faint whispers from the rear room and the soft tread of footsteps pacing back and forth. Their sudden roomers weren't sleeping much.

Dawn brought no solution to the problems of the SLA. The six comrades took over Minnie and Christine's frame home as though it were their own. They stood by the windows, watching the neighborhood begin its morning. Christine made coffee. The SLA talked among themselves. They were not over-friendly with their two hostesses, keenly aware that their shelter had been bought and paid for, and not offered to their cause.

Christine finally asked, "When you all leaving?"

"Later—tonight, after dark," Cinque answered. He had to say something.

A young girl burst through the front door. Her name is Brenda and she came by almost every morning to chat with Minnie and Christine, bubbling with talk and games for Minnie's children. But that day none of Minnie's children were there. "They're all right, they're at Grandma's house," Minnie assured her.

Cinque struck up a conversation with the young girl. "We need some food—lunch meat and bread and some beer and some cigarettes, Camels. You go get that stuff for us," he said as he pushed a twenty-dollar bill into her hand. Brenda ran the two blocks to the corner store, bought the supplies, and ran back.

The SLA women made sandwiches. They told Cinque to keep a watch out the front window. Camilla went to the two vans parked by the burned rubble behind Minnie and Christine's small house and started hauling in the five guitar cases. Neighbors watched as the blonde brought the cases into the house. Her actions seemed strange, not quite right for their neighborhood. Some of them called the police.

The morning dragged on and there was more talk. Cinque talked the most. Nobody really listened, least of all the SLA women.

Minnie and Christine walked by the bedroom where Willie Wolfe lay on the bed. He twirled a pistol on his finger, cowboy fashion. Minnie tried to talk to him, but he didn't answer. Mizmoon took off a sweater. Christine thought it was odd that she had another one on underneath.

Cinque mentioned that there were a lot of white men in business suits on the street. He looked at a clock. It was 11:00 A.M. When he opened another can of beer, he noticed it was the last. "Make another supply run for us, will you?" he asked Brenda, who had sat silently watching, fascinated by the strange people in her friends' home. She took another twenty-dollar bill from Cinque and started down the same two blocks to the grocery store. She never came back.

By noon Cinque demanded of Minnie, "Why all the pigs around here?"

Christine spoke up. "They always here, part of the neighborhood," she assured him. She didn't bother to look out the window, so she didn't see the man lying flat against the rooftop of a house across the street, a glint of metal at his side.

Mizmoon, Camilla, Nancy, and Angela sat in the kitchen, their conversation even more hushed. They didn't bother to walk to the kitchen window, so they didn't see a man easing himself down on the roof next door. He carefully placed a long-barrelled gun at his side.

Cinque was edgy. It was noon. He paced the floor, claiming he smelled "pigs around here." Christine told him again, "They come with the neighborhood." But Cinque had known the neighborhood. He had survived many a year there, snitching to the same "pigs" now and then.

He walked into the kitchen and said to the women, "We'd better split, right now. It's hot around here."

Camilla shrugged and replied, "So it's hot everywhere now." She sat down next to Mizmoon.

"That's right, it's hot everywhere. We stay here," Mizmoon said.

A decision had been reached. The women snapped open the guitar cases. Rifles, submachine guns, pistols, and revolvers were stacked under the windows, with mounds of ammunition next to them. Ugly, three-foot-long black pipe-bombs leaned against the front wall of the house, where the SLA suspected the police might attack. Molotov cocktails were tucked in between the lengths of pipe.

Christine watched with horror; it was more than her beer-weary eyes could absorb. She went off to bed, lying down to "rest for a while." So did Minnie. They had both seen pistols strapped to the sides of the women. They had seen the long-bladed hunting knives shoved down in the belts around their waists. They had seen more than they could comprehend. They understood guns and knives and weapons. But not an armory.

The SWAT (Special Weapons and Tactics) team arrived. This elite unit of the Los Angeles police force, first funded by the policemen themselves "in order to stay alive on the streets," is now an example for the nation. All members are expert marksmen; they are trained to pull triggers in a second, to obey a command without hesitation, to do combat where danger is too great for anyone else. By noon the SWAT unit was in position around 1466 54th Street. There were twenty-eight men in all, armed with rifles and tear-gas guns. Another thirty stood ready, four blocks away, for possible backup. They pride themselves, however, on not needing backup.

The trail to the cobra's lair had been surprisingly easy for the police to follow. Tickets for parking in front of the burned-out place on 53rd Street had led to the two vans, plainly visible, parked behind it. Calls from neighbors had alerted the police that a white woman had carried long cases into 1466 54th Street.

Finally, the officers had stopped Brenda, the young girl on her way to buy beer and cigarettes. She had identified the six strangers in Minnie and Christine's house. But she could not identify the Harrises or Patty Hearst.

Several neighbors were questioned. "Have you seen any of these people?" they were asked, and the familiar handful of pictures of the SLA members was displayed. Several said, "Yes, the blonde girl." Camilla stood out in Watts.

So the police took their positions: one man on a rooftop, two teams down alongside the house, and four behind it. Reserve units and a command post were set up several blocks away, with instructions not to alert the press. The area was cleared.

It was almost 2:00 P.M. when I again talked to my Los Angeles police friend by phone. He was nervous and did not want to talk. I tried a round of questions.

"Have you found exactly where they are?"

"Maybe."

I took a long shot. "Are they at two separate locations?"

"Yes, that's highly possible."

He suddenly blurted out the situation. "We're checking a burned-out duplex on Fifty-third Street and a house right behind it, the fourteen-hundred block of Fifty-fourth Street. They're somewhere between the two." He hung up.

I felt that would be the last time I would be able to reach him by phone that day. At least I had a block to work from; it was more than most of the news media had.

I persuaded KQED's librarian to get a listing of the phone numbers in the 1400 block of 53rd and 54th streets in Los Angeles. Then I called Badge to ask if events had gotten serious in Los Angeles. He snorted. "You think they're playing war games? Damned right it is—they've got them."

I didn't know how he could be so certain. A phone call to the Los Angeles police from Mrs. Mary Carr, Minnie's mother, was not the first warning the police had received, but it was the final proof.

Brenda had run into Mrs. Carr on her second trip to the store to buy more cigarettes and beer for the SLA. She had told Mrs. Carr about the strange gang in Minnie's house—a predominantly white gang with guns and knives and bombs. Mrs. Carr almost ran the block to 1466 54th Street. Inside, she saw the six

SLA members. She found Minnie half asleep on a bed and shook her awake. She helped her daughter pull on a red dress and made her promise to walk past the strangers, out the front door of her home, and down the street. It was 2:00 P.M. Mrs. Carr left, too. She went to a phone to call the police.

By 2:00 P.M. it had been confirmed—the SLA were in those two blocks, and at least some of the cobra people were in the house at 1466 54th Street.

Russin switched on the television and radio by his desk to catch any bulletin, any leak out of Los Angeles. I started dialing the phone numbers our librarian had found for the 1400 block of 53rd and 54th streets. Each call reinforced our information. It was time for the showdown for the SLA, and we had no time to get a camera crew to Los Angeles. I fumed at the decision made nine hours earlier. Now we would pay the price for KQED's budget restrictions. The grand finale of the story on which we had led the way would be played out on other stations, not our own.

One call was to an elderly woman at the corner of 54th Street and Compton Boulevard. "Yes, there sure is policemen around here. Why, there's two sitting in plain cars right in front of my house. They been there since noon. Don't know what they're watching for, but it's something going on all right."

I moved down the block. Another call, a young woman: "Yes, the cops is here all right. They told me to get outta my house. I don't get out for no one."

A robust male voice answered my next call: "They're here. Police are everywhere. I hear they're after a gang of whites that are holed up in this block."

Russin ran by my desk, asking for any confirmation, anything definite.

I replied, "Definite yes, confirmed no. The cops still aren't saying, but the people along the fourteen-hundred block of Fifty-fourth all confirm: cops are swarming all over. Some have been asked to evacuate."

It was 4:30 P.M. when I dialed the Los Angeles police department's press service. There was an immediate answer. That meant something was up. The officer was courteous. "Yes, we have assembled teams of officers. Yes, they are pinpointing the fourteen-

202

hundred block of Fifty-fourth Street." He claimed they did not know yet which house it was.

Russin was running now, from my desk to the wire machine, to his desk and back to mine again. He had become a walking news bulletin, keeping me aware of what was happening, ready to revise the "Newsroom" story for that night. The production department was ready to show any visuals we might get.

The first wirephotos came across. Cops were standing in small groups, looking away from the camera. Squad cars were dispensing officers. Here were the first pictures of the SWAT team in armor-plated vests and heavy helmets with the face masks that slide down over gas masks, making them look like mechanical monsters.

Russin said: "If the LA police catch the SLA, they'll be accused of brute force. If they don't catch them, they'll be accused of being as stupid as San Francisco's police brass."

I went back to dialing, A woman, fear thick in her throat, reported: "Lord of God, I lived through the riot but I don't think I'll live through this. I gotta get outta here, lady, I'm getting . . ." She left the phone dangling off the hook. I could actually hear the sound of running feet.

Russin shouted, "Here, Bake, get over here! It's on TV!" We crowded around the set and saw the crouching figures of uniformed men running toward houses. At one house, three children were lifted out a side window and carried under the protective arms of officers to safety, away from the silent house in the center of the screen, the house with the rusty numbers 1466. It was 5:35 P.M.

The reporter's words on the television suddenly stopped. We heard the crisp voice of authority, even more authoritative through the bullhorn that amplified it: "Come out with your hands up. This is the Los Angeles police. Come out with your hands up."

Russin looked at me, and we were thinking the same thing: Why weren't we there? He said, "Save it the best you can, Bake. I'll anchor, so come down on the set anytime during the show that you have anything to say. Try your phone calls some more."

I had started back toward my desk and the phone as the police bullhorn split the television silence. "Come out with your hands up." A lone figure, in heavy armor plating and a launcher at his shoulder, ran toward the small yellow house. He fell down on one knee and sent a cannister tumbling through the air. It crashed through the glass and spilled its tear gas inside the house. The occupants of the house replied—the screen erupted with machine gun fire and semiautomatic rifle shots. The house was an arsenal: a porcupine of guns jutted out the windows in every direction, firing at everything and anyone.

My phone rang. It was Jeff. "Jesus, Mom, it's a Vietnam fire-fight." It was difficult to talk, so we cut our conversation short.

I kept staring at the small television screen, listening to a reporter who was choking on tear gas narrate the war in the streets. The shooting seemed to go on forever. There was no let-up in the steady stream of lead death spilling out of the house. And there was no pause in the stream of fire being returned into it. We could see the wood splinter as bullets hit their target, but the firing from inside the house never slowed.

I ran back to my desk and dialed Los Angeles, grabbing the first number my hand reached from the list labeled "homes in the 1400 block of 54th Street."

A man answered, his voice barely audible above the sound of gunfire. "Yeah, I'm still here, right next door. Yeah, the police, they told me to get out, but you don't dare. You leave your house around here and someone loots it. I don't want to lose everything. Oh, my God, the walls, they keep shaking! The bullets keep hitting the house. I'm under the bed. The policeman, he told me, 'If you won't get the hell out, stay under the bed . . .' No, lady, I won't go look out my window for you for no reason." But he didn't hang up. He kept the line open. I could hear him moan, even hear the rush of prayer from his mouth close to the phone. I left the phone lying on my desk, ready to run back, to talk again to my unwilling witness.

6:15 P.M. Russin stood silent in front of the television set. He would play it by ear that evening, let "Newsroom" flow, interrupt whenever there was news from Southern California. My job was to get the news. I leaned against his desk, exhausted. Then we both jumped as the TV screen showed a black woman, in dark slacks and a white blouse, staggering out the front door directly into the firefight. The police guns went silent. The SLA kept firing. Cops rushed in, barely off their stomachs, and grabbed the woman, throwing themselves across her to screen her from bullets. They half-dragged, half-crawled their way back to the shelter provided by a stone porch next door.

"Jesus Christ, who's that? We don't have any black women in the SLA, do we?" Russin roared in my ear.

"No," I answered. "The only black is Cinque." I ran back to the open phone line. "Please, just one peek, one quick look. See who the woman was who came outside," I pleaded with him.

"Lady, I'm not about to be a target. Maybe it's one of the two women who live there." That was all I heard him say before a roar of gunfire poured through the phone into my ear. I left that phone off the hook and rushed to another desk and called the Los Angeles police. "Who was the woman?" I asked.

"We don't have any confirmation from the field yet. Commander Peter Hagen is on the scene. We hope to have word shortly."

Russin grabbed a fistful of scripts, the other news of the day that had suddenly become less newsworthy. He had to put an hour's program together. "Bake, I'm not scheduling any time for you—just come on when you have something."

I leaned closer to the television set. The reporter's voice was shaky. He said something like "the woman screamed, 'They held me!' She was a hostage." He had to be referring to the woman who had run out.

6:30 P.M. A soft cushion of black smoke oozed out the front window of the house. It looked like the heavy black smoke produced by a petroleum-product fire, the kind that hangs over oil wells and gasoline stations that erupt in a blaze. The smoke billowed out, increasing every second as Russin yelled, "Goddamnit, Bake—find out what's happening! Will the firemen go in now? What caused this fire? Get it, and get it now!"

I ran back to the open phone and the man under his bed. Yes, he had smelled the smoke. Yes, it seemed to him like a gasoline or oil fire. No fire equipment was coming.

"You're sure? You're positive? How can you tell from under your bed?"

"Goddamnit, lady, I crawled up to the window. I tell you, there's no fire truck out here. Just them bullets, all over the place."

I watched the set and made another call to the Los Angeles police. My old friend answered. "Yes, there are fire trucks standing by. No, they won't move in."

"But the house is burning, for God's sake!"

"That's right, Marilyn, and we've already been told by people who were inside that there are bombs in there. If we send in the fire fighters, and the bombs go off, it will kill all of them. We just can't send a fire-fighting team into a bomb-trapped burning house."

The flames had engulfed every wall—huge sky-shooting flames, bright from the burning old wood. The house had become an inferno. The policeman was right. I could hear bullets still being shot from the house. It was impossible—but they were still firing. Those weren't just bullets exploding in the flames, but bullets being fired from guns.

At 7:00 P.M. "Newsroom" went on the air. I ran down the back stairs and slid into the chair opposite Russin. I told as much as I knew about the fire, the bombs, and the people still inside, still firing at the cops.

"Who do they think is inside?"

I mentioned Camilla Hall. She was the one so many of the people I had talked to had been sure about. "Maybe the rest of the SLA. A gang of whites with guns was seen inside," I added.

"Is Patty Hearst in there?"

"I don't know."

I ran back upstairs to the phones and the television set. I don't know how many times during the next hour I made the run to the set and back upstairs.

A flash from the police stated that a black woman and a white woman were dead and burning on the back porch, the bullets in the bandoliers around their waists still exploding. The final sound of a bullet fired from inside the wall of flames was heard at about 7:45 P.M.—almost two hours after the first warning to "come out with your hands up."

By 8:00 P.M., when "Newsroom" went off the air, bodies were being carried out of the burned-out house—Nancy Ling Perry, Donald David De Freeze, Patricia Soltysik, Angela Atwood, and Willie Wolfe. Where was Camilla Hall? I had said on the air she was inside. Suppose what the neighbors had said was wrong. Suppose she was alive and I had announced her death.

I again called my friend of the Los Angeles police. "No, you're not wrong. We know damned well Camilla is in there somewhere, but the floor came down, all four walls fell in, and then the roof caved in on top of that. It may take days to dig her out."

By Sunday Camilla had been found.

There was a great wave of sympathy for Camilla, even among the police who had been there and had been the targets of the SLA's guns. A Los Angeles officer from the squad said, "Somehow you just knew it wasn't her idea. She was stupid to follow those others, but I guess you can't put her down for putting love above her own life."

Legends and myths were already rising like the smoke from the ruins of the small house on 54th Street. Within days, the news was that it had taken five hundred police to kill the half-dozen SLA, that the six chose death over surrender. Russin decided some hard facts were needed. Jeff and I went to Los Angeles. We searched for five days among ruins and questioned friends and witnesses and police. We came back, and I made my report on the air: The SLA had had no intention of dying.

A hole had been sawed through the floorboards at the rear of the house long before the fire had erupted. Some believe it had been sawed the night before. The six SLA members had crawled under the house when the fire started. SLA documents state clearly, "Always burn the pad." But maybe they hadn't torched this one. The fire could have resulted from a hot tear-gas cannister hitting Molotov bombs the SLA had stockpiled by the front wall or from a ricocheting bullet striking a gasoline can. We couldn't prove what had ignited the house, but we know no incendiary grenades had been issued to or used by the police that day. The rumor persists, however, that cops torched the house.

It was true that the police had held the fire trucks back—not because they had been ordered to burn the SLA, but because Christine Johnson—the woman who had run out in the middle of the firefight and been saved by the cops—had warned them, "They got the house booby-trapped with bombs."

As the house burned, the SLA had continued to fire on the police from under the floorboards. Mizmoon, Willie, and Cinque had crouched in a rear corner. Nancy, Angela, and Camilla had been hunched down in the corner near the wide entry to the crawl space below the house.

Nancy had always been terrified of being closed in. She had fought off claustrophobia by working at Fruity Rudy's sidewalk stand. She had talked to Chris Thompson about it—"Better to be dead than in a cell." She had leaned low and run from the burning house, a machine gun strapped to her arm firing in a wide arc. Police bullets had hit her with such force that her five-foot body had been sent sprawling ten feet back into the burning cell she had just escaped. Angela Atwood had followed Nancy on their final run for freedom. She hadn't made it as far as Nancy had before bullets had brought her down, too. Her finger still squeezed the trigger as she fell.

Camilla had started out, trying to push her large body through the small space her comrades had exited from so easily. She couldn't make it. She had then leaned out, firing at the police surrounding the house. Bullets smashed into her head and she fell back inside, buried under four feet of debris and rubble, where she was to lie unnoticed for two days. The remains of a cat were found next to her body. It wasn't Camilla's cat. It was Minnie Lewis's cat. A cat they had called Whitey.

People who knew the six well speculate that the dash by Nancy, Angela, and Camilla was a suicide run, meant to draw off the fire and permit Mizmoon, Cinque, and Willie to escape. If this was true, the ploy boomeranged; their comrades were trapped when their bodies blocked the only opening from under the burning house. Their gas masks were useless; there was no oxygen to filter into them. Smoke filled their lungs, bringing on lethargy, more like falling asleep than dying. Mizmoon and Willie died from smoke inhalation. Their face masks had melted into their own faces. The masks were useless relics of the war they had declared and lost.

Cinque was left alone between them. He knew what faced him if he lived—life inside prison, among prisoners who had rejected him years before. He put a revolver up to his head, fired once, and was dead.

In death, the SLA got what they never had in life—followers.

CHAPTER **16**

THE SLA DEATH WATCH began the same night that the rubble
smoldered in Los Angeles, the same night that Steven Weed arrived from San Diego. He was filmed walking dejectedly through
the smoking ruins, his head bent low, hands thrust deep in his
pockets.

Jeff and I drove across the Bay Bridge and down the East Bay
to Hayward, thirty miles south of Oakland. I was to speak at a
seminar at California State College on new careers for women,
scheduled for 8:00 P.M. I was almost two hours late. The audience of two hundred women gave me my first clue to the SLA
aftermath that would infect us all. I asked if they had heard
what happened in Los Angeles, more as a way of apologizing for
being late than of imparting information. They were fascinated,
forgetting the long wait and later forgiving the obviously ill-
prepared speech I delivered. They wanted to hear about the SLA.

After the speech and the questions and my assurance that "if I
can do it at forty-four, you can do it at any age," Jeff and I left,
warmed by the applause and the woman who followed me out-

side to say, "I never went to college either; like you, I went right to work. But now I'm not afraid to try something new. I don't need to be a clerk all my life."

Jeff and I went for a cup of coffee. For the first night since Patty Hearst's kidnapping on February 4, there was no reason to stake out street corners or to cruise salt-and-pepper neighborhoods. The cobra we had tracked had perished in Los Angeles. We "brainstormed." What would be the reaction to the SLA deaths— by radicals, by police, by average Americans? By Randolph and Catherine Hearst?

Jeff drove me home around 2:00 A.M. That's when we saw the first aftermath graffiti, spray-painted on an abandoned building not far from the hill where I live:

"Long live the cobra!"

The weekend of May 18 and 19 was a time of dental charts and long waits. The Los Angeles county coroner, Dr. Thomas Noguchi, made official identifications—he named the five whose bodies he had examined. At the Hearst Hillsborough home, there was rejoicing that Patty was not among the dead.

The flicker of joy was quickly snuffed out when the sixth body was found on Sunday. The Hearsts waited again. The police obviously hadn't told them that it was probably Camilla. When the word finally came that it was Camilla, Hearst muttered, "Oh God, thank God." Catherine's eyes were swollen and red.

For the first time Patty was not the star of the SLA saga. In death, her six comrades overshadowed her importance.

It was an eerie sensation, typing out the vital statistics for Patricia Soltysik. The day she died in the inferno was her twenty-fourth birthday. The town of Goleta reclaimed her charred remains. Neighbors who remembered only the pretty girl who had left to conquer the world a half-dozen years ago gathered around her family, forming a wall of privacy behind which they could cry.

They had been prepared. In January the FBI had informed her family that Patricia was suspected of being the brains behind the Symbionese Liberation Army. The family had cooperated, turning over to the FBI photographs of the pretty child, the letters she had written home, even the letter that arrived in the fall of 1973, warning them to "burn all my pictures and letters. You won't hear from me again." They had not obeyed. How could they destroy the last link they had to one of their own?

Patricia's brother, Fred, had gone to Berkeley, wandering on a trail not far from the one I'd traveled trying to find his sister. Ads had appeared in California newspapers—small lines under the heading "Personal"—"Mizmoon, please call home. Love, Fred."

She never did. Mizmoon was stoic. The SLA demanded no contact with family and friends. She had complied. It was a dedication few of her comrades were able to match. But Mizmoon believed in the tenets of the Symbionese as the others never could. She had helped mold them as her message to the masses, her path to importance.

On the day her remains were interred, her brother made a plea to those who would follow her teachings: "It doesn't help. It accomplished nothing."

It was the final judgment on a life that had promised so much.

In East Cleveland, Ohio, there was another funeral with another message—this the interment of Donald David De Freeze. His family of brothers and sisters and his children he had not seen for years came to pay their final respects. At last De Freeze received what he never had in life—respect.

His twenty-eight-year-old brother, Delano, stood over the coffin he claimed was not even holding the body of his brother. He eulogized him anyway. "My fallen brother died for a nation. That nation might not exist yet. But it will." Delano had sent invitations to radical leaders around the country to come and join in mourning Cinque. None came. Few even bothered to mourn.

His mother cried silently, tears coursing down her work-weary face, the earth mother standing by the ground that was reclaiming her child. She listened to her other son talking about the man she had given birth to thirty years earlier. She heard him say, ". . . We must have leaders to guide us to that nation. My brother was one." His mother turned, talking to no one in particular, and said, "I know he needed mental care, but I can't understand why he turned out like he did. My other seven children are doing fine."

It had been less than five months before that Gilbert Perry had told me, "I have nothing to do with anything like this Symbionese.

I think they're a bunch of nuts, weird, crazy. I just can't believe Nancy would have anything to do with them."

Now Perry rushed forward, declaring he had been the lawful husband of the deceased twenty-six-year-old Nancy Ling Perry, and claiming a full relationship with her, something he had avoided while she'd lived out her last months. Her parents, living out their final agony in quiet Santa Rosa, ignored the husbandly sounds issuing from the son-in-law they had always ignored. They held a private memorial service for their child. The schoolmates who remembered her gathered. There was no talk of terrorists. Her parents established a fund for Vietnam orphans in their daughter's name. Nancy at last would help the oppressed.

At Nancy's funeral in Oakland, Gilbert Perry delivered a flowery eulogy. He suddenly found new insights into the woman who had left him years ago: "My wife was a woman with a capacity for unquestionable, incalculable love, compassion, beauty, and awareness," he recited. "My wife's voice came to me out of the flames in Los Angeles. She said to me, 'Yeah, I was inside the house.' She gave me this message:

> Life is
> beautiful sometimes,
> but wait until you see—
> really see."

Perry had still another message, a tune the organ played, one he claimed Nancy had composed—"Grief for an Unknown Guerrilla." He had said to me in January, "My wife has no use for all this urban guerrilla jazz. She isn't nuts like they are." He had also said he was the musical talent in their marriage—"Nancy just listened to music."

In North Haledon, New Jersey, Lawrence De Angelis, sobbing, leaned on the arms of his son Lawrence, Jr., and another daughter, Elena, as they left the funeral service for Angela.

Angela had been only twenty-five years old—her life ending with the rejection of everything her father held dear—family, friends, and the Church. It was no comfort when the priest had said, "She died for what she believed in, just as Jesus Christ himself did."

Two hundred people paid their respects to De Angelis, most

212

of them not knowing the daughter he mourned. "She must have just run with the wrong crowd," one offered.

Meanwhile, Angela's lover, Joe Remiro, sat in a jail cell in Oakland, awaiting trial for the SLA murder of Marcus Foster. Nobody asked him what to do for Angela at her death. A guard had walked in and quietly told Remiro and his comrade—co-defendant Russell Little—that Angela, along with the other five SLA members, had perished. Recalling the incident later, the guard shook his head and said, "Remiro, he just stared. Little, he burst out crying. You know, they say he loved Nancy Ling Perry. But Remiro, he told Little to shut up and deal. Little stopped crying and shuffled the cards. They were sitting there, still playing cards when I left."

Dateline this obit "Lincolnwood, a suburb of Chicago," Russin said. It concerned the final service for twenty-nine-year-old Camilla Hall.

Her father, The Reverend George Hall, delivered the quiet words. He stood in St. John's Lutheran Church, his church. His wife Leona sat in the front pew. They had been through it before, having buried two sons and another daughter, until all that remained was Camilla. She had never broken off contact with her parents. She had managed to write them loving letters even after she had gone underground with her violent friends. Her parents still called her Candy.

Unlike their other children, whom they had lost to diseases, Camilla had died because of the overpowering love she had had for Patricia. It was small comfort for her parents during the quiet short service.

In death, twenty-three-year-old William Wolfe was the center of attention, something he had never enjoyed in life, either as the errant son of rich parents or as a guerrilla.

Willie's father, Dr. L. S. Wolfe, was determined that his son would receive in death the prominence the father felt was due him. Friends and neighbors in Allentown, Pennsylvania, told me, "Dr. Wolfe knew his son was already buried when he made that trip to Los Angeles to claim the body. He knew his ex-wife, Willie's mother, had already had the services and that Willie was interred near her home in Connecticut, but he went anyway. I think he had to do something, and he couldn't think of anything else."

Dr. Wolfe demanded that the press accompany him to the coroner's office to claim his dead son. Of course, he was told that Willie's remains had already been claimed by his mother.

Dr. Wolfe issued a statement. "I will sue the FBI for one hundred million dollars for slaughtering my son." Reporters shifted uncomfortably in the face of the charge. Hadn't anyone told Dr. Wolfe that the FBI had not been involved in the shootout? They chose not to intrude on his grief with facts.

Dr. Wolfe telephoned Randolph Hearst. Afterward, he told others, "I thought we might be able to help one another. But Hearst told me it wasn't appropriate—said we had nothing to discuss."

The doctor smarted under the social sting, the first of many. Some he hid from the press he spoke to almost daily. He paced the living room of his comfortable middle-class home in Emmaus, where a huge oil portrait of his sons hangs over the mantel. He gave out interviews, claiming his son had worked in a factory in Berkeley. It was a statement contradicted by all who knew Willie in Berkeley. "He never worked or went to school," they said.

Dr. Wolfe spoke of a fiancée, a Swedish woman named Ava, whom he had met when he had gone to Oakland and visited Willie. The visit had ended a few days before the SLA murdered Marcus Foster. He decried the brutal acts of the police in killing his son, vowing, "I will do everything in my power to put an end to this John Wayne approach to law enforcement."

Willie Wolfe was as unimposing in death as he had been in life.

PART FIVE

THE REASON

CHAPTER **17**

THE HUNT CONTINUED for the SLA trio who had escaped the flaming death of their comrades. Now Patty and the Harrises were charged with felonies from kidnapping to armed robbery.

The front pages of all the Hearst-owned *Examiner* newspapers carried a large boxed notice, addressed simply: *Urgent Message to Bill, Emily, and Patty.* It read:

> Stop running. As long as you run, you court disaster. . . . There is no safe place that you can hide. . . . Death may only be a breath away. But you can surrender and safely."

Then followed the phone number of the newspaper.

Phones rang—cranks and citizens thinking they had seen Patty. But no call came from Bill, Emily, or Patty.

I asked on television if Emily, Bill, and Patty had not violated the SLA Codes of War. Were they not required to go to the aid of a comrade in trouble? Police had privately told me that if a call had come in from Patty, from anywhere else in Los Angeles, it might well have pulled some of their forces off the house on 54th Street. But Patty had not called.

217

Hilly Rose, a communicaster for KFI Radio in Los Angeles, had interviewed me several times, primarily about my SLA stories. I started getting calls from Los Angeles area residents: "We heard you on Hilly's radio program. We think we might have seen Patty."

The police still held the sole keys for separating true leads from false ones—the dogs trained to identify Emily's and Patty's scents. So I started with them, calling the Los Angeles police.

"Any confirmed sightings?" I asked.

At first they hedged, claiming, "We're checking a dozen a day."

"But I don't want to know how many you check. I want to know how many the dogs confirm!" I replied.

They gave in. A dog had confirmed one already, on Sunday, May 19, the day Camilla's body had been found.

Anita Alcala manages and maintains an apartment complex at 260 North New Hampshire. The address is one block west of Vermont Avenue and two dozen blocks south of the place where Frank Sutton had been released by Patty and the Harrises on May 17. Mrs. Alcala was repainting a vacant apartment at 9:30 Sunday night when a white woman and a black man walked in through the open front door.

"Is there an apartment for rent?" the woman had asked.

When Mrs. Alcala said no, the woman pulled out a wad of money and said, "I'll give you five hundred dollars."

Mrs. Alcala snapped, "There's no vacancy if you paid me a thousand dollars."

The woman then jerked open her coat and shoved an automatic rifle at Mrs. Alcala, but before it was in firing position, the man had produced a knife. He jumped at her, and the knife slashed through her dress, missing her flesh by a hairbreadth. Mrs. Alcala, convinced she was about to be cut to ribbons, began screaming. The couple turned and ran out to a car at the curb. A second black man sat behind the wheel. They drove off into the night traffic.

Mrs. Alcala had examined the mug shots and said it was Patty Hearst who had drawn the rifle. The police dog confirmed that Patty had been in the room. But who were the two men with her? The policeman said, "Who knows? Probably just a couple of guys she paid a hundred bucks to, to help her rent a place. That's the SLA's method of operation, you know."

218

It meant that Patty and her two comrades had stayed within a mile of Griffith Park, where they had dumped their last kidnap victim, and they had remained there for forty-eight hours. They weren't running very fast or far.

Another sighting, the first clue that the trio might try heading back to San Francisco, had been called in by a man who lives a good fifty miles from Los Angeles, in the hills above the San Fernando Valley near Placerita Canyon, not far from a direct freeway route to San Francisco. I read the brief report from the wire service. Obviously, the reporter hadn't had much faith in the sighting. It was almost ignored in the daily wrap-up of SLA news on Tuesday, May 21.

I could see why. The man who reported he had seen Patty was eighty-three years old. That in itself was enough to make most journalists doubtful, for, unfortunately, we are brainwashed to believe that age obliterates the mind. But the Los Angeles police had mentioned several sightings they had not checked yet, all in the San Fernando Valley.

Placerita Canyon is just above the Valley, and it would be easy for me to check, even if I was hundreds of miles away. I had a good contact in the area. Scott Newhall, who had edited the *Chronicle* for years, now operates the *Signal*, a family-owned newspaper in the family-owned town of Newhall, next to Placerita Canyon. I called him, and within an hour he had a full report.

On Monday evening, May 20, at about seven o'clock, William Walls had walked down the trail from his home to the dirt road where his nearest neighbors live. He had been standing by the edge of the path, enjoying the air and the coming hush of evening, when a car turned the bend and pulled up next to him. It was an early 1960s sedan—black top with a red body, he recalls. A man was driving, with a woman next to him; another woman was in the back seat, beside a pile of old clothes and blankets.

It was the woman in the back seat who spoke. "Do you know of a motel or a hotel around here?"

"No, there's none in these parts," Walls answered.

"Well, do you know where we could rent just a room for the night?"

Walls hesitated. There was something haunting, almost known, about the smile of the young girl. But he knew no one with a short dark Afro. So he said, "Nope, no rooms for rent either."

He suggested they go to the San Fernando Valley, the nearest place for a motel. He offered directions. "It'll take you right to the Antelope Valley Freeway, and that'll take you right into the Valley."

"Oh no, we don't want to drive on any freeway," the young woman quickly replied. Then she seemed to think an explanation was in order, so she stammered, "Well, it's so crowded at this time of night, you know."

Walls knew very well it was not crowded at that time of night. Something nagged at the back of his mind—something about the girl and her two companions, something he should remember. It hit him. Of course! It was Patricia Hearst and the two terrorists being hunted by the authorities. He peered into the back seat of the car. There was no mistake about it. Remove the Afro wig and you'd have Patty. The three appeared nervous. The man behind the wheel started up the car, as if he thought they'd said enough.

"Wait, I can tell you how to get down to the Valley without going on the freeway," Walls offered. They stopped and heard him out, listening carefully to his directions—a route that only a native would know.

The girl in the back seat smiled, and Walls was further convinced of who she was. "Thanks for your help," she called as she waved her hand and the car headed up the dirt road, back toward the paved roadway.

Newhall's reporter finished, then said, "Walls called the sheriff and they finally got choppers and men up here, but there's just so much to search. There's no way of knowing if the car got through or not."

"But are you certain the old man is right?" I asked.

"He's a damned sight better source than any I know and there isn't a deputy up here that doesn't believe Old Man Walls. If he wasn't damned sure, he'd never say so."

"Did the old man have any reaction to Patty? Was he afraid of her or what?"

The reporter from the *Signal* chuckled. "Hell, no. He said, 'It's all a damned shame. She seemed like a wonderful girl.'"

I stared at a map of California spread out across my desk. Where could the trail out of Placerita Canyon lead? Toward

Death Valley? Or over the hills and to the sea? Or up San Joaquin Valley to the Sierras?

We went back to old contacts—street people in Berkeley, campus friends of Jeff's, anyone who might know where a terrorist could hide. We found no answers. I kept telephoning—to Los Angeles, San Diego, the Riverside County sheriff's office. I was striking out everywhere.

Perhaps Patty's two younger sisters would have better luck. They both tape-recorded messages to their missing sister. Television and radio stations played them, newspapers printed the texts in full.

Ann, two years younger than Patty, reminded her: "You have your whole life ahead of you." Then, with surprising candor, Patty's youngest sister, seventeen-year-old Vicki, said: "This is the only voice in the family I think you'll trust. I wouldn't lie to you. I don't want to see you die. It would be a waste. The whole thing would be a waste. I don't want to see anything happen to you. There's so much you can do and say—so just take care of yourself and just go in and go to a lawyer and everything will be all right. I just want to tell you we really love you and I really love you and want to see you again."

Her voice was nearly a sob; the words were pushed out between breaths: "You don't have to just sit around and wait for the police to come in and get you. You can go to a lawyer or go to the news media . . . but whatever you do, you're going to have to do it soon. You saw what happened in Los Angeles, and I don't want that to happen to you because I'm telling you right now that the police and the FBI are not that sympathetic anymore. I mean, they've taken a lot of trash from you guys, and I don't think they're going to sit around and take it much longer."

Even the Hearst family's servants made news. They, too, became instant Patty experts, lay psychiatrists, with quick solutions to questions about where Patty went wrong. It was a game widely played. Kathe Kellings had been the Hearst housekeeper for a decade, having joined the Hillsborough staff when Patty was ten years old. Patty was "a spoiled and temperamental child," Kathe recalled, but added that she had changed in the past few years. "Right after she moved out, she became very independent, but a nice lovely lady." When she reported that she thought she had spotted Patty in a car next to her on the freeway, the FBI ignored the sighting.

Others called press conferences. The Reverend Cecil Williams, forgotten since his early offer to act as intermediator had failed, now had Gary Ling, Nancy's brother, at his side. They asked Patty and the Harrises to surrender. Their appeal received no response.

Steve Weed was not much more effective. He volunteered to testify before the grand jury, still probing the SLA beginnings. Weed was indignant. The U.S. Attorney General for Northern California, James Browning, had become evasive when Weed asked to interview Tom Matthews. "In fact, they sneaked him in by the basement, when we both had to testify, and kept us in separate locked rooms," Weed fumed.

But Steve sent out a message to Patty—that she shouldn't despair, that all the talk about "life in prison" was only talk. "Patty Hearst will never spend a day in jail," Weed told me confidently. "Not a Hearst." He still had faith in the power of the name, even if Randolph Hearst did not. Randolph had said to me, "Why did her name have to be Hearst? I keep thinking about that." Then he quickly changed the subject.

Of all the spotlight-seekers, the journalists were the worst. My "Open Letter to the SLA," which I had aired on February 12, was branded "self-serving and gratuitous" by my colleagues. But it had been something I had wanted to say and I had used the platform on TV to say it, an advantage few have.

However, John Lester, who started out as "pool man" for the news corps parked in front of the Hearst home, topped us all. He held a phone up to the camera on the eleven o'clock news one night and told the viewers, "We've learned the phones at the radio stations that receive SLA communiqués are shut off at eight P.M." Then Lester assured the SLA that his station would keep a phone open for them until one in the morning, and he would be standing by, awaiting the SLA's ring. The phone never rang. Shortly after that Lester quit his job as a reporter and moved into the Hearst home as spokesman for the family, to make all press statements, answer all questions.

Not to be outdone, anchormen on the local KPIX news program offered to "hold any contact from the SLA in the strictest confidence. We won't violate the confidentiality of your call," they promised. They never got the chance. The SLA ignored them, too.

KRON-TV decided to make its appeal via visuals. It did a story on the free-food program, which had never been openly called "ransom." A drawing of a bulging bag of groceries was shown behind an anchorman's head. On the side of the bag was the seven-headed cobra symbol.

There were other appeals that touched the toughest reporters. One was to Emily Harris from her father, Fred Schwartz. While the parents of other SLA members were burying their children, Schwartz arrived in Los Angeles from his suburban Chicago home to plead for his daughter's life. He took a room at the Brentwood-Bel Air Holiday Inn, a vast circular tower in the sky between the two quiet rich canyons. His room looked out over the city where he thought his daughter might still be hiding. He asked the media to help him reach her. "She and her husband Bill are highly intelligent people, whom I respect very much," he emphasized. He reminded Emily of the death of her comrades and warned her that her fate could be the same. Then he said, "With your death, your causes and ideals—whatever they might be—die with you. If your ideals are worth all you've been through, they are worth living for."

He waited to hear from his fugitive daughter. He received one call. A man's voice claimed to have information that could lead to Emily. A secret meeting was arranged, and Schwartz promised not to bring the police, nor to tell anyone.

Schwartz was so anxious for the meeting that he left for the designated place an hour earlier than would normally be necessary. But he got lost on the freeway and drove for miles to find an off ramp that took him back to where he had just been. He was an hour late for his meeting. No one was waiting. Two days later there was another call. The same voice set up another meeting. This time Fred Schwartz was on time, but no one showed up.

Emily's father then put out an appeal for his daughter to surrender. He asked that she call him first. He promised to walk with her hand in his, to make sure she would not be hurt. He put his life on the line, but his offer was ignored.

Schwartz persevered. He had reason to hope. The Symbionese laws demanded that the members forsake all family ties, yet Emily had written him on February 1, after she had gone underground. He did not want to discuss the letter with the press. It had been rambling, emotional, obviously written by a distraught woman. Schwartz didn't know why; he only knew Emily had broken the SLA law once to communicate with him and he hoped she would now do so again. He waited eight days. No call ever came. He returned to Chicago, defeated.

My obsession with the SLA absorbed my life. I followed every lead, hoping one would take me to Patty and her comrades. Jeff and I went back to Los Angeles. We had three names from Emily Harris's address book. Two had the same address and phone number. The third had no address and the phone had been disconnected.

We tracked down the address on Pico Boulevard. It had previously been an office for the Peace Action Council. We gloated because everyone, including radical reporters, had been stumped when the SLA tape had sent "revolutionary greetings to the PAC." None of us had ever heard of it, not even KPFA or KSAN, the radio stations used for SLA tape deliveries. Now we knew what PAC meant but not where it was at present. The office had been closed for months. Neighbors, all black, remembered them as "a bunch of white folks in a storefront right in the middle of our district."

The Los Angeles police knew the PAC. They said of it, ". . . almost unlimited money . . . backed by some professors who leaned toward Maoist politics." They added, "We've watched them for years. They faded out when the Vietnam war ended."

Jeff found new addresses for two of the names. We went to knock on their doors. One door was opened by a kindly elderly woman, not by a cobra cultist. She was shocked to learn that her husband's name was in Emily Harris's address book. Our shock was that no one—neither cop, FBI, nor reporter—had been there before us to question her husband.

The address is a quiet upper-class duplex in Westwood. The man is a typical humanitarian. "I am for prison reform and all those things," he assured us. But he had no idea why his name and address were in Emily's book. We left, somewhat deflated.

At seven the next morning the phone rang as Jeff was entering my hotel room with coffee. It was the Westwood man. "I think it might tie in," he apologized. "I remember this now."

The previous year, in August or September, a man had asked

if he could use the Westwood man's name and address on mail from his wife, who was serving time in prison in San Francisco. He had explained that they didn't want her family to find out she was in jail. "I said 'All right.' After all, it seemed innocent enough. But the only mail that ever came was one big package. That came the first week in December. Another fellow came by to pick it up. He said he was the woman's brother. I never did know their names at all. I never even looked at the return address on that package. I haven't seen any of them since."

The third name on our list—a man whom we can call Sam— was more elusive. It was two days before Jeff tracked him down. He is a professional man in Beverly Hills, and he refused to take any of our calls.

Weeks later I jumped when Steve Weed asked me, "Have you run across a Sam anywhere?"

Why did Weed ask? "Because a good mutual friend of Patty and me got a phone call from a man who said his name was Sam, and he called because of a common friend they had. He knew too much not to have talked to someone. Maybe he talked to Patty."

I had turned over the name and address of Sam to the Los Angeles police and assumed they would have followed it up.

"When did your friend get this call from Sam?"

Weed thought a minute, then said, "Oh, about a week ago, I guess."

It had been three weeks since I had been in Los Angeles. The police obviously had not talked to Sam. Or had Sam evaded them, too? Or was Weed's Sam a different Sam? It was another of the many leads that never got followed up.

I had another meeting with Chris Thompson. He had changed some of his opinions. He talked softly of the dead SLA members. "They were worthwhile people, all of them." He said their message must not be lost. "But they were impatient. I'm working for 1976. They wanted it tomorrow." He added, "I've thought of trying to communicate with Remiro and Little. I wrote a poem for them—it's a good poem."

A new communiqué stopped us all in our tracks. This, another tape—from Bill, Emily, and Patty—had been delivered at six in the morning on June 7 to KPFK, the sister station in Van Nuys, in the San Fernando Valley, to Berkeley's KPFA.

I heard the bulletin on the radio and phoned KPFK. They told me they'd had a call. A man's voice had told them to look behind an old mattress in the alley outside their back door. There they had found the tape. By noon they had set up lines to feed it to radio and television stations across the country.

"May I hear it, too?" I asked.

There was a flap—too many requests and not enough lines. Finally the general manager came on the line. "Sure, Marilyn. We'll unplug Minnesota and let you have their line."

So I replaced a state and heard, for the first time, in Tania's own voice, the reasons behind Patty's conversion to Tania:

"Greetings to the people. This is Tania. I want to talk about the way I knew our six murdered comrades, because the fascist pig media has, of course, been painting a typically distorted picture of these beautiful sisters and brothers.

"Cujo [Willie Wolfe] was the gentlest, most beautiful man I've ever known. He taught me the truth as he learned it from the beautiful brothers in California's concentration camps.

"We loved each other so much. And his love for the people was so deep that he was willing to give his life for them. The name Cujo means 'unconquerable.' It is the perfect name for him. Cujo conquered life as well as death by facing them and fighting.

"Neither Cujo nor I had ever loved an individual the way we loved each other, probably because our relationship wasn't based on bourgeois, fucked-up values, attitudes, and goals. Our relationship's foundation was our commitment to the struggle and our love for the people. It's because of this that I still feel strong and determined to fight.

"I was ripped off by the pigs when they murdered Cujo— ripped off the same way that thousands of sisters and brothers in this fascist country have been ripped off of people they love. We mourn together, and the sound of gunfire becomes sweeter.

"Gelina [Angela Atwood] was beautiful—fire and joy. She exploded with the desire to kill the pig. She wrote poetry—some of it on the walls of Golden Gate—all of it in the L.A. pig files now. It expressed how she felt. She loved the people more than her love for any one person or material comfort, and she never let her mind rest from the strategies that are the blood of the revolution.

"Gelina would have yelled, 'Firepower to the people' if there wasn't the necessity to whisper the words of revolution. We laughed and cried and struggled together. She taught me how to fight the enemy within through her constant struggle with bourgeois conditioning.

"Gabi [Camilla Hall] crouched low with her ass to the ground. She practiced until her shotgun was an extension of her right and left arms—an impulse, a tool of survival. She understood the evil in the hearts of the pigs and took the only way that could demoralize, defeat, and destroy them. She meant to touch people with a strong—not delicate—embrace.

"Gabi taught me the patience and discipline necessary for survival and victory.

"Gelina wanted to give meaning to her name and on her birthday she did.

"Zoya [Patricia Soltysik], female guerrilla, perfect love and perfect hate reflected in stone-cold eyes. She moved viciously and with caution, understanding the peril of the smallest mistake. She taught me, 'Keep your ass down and be bad.'

"Fahizah [Nancy Ling Perry] was a beautiful sister who didn't talk much but who was the teacher of many by her righteous example. She, more than any other, had come to understand and conquer the putrid disease of bourgeois mentality. She proved often that she was unwilling to compromise with the enemy because of her intense love for freedom. Fahizah taught me the perils of hesitation, to shoot first and make sure the pig is dead before splitting. She was wise and bad, and I'll always love her.

"Cinque loved the people with tenderness and respect. They listened to him when he talked because they knew that his love reflected the truth and the future. Cin knew that to live was to shoot straight. He longed to be with his black sisters and brothers, but at the same time he wanted to prove to black people that white freedom fighters are comrades in arms.

"Cinque was in a race with time, believing that every minute must be another step forward in the fight to save his children. He taught me virtually everything imaginable, but wasn't liberal with us. He'd kick our asses if we didn't hop over a fence fast enough or keep our asses down while practicing. Most importantly, he taught me how to show my love for the people. He helped me see that it's not how long you live that's important, it's how you live, what we decide to do with our lives.

"On February 4th, Cinque Mtume [De Freeze] saved my life.

"The Malcolm X combat unit of the SLA was a leadership training cell under the personal command of General Field Marshal Cinque. General Tico [William Harris] was his second-in-command. Everything we did was directed toward our development as leaders and advisers to other units. All of us were prepared to function on our own if necessary until we connected with other combat units.

"The idea that we are leaderless is absurd as long as any SLA elements are alive and operating under the command of our general field marshal.

"It's hard to explain what it was like watching our comrades die, murdered by pig incendiary grenades, at the cowering of pigs facing a fire team of guerrillas, and the only way they could defeat them was to burn them alive. It made me mad to see the pigs looking at our comrades' weapons, to see them holding Cujo's .45 and his watch, which was still ticking. He would have laughed at that.

"They gave no surrender. No one in that house was suicidal—just determined and full of love.

"It was beautiful to hear [unintelligible]. He understands.

"Gabi loved her father, and I know that much of her strength came from the support he gave her. What a difference between the parents of Gabi and Cujo and my parents.

"One day, just before the last tape was made, Cujo and I were talking about the way my parents were fucking me over. He said that his parents were still his parents, because they had never betrayed him. But my parents were really Malcolm X and Assata Sakur. I'll never betray my parents.

"The pigs probably have the little old man monkey that Cujo wore around his neck. He gave me the little stone face one night.

"I know that the pigs are proud of themselves. They've killed another black leader. In typical pig fashion, they have said that Cinque committed suicide. What horseshit. Cin committed suicide the same way Malcolm [X] and [Martin Luther, Jr.] King and Bobby [Kennedy] and Fred [Hampton] and Jonathan [Jackson] and George [Jackson] did. But no matter how many leaders are killed, the pig can't kill their ideals. I learned a lot from Cin and the comrades who died in that fire, and I'm still learning from them. They live on in the hearts and minds of millions of people in fascist America. The pigs' actions that Friday evening showed just how scared they really are. They would have burned and bombed that entire neighborhood to murder six guerrillas.

"The SLA terrifies the pigs because it's called all oppressed people in this country to arms, to fight in a united front to overthrow this fascist dictatorship. The pigs think they can deal with a handful of revolutionaries, but they know they can't defeat the incredible power which the people, once united, represent.

"It's for this reason that we get to see, live and in color, the terrorist tactics of the pigs. The pigs say, 'You're next.' This kind of display, however, only serves to raise the people's consciousness and makes it easier for our comrade sisters and brothers throughout the country to connect.

"I died in that fire on Fifty-fourth Street, but out of the ashes I was reborn. I know what I have to do. My comrades didn't die in vain. The pig lies about the advisability of surrendering have only made me more determined. I renounced my class privilege when Cin and Cujo gave me the name Tania. While I have no death wish, I have never been afraid of death. For this reason, the brainwash-duress theory of the pig Hearsts has always amused me.

"Life is very precious to me, but I have no delusions that going to prison would keep me alive, and I would never choose to live the rest of my life surrounded by pigs like the Hearsts. I want to free our comrades in this country's concentration camps, but on our terms, as stated in our Declaration of Revolutionary War—not on the pigs' terms.

"Death to the fascist insect that preys upon the life of the people."

CHAPTER **18**

So IT HAD BEEN love that had turned pretty Patty Hearst into
a terrorist.

Actually, Jeff, Russin, and I, sitting in our cars during the
long dreary stakeouts, had even considered that. It had been
a game to play: Which SLA member did Patty love? I had
leaned toward Cinque, who would have been a unique experience for a girl like Patty, the total reversal of all she had
known as a Hearst. We'd made the usual cheap jokes—about how
Patty would come home in nine months and present her father
with Cinque, Jr., son of Cin.

But Patty and Cinque were too different from each other to
love. They didn't even speak the same language. All along it had
been Willie Wolfe. We had heard it in her own words. She
had fallen in love with Cujo. And now, with twenty-twenty hind-
sight, it seems so obvious.

They came from similar backgrounds, families of money, comfort, and indulgence. Patty had left home to live in Berkeley,
taking her father's credit cards with her. Willie had left home to

live in Berkeley, bringing with him his shares of Standard Oil of New Jersey. He was somewhat shy, with an inborn arrogance, and soft-spoken. He was somewhat like Steve Weed, the fiancé he replaced in Patty's affections.

Chris Thompson had known Willie Wolfe since 1971. They had lived together since 1972. I asked Thompson to describe Cujo, but the verbal portrait Chris drew did not fit the profile given by Tania.

"Willie? Why, he was just a rich man's son, that's all," Chris answered. He smiled, remembering Willie. "He'd mainly just lay on the bed, not doing anything, maybe reading comic books; he liked those. Or he'd watch television. He liked that too. Oh, some of the programs he watched were good—nature programs, things on China. But he watched a lot of junk too. He was lousy, I mean he didn't take care of himself. He only took baths periodically. He was very lazy, with a sort of prep-school personality."

Thompson continued, "He was like a kid brother who you tell to tidy up his room a dozen times but five hours later, it still isn't done. You can't sock him in the mouth—it won't do any good anyway. Even if you want to."

Thompson got down to instances. "There was this cart that we wanted Willie to put wheels on and fix a gas hose into it. It was no big deal, a few hours' work at the most. We were going to use the cart to sell Chinese food along Telegraph Avenue, you know, a street-vendor thing. We were all living at Peking Man House together. And as Willie didn't work or go to school, we told him to do it. We explained exactly how to put those wheels on and get that hose inside the cart. We kept after him, day after day, but would you believe it was five months—that's right, five months—before he ever got around to it? That was Willie, always putting things off."

I tried to imagine Patty with that young man. He was "bland as Pablum," Chris Thompson said. Willie was everything Patty had been taught was a "man": a product of wealth, upper-middle class, a private school in Northfield, Massachusetts, where the dean remembered him as "thoughtful, articulate, and concerned." But never violent.

I remembered a young woman who had sold Willie a car on April 12, three days before the bank robbery. She had called him "one of the nicest fellows I'd ever met." In fact, she made it clear that she would not have turned down a date with the freckle-faced twenty-three-year-old had he asked for one. "He was so open, so friendly, told me how he'd lived in the woods for a while with friends and then a commune and how he loved people."

She also remembered how free he had been with money. "I was going to ask six hundred dollars for the car. It was a 1962 Karmann Ghia, not in very good shape. But he offered me seven hundred dollars and when I hesitated he said he'd pay seven hundred fifty, almost like he was willing to pay any price."

Willie had gone to Berkeley in 1971, his head full of Marx and Mao; but he had few original political philosophies. Willie never seemed to think out his own view. He enrolled in the University of California, with archeology and astronomy his subjects, but he never went to class. Within a month, he moved out of the campus dormitory into the Peking Man House commune. There he could listen to others talk of Mao and nod his head in agreement, without having to read the words first. Peking Man House residents were the heavies of the Berkeley Maoists. They knew the polemics of the Chairman, whether Willie did or not.

Willie then discovered the Black Cultural Association, a prison program to aid black men behind bars. It was tailor-made for Willie. It gave him the chance to sit and rap with the hard men who had pulled big crimes and who were now doing time. They were Willie's heroes—not his father and uncle and grandfather and brothers, who had all gone to Yale, but men who talked about murder as though it were a game.

Willie probably told Patty about the days he had lived in Harlem with a man named Michael Carrerras. Going to Harlem had been daring, but it was not on a par with robbing a bank or murdering a man. In an interview with a Pennsylvania newspaper, the Allentown *Morning Call*, Carrerras described Willie as "an American Tragedy . . . looking for a life with a little deprivation. When you've had it easy, maybe you feel guilty because you haven't been able to experience life in the raw."

Neither Willie nor Patty had ever known life in anything but its highly refined state. They found new life, and each other, in the filth of the Golden Gate Avenue apartment, in the excitement of a bank holdup, in the drama of seeing their names and faces on television screens and in the massive hunt for them.

If Patty really loved Willie, why didn't she take action to save his life? Maybe the Harrises wouldn't let her. Maybe she is harboring the knowledge that it was the parking tickets that Emily Harris left lying around that led the police to her lover and her lover to his grave?

There is nothing in the pictures of Willie Wolfe to excite the glands, no charismatic sex appeal. When I asked Chris Thompson who had been Willie's girlfriend in Berkeley, Chris said, "He never had one."

"What did he do for sex?" I asked.

"The same as he did for everything else—nothing."

Weed had described Patty as "always very affectionate—she needed physical comfort, she liked to be touched. I can understand in this situation, held by the SLA, she would need it more than ever." Then Weed had looked almost embarrassed as he added, "Of course, she didn't take her birth control pills with her when they kidnapped her."

Willie's father has described his son as "an angel, the gentlest person ever born." The words are not too removed from Randolph Heart's description of his daughter—"this lovely, beautiful child."

Other members of Willie's family saw him in a more realistic light. His sister Roxanna told the Allentown *Morning Call*, "Willie was overwhelmed by the problems of the world, but he didn't have the wisdom that comes with years . . . that lets you know how to deal with such things." She added, "He was in that house in Los Angeles because he was committed. He was always an idealist; he always wanted to help."

Willie had hitchhiked home for Christmas in 1973, leaving behind his roommates, Joe Remiro and Russell Little, and leaving with Nancy Ling Perry the car his father had bought him. Roxanna remembers Willie's arrival. He was wearing a Chinese workingman's jacket and a small cap, which she jokingly called his "Willie-we-the-people-skullcap." They had long talks. Willie again spoke to her of his ideals, but there was a new tone, a certain braggadocio, as he said, "I have friends who are going to be dead or in jail in five years."

233

His mother gave him a substantial check as a Christmas present. Willie said he would use it to go to Sweden to marry Ava. It was a lie. On January 10, Willie got a phone call from Oakland. He left his family home within the hour, taking a bus to New York. The phone call had been to warn him that Remiro and Little had been arrested, that the Clayton safe house had to be burned, and that the SLA had to go underground. Willie went, leaving behind his mother's check.

On February 4, Patty came into Willie's life, first as captive, then as lover. Steve Weed said he is not jealous of Willie. "I just don't believe there was really anything in it," he shrugged, adding, "You have to understand, Patty is a very accommodating girl, generous to everyone. Of course she'd go for Willie, but she sure wouldn't like Bill Harris. She hates short men. Willie was six feet tall, Harris is barely five-feet-seven."

Weed puzzles over the new love of his former fiancée. "She always liked older men, men who could teach her something. She had a teacher complex; in fact she had her first lover when she was just fourteen, a twenty-six-year-old man. She said he'd been her sexual teacher."

Weed described his visit to Willie Wolfe's house, his talk with Willie's father, who even now will not admit his son's SLA membership. "Dr. Wolfe really trips out on Patty being in love with Willie," said Weed. "But he seems to be suffering from a lot of guilt. He kept telling me not to feel guilty. I wanted to say to him, 'Don't look at me, look at yourself.' "

But Weed still has not actually listened to Patty's voice on tape telling how she and Cujo loved one another as neither had ever loved before. "I don't know if I want to hear it," he mumbled. "One of our friends did, and she said, for the first time, it sounds like Patty. I mean the way she talks and all. But it's some kind of a perversion of Patty, like a monster made out of a human you know." Then, almost in admiration, he added, "But Patty always was the one in her family that had spunk."

If any faint hope remained for Randolph and Catherine Hearst that Patty had been brainwashed, coerced, or drugged, the June 7 tape destroyed it.

And perhaps now we can understand the confusion on April 2, when a letter stated Patty's release date would be announced within seventy-two hours. Had Patty asked Willie to leave with her? Had he refused? Is that why she stayed?

Now Patty has had the perfect love affair and the perfect lover. He died, in a dramatic finale, at the height of the affair. This, more than the rhetoric and guns, more than the revolutionary commitment and the inferno death, is what makes Patty truly dangerous. She mourns the dead lover who can never rise from the ashes. She stays true to him so as not to dishonor his death. And staying true means remaining what he named her: Tania.

CHAPTER **19**

Is THE SYMBIONESE still alive and well underground? This is a difficult question to answer. It involves too many subjective elements, such as what is meant by "alive and well?" And what is the army, Symbionese style? As for the rash of communiqués that came forth as the embers died at the 54th Street house, few are given any importance. In one of Charles Bates's public statements, he said, "Everyone wants to be a field marshal." That does seem to be the driving force behind most of the communiqués, which range from a penciled, misspelled one sent to a Sacramento radio station by a Field Marshal Pax, claiming six policemen would be killed, to lengthy dissertations by other field marshals, each claiming to be the new voice of the Liberation Army.

There has been one among the barrage that the FBI and police believe might actually have been authored by persons once close to the core of the SLA. It followed the SLA's well-traveled path—delivery to Berkeley's KPFA radio station. The taped message was from a General Field Marshal Cabrella, a woman. She spoke of changing the code of the Liberation Army, restricting all safe houses to no more than three comrades in residence at any one time, explaining, "Six soldiers are too many comrades to lose in one attack." And she ended by calling the six SLA dead not only comrades "but close friends."

The tape has an authentic air about it. It is known that some radical women who were close to the SLA are still in the East Bay Area. Some spend their time at karate lessons, meeting nightly to perfect their skills. Others use the same rifle range where the SLA practiced shooting. Both the radicals and the police agree that another terrorist group is most likely to form in Berkeley, a city that casts a mild eye on such actions.

Can Patty hide in the underground for long? She might. Bernadette Dorhn—remember her?—has been underground for five years now. She was one of the FBI's most wanted. They don't like to talk about her Weatherwoman activities now, since they never found her.

Thero Wheeler, the man the FBI believes was Cinque's companion in the Patty Hearst kidnapping, disappeared immediately after the abduction. Today, those who knew him well say he is hiding in San Francisco's Fillmore district and has totally disavowed the SLA.

The underground is anywhere one can pass as someone else— Topeka, Des Moines, Nantucket, Palm Beach, San Fernando Valley, or San Francisco. It's anywhere a criminal professing radical politics hides out.

Who was the woman with the two men who kidnapped Patty Hearst? Steven Weed, the only one besides Patty herself who saw the woman, says it could have been Angela Atwood, but he isn't sure. And who was the third member of the trio that gunned down Marcus Foster? Two of the three—Little and Remiro— are awaiting trial, charged with that killing. The third member was described as petite—around five feet, and less than a hundred pounds. Witnesses say it may have been Nancy Ling Perry who hid behind the tree with a sawed-off shotgun and fired the first blast that cut Marcus Foster down.

Did the Symbionese snake grow out of the Venceremos collapse? First, one would have to believe that Venceremos is dead. This radical group, four of whose members are already charged with murder in one prison escape, doesn't disband like a defunct

Rotary Club. Members slide into another group, operate under another dramatized title, carry on the same illegal activities, all in the name of saving the people.

Was drug distribution on school grounds the real motive behind the Marcus Foster murder? Was all the SLA revolutionary rhetoric simply used to cover up the true purpose? At first I believed so, and I still don't discount it. I have talked to close associates of Foster's, who claim he had information that could have brought about the collapse of the drug business in the East Bay. They say that just before he was killed he had expressed his intention of going after the drug dealers.

There is no doubt that Nancy Ling Perry was into heavy drugs. Even in the spring of 1973, when she had supposedly turned off drugs to help the revolution, a former lover said: "She still paid a hundred dollars for a tiny bottle of opium oil. She loved the stuff." Nancy didn't make that kind of money selling juice at Fruity Rudy's; she had to have other income, obviously one she could not divulge. It may have come from drug sales.

Joe Remiro was reported to have been a drug user, and though the U.S. Army refuses to reveal the full record, it has been said that he was faced with disciplinary action because of involvement with drugs while in the service.

It is quite possible that drugs may yet prove to be the egg that hatched the cobra.

Did the FBI botch the SLA case? Yes, but so did the news media.

The FBI failed to put Camilla Hall under surveillance in mid-February, when they learned she was Mizmoon's lover; they believed then that Mizmoon was the brains of the SLA. The only action they took was to notify the bank downstairs in their building, where Camilla had an account, to call them if she came in to make a substantial withdrawdal. When, on March 1, Camilla closed her account, in which there was about $1,500, the bank never phoned upstairs to the FBI.

Charles Bates has worried about his public image and about reassuring Randolph Hearst, instead of encouraging his agents. And Frick and Frack have only been concerned with "how it would go down in the public eye." They never hesitated to mislead reporters, to withhold information, or simply to ignore proffered leads.

What about the Berkeley, Oakland, and San Francisco police? Their biggest handicap was that the FBI refused to share any information with local police departments. Policemen were reduced to watching newscasts to get leads that the FBI had sat on for weeks. In fact, the FBI has not always shared its information with its own agents. One agent might spend weeks looking for a certain woman, without being told that the man he kept running into was the object of another search by a different FBI agent.

Bates was convinced that his bureau's prestige was at stake, and he wanted to hang on to that diminishing prestige by solving the Hearst kidnapping single-handedly. He didn't solve it at all. It was the SLA's own carelessness, in leaving parking tickets lying around their safe houses, that trapped them.

And is the SLA saga over, or will there be still more indictments, other arrests? There has been a major haggle going on over new indictments, possible charges against the fringe characters who helped the SLA. The politically minded leaders of law enforcement want to forget the whole thing. They are convinced that any further probe would turn the six SLA dead into national folk heroes. Younger, less political lawmen would like to move for a clean sweep.

The news media have not come to grips with the fact that they were the real captives of the kill-cult. They paid the highest ransom and are still not free. Isn't it a form of ransom when hours of prime time on television and radio are preempted to play the rambling rhetoric of a gang of killers, all in the name of protecting Patty Hearst? Isn't it submitting to extortion when newspapers turn over their front pages to the preachings of terrorism, and claim they are doing it just to save one girl's life? Why did no newscaster demand that he be given the right of instant analysis after every SLA communiqué? It is a right we have fought to uphold when it comes to President Nixon's speeches. It is a right we should uphold whenever airtime is turned over to the use of one person or party or gang.

It became ludicrous when reporters didn't want to include mention of the Marcus Foster murder in their SLA stories. They tried to bury the murder with the victim, instead of putting the responsibility on the killers who claimed it, the Symbionese Liberation Army.

If the news media don't deal with the truth now, it may be too late for another chance. Already graffiti are proliferating on Berkeley's walls:

Six burned, so you can learn, scrawled in red paint across a vacant storefront.

Sisters for the SLA, signed with the symbol for female, on a door to a men's room.

The SLA . . . the tip of the iceberg, in three-foot-high letters across the street from a campus hamburger stand.

And scribbled across the side of Berkeley High School, the ultimate cop-out: *Only those who do nothing never make mistakes. Right on, SLA!* It is an obvious excuse for the murder of Marcus Foster, written on the walls of a school filled with children he worked most of his life to help.

Sunday memorial services for the SLA dead, which first attracted only forty or fifty people, now draw up to four hundred. The same people who abhorred SLA violence now attend picnics and rallies at which the SLA is extolled.

And then there are the posters—not the Patricia Campbell Hearst *Wanted* handbills found on post-office walls, but rather the full-color posters rushed into print by a promoter who saw a chance to make a fast buck—Patty as Tania in front of the SLA flag with its seven-headed cobra rising from one thick coiled body. The caption reads: "We love you, Tania."

INDEX